The FLOWER EXPERT
Dr. D.G. Hessayon

Previous Impressions	1,600,000
9th Impression	**100,000**

Other books in the EXPERT Series:

THE ROCK & WATER GARDEN EXPERT

THE GARDEN DIY EXPERT

THE BEDDING PLANT EXPERT

THE GARDEN EXPERT

THE TREE & SHRUB EXPERT

THE ROSE EXPERT

THE LAWN EXPERT

THE VEGETABLE EXPERT

THE HOUSE PLANT EXPERT

THE HOME EXPERT

THE FRUIT EXPERT

Acknowledgements
The author wishes to acknowledge the painstaking work
of Jane Roche and Mary Hicks. Grateful acknowledgement
is also made for the help or photographs received from
Joan Hessayon, Angelina Gibbs, A-Z Botanical Collection Ltd,
Pat Brindley, Harry Smith Horticultural Photographic
Collection and Michael Warren.

John Woodbridge provided both artistry and design work.
Deborah Achilleos, Gabrielle Smith and Norman Barber
prepared the paintings for this book.

pbi PUBLICATIONS · BRITANNICA HOUSE · WALTHAM CROSS · HERTS · ENGLAND

Contents

Printed and bound in Great Britain by Jarrold & Sons Ltd., Norwich

ISBN 0 903505 19 3

CHAPTER 1

FLOWERS IN THE GARDEN

Above all else, the garden is a place for flowers. Part of this display is provided by roses, climbers and flowering shrubs and trees – plants which produce woody stems and so form the basic upright skeleton of the garden throughout the year.

But in practically every garden we ask for more. In tiny plots there is just not enough space for an adequate range of shrubs to give floral colour from early spring to late autumn. In large estates there is a need for flowers which cannot be met by woody plants alone. There are bright spring carpets to provide, beds to fill, rockeries to clothe and borders to furnish. For all these uses, from filling tiny cracks between paving stones to displaying plate-sized blooms against clipped hedges, we turn to the herbaceous group of flowering plants. These are the annuals, biennials and perennials which die down in the winter, disappearing beneath the soil outdoors or waiting indoors as plants, bulbs or seeds until the garden awakens in spring. The purpose of this book is to provide information on the selection, care and propagation of this vast range of plants – the garden flowers.

The traditional pattern is to use Snowdrops to herald in the New Year, followed by the yellows and blues of clumps of Daffodils and Crocuses growing in the grass or underneath trees. A little later the flower beds produce their spring livery – the biennials such as Wallflowers and Forget-me-nots and bulbs such as Tulips now burst into bloom. The rockery is also bright in April with its sheets of Aubrietia, Arabis and Alyssum saxatile – many gardens are aglow with flowers in spring, but early summer is sometimes a rather barren time. In midsummer we see flowers in their full glory – the border displays its perennials in tiered rows, with Delphiniums and Achillea at the back, Campanulas, Phlox and Shasta Daisies in the middle and Pinks, Catmint, Geum, etc at the front. In contrast to this informal muddle of perennials in which flowers come and go at various times, there are the summer beds now rid of their spring Tulips and Wallflowers. Here we find the fussy and formal lines or blocks of half hardy annuals which were bedded out in late May or early June. Yellow French Marigolds and multicoloured Snapdragons are used to break up the pattern of red, white and blue – Geraniums (or Salvias), Alyssum and Lobelia. Autumn is the time for Chrysanthemums, Dahlias and Michaelmas Daisies – reds, yellows and mauves before the flower garden goes to sleep.

So the traditional floral year goes round, beginning with the Snowdrops and ending with the Michaelmas Daisies. Colourful, yes, but so often commonplace. Once there was a good reason for having a garden filled with the same plants as everybody else. Before the Second World War our seeds were bought at the local garden shop where only the popular varieties were stocked, and perennials for the border were chosen from the narrow selection on offer at these shops or from the mail order companies which advertised in gardening magazines. The keen gardener sent for catalogues, but for most of us the choice was a limited one.

We now live in a completely different horticultural world. The large garden centre offers a vast range of seeds, border perennials, rockery plants and bulbs. It is not just a matter of having more plants on display – in recent years there has been a flood of new types. Of course there are now wider colour ranges – Tagetes in every shade from palest yellow to deepest brown instead of just a few yellow and maroon varieties.... Day Lilies in a rainbow of colours instead of the dull oranges of yesteryear. But new varieties mean more than just new colours – many have been bred to cater for today's smaller garden, so that sturdy dwarfs of old favourites such as Sweet Pea and Sunflower are now available.

This means that every garden can be made more interesting by introducing new varieties and uncommon plants to go alongside the established favourites. In this way the garden can be kept in bloom all year round – there are Chionodoxas and Winter Aconites as well as Snowdrops to herald in the year and there are Nerines, Colchicums and Cyclamens as well as Michaelmas Daisies to bid it goodbye.

Of course you need some spirit of adventure, but you must never be foolhardy. It is sheer folly to buy a packet of seeds or a container-grown plant just because you like the picture on the packet or label. You must first find out whether it is right for your garden.

And that is the purpose of this book. In its A-Z sections you will find the likes and dislikes of all sorts of out-of-the-way plants, together with details of uncommon varieties of popular plants. Of course the mainstays of the traditional garden must not be forgotten. The well-loved plants of Victorian times have a place here, as they have in your garden.

Choosing the right type

The blessing of the modern garden centre is also its drawback. No longer do you have to make your selection from a small group of plants if you want to take them home with you – here you will find countless varieties all waiting to be bought.

What a blessing to have so many lovely flowers to choose from. . . . but it is so easy to lose your way and be stuck for choice. To avoid the pitfalls, ask yourself the following 5 questions. The answers will guide you to the right section of the book, and there you will find the A-Z guides. For each plant you will find the answers to the questions you need to ask – What height will it reach? Will it thrive or even survive in the spot I have in mind? When will it flower? Does it need winter protection? . . . and so on. In these A-Z guides you cannot look up Snapdragon, Sunflower or Stocks – the plants are listed under their latin names. Look up common names in the Index (pages 157-160).

Now you should be in a position to make your choice. Of course the picture and the description in the catalogues or on the label must appeal to you, but do remember that these descriptions dwell on the good points of the variety in question. The A-Z guides will also tell you the limitations and these should not be ignored. Some flowers, like some people, are both difficult and dull!

QUESTION 1: DO I WANT IT TO BE A PERMANENT FEATURE?

ANNUALS & BIENNIALS

A hardy annual (HA) is a temporary visitor. It grows from seed and then flowers and dies all in a single season. The seeds are sown in the open in spring.

A half hardy annual (HHA) also grows from seed, flowering and dying all in a single season. It is another temporary visitor, used for summer bedding. It is not as easy to grow as a hardy annual — the seedlings must be raised indoors in spring and planted out when the danger of frost is past.

A hardy biennial (HB) grows from seed, producing stems and leaves in the first season and flowering in the next. After flowering the plant dies. It is a temporary visitor used for spring bedding and for filling gaps in the border. The seeds are sown in the open in summer.
See pages 7–40

ROCKERY PERENNIALS

A rockery perennial (RP) will live in the garden for years, the stems dying down each winter and new shoots appearing in spring. It is a permanent resident — at home, of course, in the rock garden but also grown in the alpine house, sink garden and front of the small border.
See pages 86–107

Hollyhock, Sweet William, Foxglove and Wallflower quickly decline if grown as permanent residents in the border. It is much better to grow them as biennials. Some half hardy perennials (Antirrhinum, Petunia and Nemesia) produce a poor floral display if planted out in spring for a second year — they are therefore grown as half hardy annuals.

The dividing line between the rockery perennial and border perennial is an indistinct one. It is based on height — herbaceous perennials which grow less than 1 ft high are generally called rockery perennials and those over 1 ft high are border perennials, but there are exceptions.

BORDER PERENNIALS

A herbaceous perennial (HP) will live in the border for years, the leaves and stems dying down each winter and new shoots appearing each spring. It is a permanent resident — the basic ingredient of the herbaceous border, island bed and mixed border.
See pages 41–81

Several border perennials form bulbs or bulb-like storage organs below ground — Agapanthus and Kaffir Lily are examples. They are not included with the bulbs because they are generally sold and transplanted as growing plants.

A half hardy perennial (HHP) is not fully hardy and needs to spend its winter in a frost-free place. It is therefore a regular visitor rather than a permanent resident in the garden, overwintering indoors as green plants (Pelargonium and Fuchsia), tubers (Dahlia) or as roots (Chrysanthemum).

BULBS

A bulb (more correctly a bulbous plant) produces an underground fleshy storage organ which is offered for sale for planting in the garden. Included here are the true bulbs, corms, tubers and rhizomes.

Some bulbs are permanent residents. They can be left in the ground for years, producing flowers each season. Lifting is only required when overcrowding threatens the quality of the display — examples are Crocus, Snowdrop and Narcissus. The remainder are regular visitors, growing in the garden for part of the year and resting indoors as dormant bulbs until planting time comes round again. Examples are Gladiolus, Tuberous Begonia and Tulip.
See pages 108–123

HOBBY PLANTS

A hobby plant is a genus with sufficient variety and complexity to warrant a specialist national society and one which calls for considerable skill in maintaining a representative collection in peak condition. In this book a bulb (Lily) and several half hardy perennials (Chrysanthemum, Dahlia, Fuchsia and Pelargonium) have been chosen, but there is a strong case for treating Sweet Peas, Carnations and Irises as hobby plants.
See pages 131–145

As the chart above shows, there are temporary visitors, regular visitors and permanent residents from which to make your choice. The appeal of growing permanent residents is, of course, a strong one but the word 'permanent' can be deceptive – many of them need to be lifted and divided every few years.

QUESTION 2: WHERE WILL IT HAVE TO LIVE?

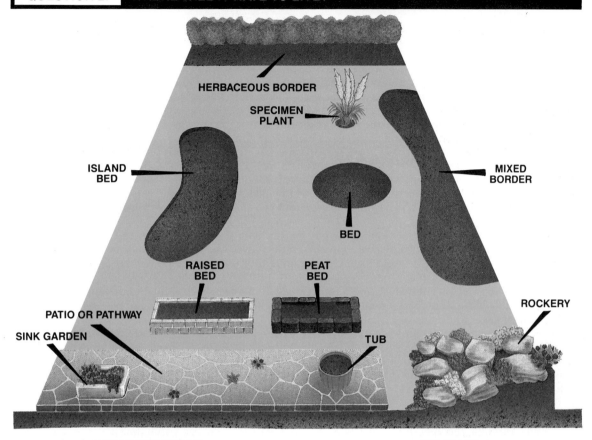

HERBACEOUS BORDER
In the early years of the 20th century the herbaceous border was an essential feature of the larger garden. It was long and narrow with a backcloth of a wall or clipped hedge. Border perennials were used in tiers, with tall-growing varieties at the back and clumps of low-growing plants at the front. See page 42.

MIXED BORDER
The mixed border has taken over from the herbaceous border as the most popular way of growing border perennials. Gone are most of the slavish rules, and the flowering season has been extended by including other types of plants. Like all borders it is designed to be viewed from 2 or 3 sides and not from all angles, and the shape is often irregular and no longer strictly rectangular. The usual pattern is a framework of flowering shrubs and decorative evergreens. Roses and border perennials form large and colourful patches and close to the front a number of pockets are left to be filled with bulbs and annuals. See page 42.

ISLAND BED
The island bed is a modern variation of the traditional herbaceous border. Like its illustrious predecessor it is designed for border perennials, with the tallest at the centre and the shortest around the edge. Like all beds it is designed to be seen from all sides and the shape is often irregular. See page 42.

SPECIMEN PLANT
A specimen plant is grown to be admired on its own as distinct from being grouped with other plants — its role is to serve as a focal point. Obviously great care must be taken in its selection and maintenance, and the usual choice is a shrub or tree. Several border perennials make excellent specimen plants — examples are Agapanthus, Cortaderia and Paeonia.

BED
A bed is a planted area which is designed to be viewed from all sides. The flower bed is the traditional home for annuals, biennials, bulbs and hobby plants — the occupants are usually planted ('bedded out') in autumn for a spring display and in late spring for a summer show. See page 7.

RAISED BED
A raised bed is similar in use to an ordinary flower bed but the sides are made up by a retaining wall and the space within filled with free-draining soil. The raised bed is particularly useful where the drainage of the garden soil is poor or where age or infirmity makes stooping by the gardener difficult.

PEAT BED
A peat bed is a variation of the raised bed. The retaining wall is made up of peat blocks and the in-fill is a compost in which the peat content is greater than the soil fraction. An excellent home for lime-hating plants — grow alpines or ferns in the cracks between the blocks.

TUB
A useful way of growing showy annuals or bulbs close to the house. Alternatively use it for a bold specimen plant. If you have a greenhouse or conservatory, tubs can be used for half hardy or tender perennials — the containers are moved indoors in October and brought out again in June. Remember that tubs require regular watering.

SINK GARDEN
A sink garden is made from an old stone sink in which the drainage hole has been covered with perforated zinc and which has been filled with a free-draining compost. Glazed sinks should have the outer surface covered with a more natural-looking coating. It is used for growing miniature rockery perennials, dwarf conifers and miniature bulbs. See page 86.

PATIO OR PATHWAY
A pathway is a hard-surface area which leads somewhere. A patio doesn't — it is basically an outdoor extension of the living room. Cracks between the stones can be filled with a variety of mat-forming rockery perennials. See page 86.

ROCKERY
A rockery or rock garden is a planted area devoted to rockery perennials, dwarf conifers and bulbs. Low growing annuals are frequently used to supplement the summer display. Ideally it should imitate a natural stone outcrop. See page 86.

QUESTION 3 : DO I WANT A POPULAR PLANT OR A RARITY?

Many of the plants in the A-Z guides are distinctly common – you will find them in gardens everywhere. Before rejecting these over-popular plants, remember that they are inexpensive, easy to obtain and have proved their ability to flourish under all sorts of conditions. Rarities, on the other hand, can be expensive, difficult to find and are often quite temperamental. As a general rule it is unwise to stick slavishly to either group – you don't want a garden filled with nothing but everyday plants nor do you want a botanical garden. A good plan is to have a framework of modern varieties of old favourites and then a number of unusual plants which you might not have seen before, but which the A-Z guides say are suitable for your site. In that way you will blend reliability with novelty.

QUESTION 4 : WHAT WILL THE GROWING CONDITIONS BE LIKE?

Think about the climate and soil before you make up your shopping list. Some features you will be able to alter to suit the plant – you can make a soil less acid by adding lime and you can add peat to increase acidity. But there are features you cannot change and you therefore have to choose plants which are right for the conditions.

Most hardy annuals are undemanding except for sunlight – when grown in the shade the stems become lanky and the floral display poor or even absent. There is no built-in supply of food reserves in roots, stems or bulbs to keep these plants going – for annuals it is a short life and it must be a sunny one. If the site is shady, look through the A-Z guide (pages 7-40) for exceptions to the sun-loving rule. Pot Marigold, Cornflower, Virginia Stock and Nasturtium will thrive in partial shade, but biennials tend to be more shade tolerant than hardy annuals – Bellis, Foxglove, Honesty, Forget-me-not and Pansy will all grow in shade.

An outstanding annual for growing under trees is the Bedding Begonia, but it is a half hardy annual, and for all this group there is another problem – the killing effect of frost. Don't set out any plants from the HHA group before early June if your location is subject to late frosts.

With border perennials the need for well-drained soil is greater than it is for most annuals – the cause of winter death is much more likely to be due to roots rotting in waterlogged soil rather than roots killed by frost. This does not mean that you can ignore the frost problem – avoid the cold-sensitive ones like Eremurus and Agapanthus if you live in an exposed northerly district.

Looking through the A-Z guide (pages 41-81) you will find border perennials for almost every situation. Some, like Globe Flower and Tradescantia, will grow in wet soil – others such as Catananche thrive best on a dry, sandy site. Many will flourish in shady situations – see page 68.

There is no point in picking choice rockery perennials unless you can provide a well-drained site – with this group of plants the need for free-draining soil is paramount. Once again think of the growing conditions before buying – some rockery plants need full sun and others need a north-facing situation. Some are planted in open ground, others in crevices and a few must be grown vertically in the cracks between rocks or bricks.

Annuals generally need sun and rockery perennials must have good drainage, but there are no general rules for bulbs. Of course they appreciate reasonable soil but on looking through the A-Z guide (pages 108-123) you will find varieties ranging from Snowdrops, which will grow anywhere, to Ixia and Sparaxis, which are out of the question in cold districts.

QUESTION 5 : HOW MUCH DO I WANT TO SPEND?

Obviously, as little as possible – but you will not save money in the long run if you buy poor quality stock. If you have an established garden then the cheapest way of obtaining new plants is to divide up perennials and use seeds saved from last year. Every good gardener does increase his plants in this way, but every good gardener also regularly buys new plants, for that is one of the pleasures of gardening.

Look at the list of planting materials on page 125. Seeds are the cheapest way of producing summer colour – it is more expensive to buy them as bedding plants in trays ('flats') and even more expensive to buy them as seedlings in individual pots. Sow seeds for annuals and biennials, but remember that you can also raise many border and rockery perennials from seed. Inexpensive, of course, but you will need patience as you wait for them to reach flowering size.

Collections of rooted cuttings are a cheap way of starting a herbaceous or mixed border. If money is short then leave spaces which you can fill with annuals grown from seed until you can afford to buy choice plants to fill the gaps. Many perennials can be bought as container-grown plants in flower – an expensive but satisfactory way of adding instant colour to the garden.

CHAPTER 2
ANNUALS & BIENNIALS

The standard clear-cut definitions of annuals and biennials are given on page 4. Annuals grow from seed and they flower and die all in a single season – the hardy ones can be sown in the open in spring and the half hardy ones are raised indoors and then planted out when the danger of frost is past. The hardy biennials are also grown from seed, but with these plants only stems and foliage appear in the first season – you have to wait until the following season for the flowers.

In practice the dividing lines between the groups are a little ragged. Hardy annuals are sometimes treated as biennials, being sown in autumn to provide an unusually early floral display in the following season. Half hardy annuals can be sown outdoors in May to give an unusually late floral display. A few biennials, such as Hollyhocks and Pansies, are often left to grow as perennials in the border.

Despite this slight overlapping, the annuals and biennials are a distinct and invaluable collection of plants for any garden. They are raised from seed, so that large numbers can be produced at a reasonable price, and they have many uses. Filling tubs and window boxes, decorating hanging baskets, covering gaps in borders and beds, providing cut flowers, adding splashes of colour to the rockery and, above all, the provision of planting material for bedding out schemes.

A bedding plant is generally an annual or occasionally a biennial or perennial which is raised under glass or in a nursery bed and then planted out elsewhere as a temporary occupant to provide a colourful display. So the term describes a *use* and not a *type* of plant – a Geranium kept indoors is a 'flowering house plant'; the same variety planted outdoors is a 'bedding plant'.

We shall never know where the first large-scale bedding schemes were created – both France and Germany claim the honour. What we do know is that by 1840 the formal flower bed was firmly established in Britain and by 1870 it had become a craze. The fashionable competed with each other to produce the most dazzling, ornate and expensive displays. Colours clashed, beds grew more and more bizarre and costs soared. Reaction was inevitable and quite suddenly the formal bed became the symbol of bad taste. The gardening gurus ruled that bedding plants were no longer to be used, but park and home garden bedding refused to die. In recent years the noisy criticism has abated and about half of all gardeners buy bedding plants each year.

The problem is that little imagination or variety is used in the bedding schemes found in the average garden. Dutifully every autumn we plant out the Tulips and cover them with Wallflowers and an edging of Forget-me-nots. When they come out in late spring we are ready to plant out the red Geraniums or Salvias with a frill of Alyssum and Lobelia. Even in Victorian times there were critics – "The common disposition of red, white and blue is better adapted to delight savages than represent the artistic status of civilised people."

This criticism is too hard – you are perfectly entitled to have the common-or-garden quilt of red, white and blue or French Marigolds with Ageratum if you feel it is part of your gardening year. But nowadays there are so many new and eye-catching varieties to choose from that you might try a more adventurous scheme. The choice is up to you – a traditional floral tapestry or a bed filled with a single variety, but either way there are general rules to remember. Most annuals adore sunshine and dislike rich soil – do not site an annual bed under trees unless you are prepared to choose from the limited range of shade-lovers. Annuals involve a lot of work – sowing, pricking out, weeding, watering, dead-heading and so on. They are a way to save money but not time. Try to plant them in groups and not as single plants which tend to get lost amongst the greenery in the garden. Place the largest varieties in the centre of the bed or at the back of the border, but do not stick slavishly to this rule.

It is stupid for anyone to pronounce that annuals should not be grown in the garden, but it is equally wrong to try to create a garden with annuals alone. The most ardent critics of these short-lived plants missed the major drawback – the chart on page 17 shows that there is little in bloom before June, and page 33 reveals that there is virtually nothing in flower after October. A garden needs a much longer floral season than that, and so we must turn to the bulbs, perennials and shrubs for help.

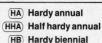

KEY TO SYMBOLS USED
IN THE A–Z GUIDE

(HA) **Hardy annual**
(HHA) **Half hardy annual**
(HB) **Hardy biennial**

Acroclinium roseum grandiflorum

ACROCLINIUM
Everlasting Flower
(HA)

This Australian flower is often called Acroclinium in the seed catalogues, but its proper latin name is Helipterum. The strawy-petalled, Daisy-like flowers are borne on slender stems, and they belong to a group of 'everlasting' flowers which can be cut and dried for winter decoration. The blooms may be single, semi-double or double.

VARIETIES: You will usually find Acroclinium offered as **'Large-flowered Mixed'** — such seed packets contain **A. roseum grandiflorum** and will provide a fine display of white and rose-pink flowers. Other species are less common — **A. humboldtianum** (yellow), **A. roseum** (rose) and **A. manglesii** (white and red). Cut stems for drying before flowers are fully open.

SITE & SOIL: Any well-drained garden soil will do — thrives best in full sun.

PLANT DETAILS: Height 15 in. Spacing 6 in. Flowering period July – September.

PROPAGATION: Dislikes root disturbance. Sow seeds in April where they are to flower. Thin to required spacing.

A. roseum

Ageratum houstonianum

AGERATUM
Floss Flower
(HHA)

Ageratum is seen everywhere during the summer months. The compact plants and the neat powder-puff flowers cover bare patches in borders, edge formal beds and brighten up window boxes. This popularity is largely due to the free-flowering habit and the long flowering season. The display will last until the frosts arrive if you dead-head regularly and water copiously in dry weather.

VARIETIES: The blue and mauve varieties of **A. houstonianum** are the most popular. There is **'Blue Mink'** (azure-blue), **'Blue Angel'** (lilac-blue) and **'Blue Blazer'** (deep blue). The 1½ ft **'Blue Bouquet'** is the giant, and the non-blues include **'Summer Snow'** (white) and **'Fairy Pink'** (rose).

SITE & SOIL: Any reasonable garden soil will do — thrives in sun or light shade. Dislikes windy, exposed sites.

PLANT DETAILS: Height 8 in. Spacing 8 in. Flowering period June – October.

PROPAGATION: Follow the Half Hardy Annual technique (page 82). Plant out when the danger of frost is past.

A. houstonianum
'Blue Mink'

Agrostemma githago 'Milas'

AGROSTEMMA
Corn Cockle
(HA)

Corn Cockle is not a popular garden flower, and it is even less popular with the farmer when it appears as a weed in his fields. But it is an excellent cottage garden plant, bearing large flowers on top of slender stems which withstand both wind and rain. The Corn Cockle is recommended for cutting.

VARIETIES: The weed **A. githago** bears narrow hairy leaves and bright magenta flowers which close at night. The variety most commonly grown as a garden plant is **A. githago 'Milas'** which came from Turkey. Its pale lilac flowers fade to white at the centre — they measure 2 in. across and provide unusual specimens for flower arranging. Gather the blooms when they are fully open.

SITE & SOIL: Any reasonable garden soil will do — thrives best in full sun.

PLANT DETAILS: Height 2½ ft. Spacing 1 ft. Flowering period June – August.

PROPAGATION: Dislikes root disturbance. Sow seeds in autumn or early spring where they are to flower.

A. githago

A. githago
'Milas'

ALTHAEA

Hollyhock
(HA), (HB) or (HP)

The familiar Hollyhock is the giant of the flower garden, its tall spires of large, funnel-shaped flowers providing summer colour at the back of herbaceous borders or in cottage gardens. Nearly all colours apart from blue are available. It can be grown as a perennial but rust disease soon ruins older plants — it is better to treat it as a biennial or to grow one of the annual varieties.

VARIETIES: A. rosea is the Common Hollyhock and there are both single and double varieties from which to make your choice. **'Chater's Double'** is the one most usually grown. If you want to grow Althaea as an annual then choose an early-flowering variety such as **'Majorette'** or **'Summer Carnival'**.

SITE & SOIL: Any reasonable garden soil will do — thrives in a sunny, sheltered spot. Stake on exposed sites.

PLANT DETAILS: Height 6–9 ft (annual vars. 3–6 ft). Spacing 2 ft (annual vars. 15 in.). Flowering period July–September.

PROPAGATION: Take cuttings in autumn or sow in June — follow the Biennial technique (page 83). Sow annual varieties under glass in February.

A. rosea

A. rosea 'Powder Puffs'

Althaea rosea 'Chater's Double'

ALYSSUM

Sweet Alyssum
(HA)

Some experts feel that too much Alyssum is grown, but without it many of our small gardens would be poorer. The dwarf cushions are covered with tiny, honey-scented flowers throughout the summer, and it is used to edge flower beds, fill the spaces between paving stones, cover bare patches in rockeries and clothe window boxes. Trim off dead blooms with scissors to ensure continuous flowering.

VARIETIES: Most people choose a white variety of **A. maritimum** (proper name **Lobularia maritima**). The low-carpeting ones are **'Carpet of Snow'** and **'Minimum'** — the popular **'Little Dorrit'** is more upright. For a change pick a coloured variety — there are **'Oriental Night'** (deep purple), **'Rosie O'Day'** (pink) and **'Lilac Queen'** (deep lilac).

SITE & SOIL: The soil should be well drained but not rich — thrives best in full sun.

PLANT DETAILS: Height 3–6 in. Spacing 9 in. Flowering period June–September.

PROPAGATION: Sow seeds in compost under glass in February or in April where they are to flower.

A. maritimum 'Minimum'

A. maritimum 'Rosie O'Day'

Alyssum maritimum 'Little Dorrit'

AMARANTHUS

Love-lies-bleeding
(HHA)

The standard way to use Love-lies-bleeding is to plant one or a small group as a centrepiece in a formal bedding scheme. During the summer months the 18 in. long tassels of tiny blooms are a spectacular feature, recommended for use in flower arrangements. Keep the plants well watered during dry spells to prolong flower life and to ensure an attractive autumn display of red stems and bronzy leaves.

VARIETIES: A. caudatus is a tropical plant, but in the warmer areas of Britain it can be treated as a hardy annual. The basic species bears large green leaves and crimson tassels, but you can buy seeds of the variety **atropurpureus** which has dark red tassels or **viridis** which produces pale green flowers.

SITE & SOIL: Any well-drained garden soil will do — thrives best in full sun.

PLANT DETAILS: Height 3 ft. Spacing 2 ft. Flowering period July–October.

PROPAGATION: Follow the Half Hardy Annual technique (page 82). Plant out when the danger of frost is past.

A. caudatus

Amaranthus caudatus

ANCHUSA
Anchusa
(HA)

Anchusa is usually grown as a perennial in the herbaceous border, but there is a dwarf annual species which is excellent for bedding or window boxes. The bushy plant bears branching stems which are covered with starry blue flowers in midsummer. The secrets of success are to dead-head regularly, keep well watered and spray against mildew if white spots appear.

VARIETIES: The variety of **A. capensis** to choose is **'Blue Angel'**. The dark blue, Forget-me-not-like flowers are borne in great profusion. The leaves are narrow and hairy and the plant grows only 9 in. high. Taller varieties are **'Bedding Blue'** (1½ ft, sky blue) and **'Blue Bird'** (1½ ft, indigo blue).

SITE & SOIL: Any well-drained garden soil will do — thrives best in a sunny, open situation.

PLANT DETAILS: Height 9 in. or 1½ ft. Spacing 9 in. Flowering period July–August.

PROPAGATION: Sow seeds in September or April where they are to flower. Thin to required spacing.

Anchusa capensis 'Blue Angel'

A. capensis 'Blue Angel'

ANTIRRHINUM
Snapdragon
(HHA)

As children we learnt to recognize the tall spike of the simple Snapdragon with its lipped tubular flowers, but these days there is a wide variety of flower shapes, colours and plant heights. This garden favourite is really a perennial which will withstand short periods of frost, but it is usually grown as a half hardy annual. When the plants are about 3 in. high, pinch out the growing points to encourage bushiness. Stake tall varieties if the site is exposed and remove faded spikes to prolong the flowering season.

VARIETIES: Our garden Snapdragons are varieties of **A. majus**. There is the *Tall* group which provides flowers for bold bedding schemes and cutting — in the catalogues you will find **'Apple Blossom'** (pink), the vigorous Rocket hybrids and the Azalea-flowered types such as **'Madame Butterfly'** with trumpet-like blooms. The *Intermediate* group is the most popular — **'Coronette Mixed'** is generally considered to be the finest of all but you can choose **'Rembrandt'** (scarlet and gold), **'Black Prince'** (deep crimson) or one of the Hyacinth-flowered varieties. The *Dwarf* group is used for edging or carpeting — pick **'Magic Carpet'**, **'Floral Carpet'** or **'Tom Thumb Mixed'**. Choose a rust-resistant variety if this disease is a problem in your area.

SITE & SOIL: Any well-drained garden soil, but light or medium land is preferred. Choose a sunny spot.

PLANT DETAILS: Height 3–4 ft (Tall Group), 1½ ft (Intermediate Group) or 6–9 in. (Dwarf Group). Spacing 1½ ft (Tall Group), 1 ft (Intermediate Group) or 9 in. (Dwarf Group). Flowering period July–October.

PROPAGATION: Follow the Half Hardy Annual technique (page 82). Alternatively sow seeds outdoors in July and plant the seedlings in September where they are to flower. This Biennial technique gives earlier flowers, but it is not suitable for cold and exposed sites.

Antirrhinum majus 'Madame Butterfly'

Antirrhinum majus 'Coronette Mixed'

A. majus 'Rembrandt'

A. majus 'Fiery Red'

Antirrhinum majus 'Magic Carpet'

ARCTOTIS African Daisy
(HHA)

A showy plant with large Daisy-like flowers borne on long stems. These flowers are often recommended for cutting, although they close in the evening. When the plants are about 5 in. high, pinch out the growing points to encourage bushiness. If you dead-head regularly and support the stems with twigs the eye-catching display should last until the first frosts arrive.

VARIETIES: You will find two basic groups in the catalogues. **A. grandis** produces flowers with white or pastel petals surrounding a central blue disc, and although attractive this group is less popular than **A. hybrida**. This latter group is usually sold as **'Large-flowered Hybrids'**, producing 4 in. flowers in many brilliant colours.

SITE & SOIL: Any soil apart from heavy clay will do — thrives best in full sun.

PLANT DETAILS: Height 1½ ft. Spacing 1 ft. Flowering period July–October.

PROPAGATION: Follow the Half Hardy Annual technique (page 82). Plant out when the danger of frost is past.

A. hybrida

A. grandis

Arctotis hybrida

BARTONIA Blazing Star
(HA)

If you have sandy soil, this easy-to-grow plant is an excellent choice. The glistening yellow flowers are 2 in. across and are borne in profusion throughout the summer. The feathery stamens and golden petals give the plant the appearance of a miniature St. John's Wort, and this annual from California deserves to be much more widely grown.

VARIETIES: You will find Blazing Star listed in the catalogues as **Bartonia aurea**, although its modern latin name is **Mentzelia lindleyi**. The succulent stems bear long, much-divided leaves and the flowers are slightly fragrant. The only drawback is seen in dull weather — the flowers close when the sun isn't shining.

SITE & SOIL: Thrives best in dry, sandy soil and an open, sunny situation.

PLANT DETAILS: Height 1½ ft. Spacing 9 in. Flowering period June–September.

PROPAGATION: Sow seeds in April where they are to flower. Thin to required spacing.

B. aurea

Bartonia aurea

BEGONIA Bedding Begonia
(HHA)

The Bedding or Fibrous-rooted Begonia is one of the most useful of all summer bedding plants because it can thrive where most annuals are distinctly unhappy — in the shade under trees. The plants will provide rich colour even when they are in shadow for much of the day provided you follow these rules — buy good stock, don't plant out until June, enrich the soil with humus and water when it is dry.

VARIETIES: B. semperflorens is available in a wide range of flower colours (white, pink, red), leaf colours (green, copper, bronze) and heights. Dwarf varieties are the most popular and include **'Organdy'** (mixed colours, green leaves), **'Cocktail'** (mixed colours, bronze leaves) and **'Thousand Wonders White'** (white flowers, green leaves). The best tall Begonia is **'Danica'** (large red or pink flowers, red leaves).

SITE & SOIL: Thrives best in humus-rich soil and partial shade.

PLANT DETAILS: Height 6 in.–1½ ft. Spacing 5–15 in. Flowering period June–September.

PROPAGATION: Follow the Half Hardy Annual technique (page 82). Usually bought as bedding plants — propagation from seed is not easy.

B. semperflorens

Begonia semperflorens 'Organdy'

BELLIS
Daisy
HB

The familiar Daisy on the lawn has given rise to a large number of garden varieties over the years. There are red and pink ones as well as the native white colour, and there are double varieties in which the central yellow disc has been obliterated. Daisies are useful for edging beds and for planting in window boxes. It is a perennial plant which can be kept from year to year, but it is usually grown as a biennial.

VARIETIES: There are several delightful dwarf varieties of **B. perennis** for carpeting, edging or growing in the rockery — **'The Pearl'** (white), **'Dresden China'** (pink) and **'Rob Roy'** (red). **'Pomponette'** produces pompon-like buttons and the **'Monstrosa'** types produce large double blooms in white, pink or red.

SITE & SOIL: Any reasonable garden soil will do in sun or partial shade.

PLANT DETAILS: Height 3–6 in. Spacing 6in. Flowering period March–July.

PROPAGATION: Divide plants in spring or sow seeds in May — follow the Biennial technique (page 83).

Bellis perennis

B. perennis
Single variety

B. perennis
Double variety

CALCEOLARIA
Slipper Flower
HHA

The Slipper Flower was a favourite bedding plant in Victorian times but it is no longer popular. You will find only one or two varieties listed in the seed catalogues and some books on garden annuals don't even mention them. But the bright masses of pouched flowers provide a colourful display all summer long when planted in tubs, window boxes or flower beds.

VARIETIES: Sowing a **C. multiflora** seed mixture will produce plants with large flowers in varied and brilliant colours; these hybrids are more commonly used as pot plants than bedding ones. The old yellow Bedding Calceolaria was **C. rugosa** — a much improved modern hybrid is **'Sunshine'**.

SITE & SOIL: Any reasonable garden soil will do — thrives best in full sun.

PLANT DETAILS: Height 1 ft. Spacing 9 in. Flowering period June–October.

PROPAGATION: Follow the Half Hardy Annual technique (page 82). Usually bought as bedding plants — propagation from seed is not easy. In autumn pot up plants and overwinter under glass.

Calceolaria 'Sunshine'

C. multiflora

CALENDULA
Pot Marigold
HA

This old garden plant was once widely used as a kitchen herb but now it is grown as a trouble-free, summer-flowering annual. Like radishes in the vegetable garden, the Pot Marigold is a favourite starter plant for young children. A pinch of seed in spring and in about 10 weeks masses of flowers appear above the hairy, pungent leaves. Pinch out growing points on young stems to encourage bushiness.

VARIETIES: There are now many variations on the flat, orange flowers borne on the old-fashioned **C. officinalis** of the cottage garden. The colours range from the 1½ ft **'Lemon Queen'** (yellow) to the 2 ft Chrysanthemum-like **'Geisha Girl'** (reddish-orange). **'Radio'** has orange, fluted petals and **'Art Shades'** has pastel flowers — apricot, cream, etc. The best compact variety is the 1 ft **'Fiesta Gitana'**.

SITE & SOIL: Thrives best in poor soil in sun or partial shade.

PLANT DETAILS: Height 1–2 ft. Spacing 1 ft. Flowering period June–October.

PROPAGATION: Sow seeds in September or March where they are to flower. Thin to required spacing.

Calendula officinalis 'Fiesta Gitana'

C. officinalis
'Lemon Queen'

C. officinalis
'Orange King'

CALLISTEPHUS

China Aster, Annual Aster
(HHA)

Chinese Asters (C. chinensis) provide late summer and autumn colour in flower beds and long-lasting blooms for indoor decoration. The leaves are hairy and deeply lobed, and the flowers look like large Daisies or small Chrysanthemums. You will find a bewildering selection in the seed catalogues — dwarf and tall, single and double, and a wide variety of flower shapes and colours. Callistephus is almost hardy — it is usually bedded out in May but in mild districts the seeds can be sown outdoors in spring. Never grow this plant on the same spot year after year — there is a danger of disease. For really good results, spread a mulch around the stems, dead-head regularly and stake tall varieties.

VARIETIES: The *Single* group includes the old-fashioned types — **'Super Chinensis'** (2 ft) is the one to choose. The *Dwarf* group is extremely useful where space is limited — pick **'Milady'** (10 in.), **'Pinocchio'** (9 in.) or **'Pepite'** (12 in.). At the other end of the scale is the 2½ ft *Tall* group — **'Princess Giant'**, **'Perfection'** and **'Giants of California'**. There are several flower forms — the *Ball* group has fully double, globular flowers — **'Miss Europe'** is a good example. The *Chrysanthemum-flowered* group includes the well-known **'Duchess'** variety; the *Ostrich Plume* group with its feather-like petals is popular for bedding. Finally there is the button-like *Pompon* group which includes **'Pirette'**.

SITE & SOIL: Any well-drained garden soil will do if adequate lime is present. Thrives in a sunny, sheltered spot.

PLANT DETAILS: Height 9 in. – 2½ ft. Spacing 9 in. – 1½ ft. Flowering period August – October.

PROPAGATION: Follow the Half Hardy Annual technique (page 82). Alternatively in mild areas sow seeds outdoors in mid April.

Callistephus chinensis 'Miss Europe'

C. chinensis
Single group

C. chinensis
Ostrich Plume group

C. chinensis
Chrysanthemum group

C. chinensis
Pompon group

C. chinensis
Ball group

Callistephus chinensis 'Duchess Crimson'

CAMPANULA

Canterbury Bell
(HB)

The Canterbury Bell has been grown in British gardens for hundreds of years. Above the wavy-edged, hairy leaves numerous spikes of bell-shaped flowers appear. The blooms may be single, semi-double or double and the colours range from white and rose to mauve and blue. Protect the plants from slugs in winter — stake the stems and dead-head the faded flowers in summer.

VARIETIES: The Canterbury Bell is **C. medium** and the most popular variety is **C. medium calycanthema**. This is listed as **'Cup and Saucer'** in the catalogues, so-called because of the shape of the semi-double flowers borne on this 2½ ft plant. A much more compact Canterbury Bell is the single **'Bells of Holland'** (1½ ft). The giant amongst biennial Campanulas is the 4 ft **C. pyramidalis.**

SITE & SOIL: Any well-drained garden soil will do — thrives in a sunny spot which receives a little shade during the day.

PLANT DETAILS: Height 1½ – 2½ ft. Spacing 1 ft. Flowering period May – July.

PROPAGATION: Sow seeds in May or June — follow the Biennial technique (page 83).

Campanula pyramidalis

C. medium calycanthema

Celosia argentea 'Cristata'

CELOSIA
Celosia
(HHA)

Celosia is one of the aristocrats of the bedding plant world. The large and brightly coloured flower-heads are crested or plumed, adding a luxury touch to the flower beds or an indoor arrangement. You must not forget, however, that all the Celosias are tender, so they require a warm and sheltered spot and must not be planted out until they have been properly hardened off and all danger of frost is past.

VARIETIES: The plumed one is **C. argentea 'Plumosa'** (Prince of Wales' Feathers). They range in height from the dwarf **'Geisha'** (9 in.) to the stately **'Thompson's Magnifica'** (2 ft). The crested variety is **C. argentea 'Cristata'** (Cockscomb). Choose the compact **'Jewel Box'** (9 in.) or **'Chanticleer'** (9 in.). The Celosia colours are red, yellow and orange.

SITE & SOIL: The soil should not be heavy and the site should be warm and sunny.

PLANT DETAILS: Height 9 in. – 2 ft. Spacing 9 in. – 1 ft. Flowering period July – September.

PROPAGATION: Follow the Half Hardy Annual technique (page 82). Plant out when the danger of frost is past.

C. argentea 'Plumosa'

CENTAUREA
Cornflower
(HA)

Cornflower was once a common farmland weed, but careful selection and breeding has turned it into a colourful annual for flower bed or cutting. Wiry stems bear sprays of flowers in pink, red, purple, white or the original blue. The greyish green leaves make a pleasant change from the standard green foliage of most annuals. Stake tall varieties and dead-head regularly.

VARIETIES: The *Tall* group of **C. cyanus** reaches 2½ – 3 ft. **'Blue Diadem'** is a good choice with its large, deep blue flowers and so are **'Blue Ball'** and **'Red Ball'**. The *Dwarf* group grows only about 1 ft high — the best one to pick here is **'Polka Dot'** but the old favourite is the blue **'Jubilee Gem'**. **C. moschata 'Sweet Sultan'** produces powder-puff-like flowers in a wide variety of colours, including yellow.

SITE & SOIL: Any well-drained garden soil will do — thrives in sun or partial shade.

PLANT DETAILS: Height 1 or 2½ ft. Spacing 9 in. or 1 ft. Flowering period June – September.

PROPAGATION: Sow seeds in September or April where they are to flower. Thin to required spacing.

Centaurea cyanus 'Polka Dot'

C. cyanus 'Blue Diadem'

CHEIRANTHUS
Wallflower
(HB)

Bulbs, Forget-me-nots, Primroses and Wallflowers are the low-growing heralds of spring. Millions of Wallflowers are planted every year during October and the flowers on the erect spikes open in March or April (Wallflower) or May (Siberian Wallflower). Pinch out the tips of young plants before transplanting them in their final quarters. Grow them close to the house to enjoy the fragrance.

VARIETIES: The Wallflower (**C. cheiri**) is the one which is usually grown. Large-flowering types include such old favourites as **'Cloth of Gold'** (yellow, 1½ ft) and **'Vulcan'** (deep crimson, 1 ft), but many other colours are available — pink, purple, orange, white, cream, etc. For small beds pick **'Tom Thumb Mixed'** (9 in.). The Siberian Wallflower (**C. allionii**) is available in yellow or orange.

SITE & SOIL: Any reasonable garden soil with adequate lime will do. Choose a sunny spot.

PLANT DETAILS: Height 9 in. – 2 ft. Spacing 8 in. – 1 ft. Flowering period March – May.

PROPAGATION: Follow the Biennial technique (see page 83). Plant out firmly in October.

Cheiranthus cheiri 'Cloth of Gold'

C. cheiri 'Vulcan'

CHRYSANTHEMUM

Annual Chrysanthemum
(HA)

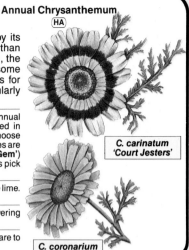

The Annual Chrysanthemum is overshadowed by its showy perennial relatives and is much less popular than it deserves. In flower from midsummer to autumn, the bushy plants are well branched and the blooms of some varieties are extremely colourful. Cut the flowers for long-lasting indoor decoration. Dead-head regularly and spray against greenfly.

VARIETIES: **C. carinatum** (**C. tricolor**) is the showy Annual Chrysanthemum. The flowers are often boldly zoned in bright colours surrounding a dark central disc. Choose **'Court Jesters'** or **'Rainbow Mixture'**. Double varieties are available. The Crown Daisy (**C. coronarium 'Golden Gem'**) produces flat yellow buttons; for white-petalled flowers pick **C. spectabile 'Cecilia'**.

SITE & SOIL: Thrives best in light soil containing adequate lime. Choose a sunny spot.

PLANT DETAILS: Height 1½–2 ft. Spacing 1 ft. Flowering period July–September.

PROPAGATION: Sow seeds in March or April where they are to flower. Thin to required spacing.

C. carinatum 'Court Jesters'

C. coronarium

Chrysanthemum carinatum 'Court Jesters'

CLARKIA

Clarkia
(HA)

This popular and easy-to-grow annual may seem as if it has been on the British gardening scene from earliest times, but it was not discovered until the last century. The flowers look like miniature Hollyhocks and are borne on upright spikes from early summer. Plant Clarkias in bold groups and support the stems with twigs. Remove the leaves from cut flowers before placing in water.

VARIETIES: The usual Clarkia is **C. elegans**. Flowers are semi-double or double and shades of red, pink, purple and white are available. **'Bouquet Mixed'** (2 ft) is a popular variety bearing blooms which are 2 in. across. **C. pulchella** (1 ft) is a smaller and more dainty plant with white, rose or lilac flowers.

SITE & SOIL: Thrives best in light or medium soil which is slightly acid. Choose a sunny spot.

PLANT DETAILS: Height 1½–2 ft. Spacing 1 ft. Flowering period July–October.

PROPAGATION: Dislikes root disturbance. Sow seeds in April where they are to flower. Thin to required spacing.

C. elegans

Clarkia elegans

CLEOME

Spider Flower
(HHA)

The Spider Flower is a must if you like to see the unusual and the exotic in your garden. The large bushy plant is equally at home as a dot plant in the centre of a flower bed or as a gap-filler in the shrubbery. The scented flowers bear long stamens which give the blooms a spidery appearance. Keep watch for greenfly on young plants.

VARIETIES: All the garden specimens are varieties of **C. spinosa** — the latin name refers to the thorns at the base of the leaves. A white variety (**'Helen Campbell'**) is available, but the usual flower colour is pale purple or rose. **'Pink Queen'** and **'Rose Queen'** are popular types — for a mixture of colours grow **'Colour Fountain'**. Look for the dwarf yellow novelty **'Golden Sparkler'**.

SITE & SOIL: A fertile, well-drained soil is necessary. Choose a sunny spot.

PLANT DETAILS: Height 3–4 ft. Spacing 1½ ft. Flowering period July–September.

PROPAGATION: Follow the Half Hardy Annual technique (page 82). Plant out when the danger of frost is past.

C. spinosa

Cleome spinosa

Cobaea scandens

COBAEA Cathedral Bell
(HHA)

The Cathedral Bell or Cup-and-Saucer Vine is an outstanding example of the small group of plants which are grown as annual climbers. It may survive the winter in mild districts but the usual practice is to discard the plants in late autumn. Cobaea grows rapidly, climbing by means of tendrils and bearing bell-like flowers. These blooms are green at first, later turning purple.

VARIETIES: There is one species — **C. scandens**. The prominent flowers are about 3 in. long and are borne throughout the summer. Cobaea is sometimes flower shy — make sure that the plants are properly hardened off before planting out, watered freely in dry weather and not overfed. A few catalogues list a yellowish green variety (**C. scandens alba**).

SITE & SOIL: Any well-drained garden soil will do — thrives best in full sun.

PLANT DETAILS: Height 10 ft. Spacing 2 ft. Flowering period July – October.

PROPAGATION: Follow the Half Hardy Annual technique (page 82), sowing the seeds edge-wise. Plant out when the danger of frost is past.

C. scandens

Convolvulus tricolor 'Blue Flash'

CONVOLVULUS Dwarf Morning Glory
(HA)

A bushy plant, not a climber like its notorious close relative the Common Bindweed. It thrives in poor, sandy soil and produces an abundance of eye-catching flowers. Each one is a wide-mouthed trumpet, brightly coloured with a yellow or golden heart. Unfortunately the glory is short-lived — the flowers open in the morning and fade in the evening. Dead-head regularly and water in dry weather.

VARIETIES: Several varieties of **C. tricolor (C. minor)** are available. **'Royal Ensign'** (1½ ft, dark blue with gold centre) is an excellent choice and so is **'Crimson Monarch'**. **'Blue Flash'** (9 in.) and **'Rainbow Flash'** are more compact plants — they are suitable for window boxes as well as the front of the bed. The climber **Ipomoea purpurea** is sometimes listed as **C. major.**

SITE & SOIL: Any well-drained garden soil will do. Choose a sunny situation.

PLANT DETAILS: Height 9 in. or 1½ ft. Spacing 6 or 9 in. Flowering period June – September.

PROPAGATION: Sow seeds in September or March where they are to flower. Thin to required spacing.

C. tricolor 'Royal Ensign'

Coreopsis tinctoria 'Dwarf Dazzler'

COREOPSIS Tickseed
(HA)

These free-flowering plants bear large, Marigold-like blooms on long stems. They are good for cutting and will succeed in most situations, but Coreopsis does not like heavy clay and produces few flowers in shady conditions. Tall-growing varieties should be staked and faded blooms removed regularly. The colour range is limited — the flowers are yellow with red or brown in various combinations.

VARIETIES: The annual Coreopsis is sometimes listed as Calliopsis in the catalogues. The species **C. tinctoria** has given rise to a number of garden varieties — **'Dwarf Dazzler'** has become the favourite one (1 ft, crimson flowers with broad golden edges). **C. drummondii** has the popular variety **'Golden Crown'** (2 ft, golden flowers with deep red centres).

SITE & SOIL: Thrives best in light or medium soil. Choose a sunny spot.

PLANT DETAILS: Height 1 or 2 ft. Spacing 1 ft. Flowering period July – September.

PROPAGATION: Sow seeds in April where they are to flower. Thin to required spacing.

C. drummondii 'Golden Crown'

C. tinctoria 'Dwarf Dazzler'

COSMOS   Cosmea
(HHA)

Cosmea is a popular annual which is easily recognised by its slender shape, delicate ferny foliage and large flowers which look like single Dahlias. Grow it in pots or flower beds for cutting or for a summer-long display outdoors. Stake tall varieties and remove dead blooms to prolong the flowering season.

VARIETIES: Most garden Cosmeas are varieties of **C. bipinnatus.** The usual choice is **'Sensation Mixed'** — 3 ft tall with white, pink or red flowers. The red-and-white patterned **'Candy Stripe'** is more eye-catching. The varieties of **C. sulphureus** have bright flowers and wider leaves. Choose from **'Sunset'** (3 ft, orange, semi-double), **'Klondyke'** (2 ft, orange, double) or the new dwarf **'Sunny Gold'** (1 ft, orange, double).

SITE & SOIL: Any well-drained garden soil, but light or medium land is preferred. Choose a sunny spot.

PLANT DETAILS: Height 1–3 ft. Spacing 1½ ft. Flowering period July–October.

PROPAGATION: Follow the Half Hardy Annual technique (page 82). In mild districts sow seeds outdoors in May.

Cosmos sulphureus 'Sunset'

C. bipinnatus 'Sensation'

Flowers for Every Season

JANUARY–MAY
(for JUNE–JULY see page 21)
(for AUGUST–SEPTEMBER see page 35)
(for OCTOBER–DECEMBER see page 33)

The flowering period for nearly all annuals and biennials lies somewhere between the beginning of June and the end of October. However, by careful selection you can have flowers in the annual bed or border almost all year round. For each month there is a list of annuals and biennials which can be expected to be in full bloom — remember that some of these plants may come into flower earlier and can continue to bloom for many weeks afterwards.

JANUARY
Viola

FEBRUARY
Viola

MARCH

| Bellis | Matthiola |
| Cheiranthus | Viola |

APRIL

Bellis	Matthiola
Cheiranthus	Myosotis
Lunaria	Viola

MAY

Bellis	Lunaria
Campanula	Malcolmia
Cheiranthus	Myosotis
Iberis	Viola

DAHLIA   Bedding Dahlia
(HHA)

The knee-high Bedding Dahlia with its 2 in. blooms has to look up to its tall and illustrious cousin the Border Dahlia, with flowers which can be as large as dinner plates. The lowly annual varieties should not be regarded as poor relations, however, as they are as bright and long-lasting as anything in the flower border. Dead-head faded blooms but do not disbud the plants.

VARIETIES: The old favourites are the **'Coltness Hybrids'** — 1½ ft, very free-flowering single blooms in a wide colour range. If you want double flowers and a more compact plant, pick **'Rigoletto'**, the bronze-leaved **'Redskin'** or the early-flowering **'Figaro'**. **'Dandy'** (2 ft) has collerette flowers — large petals with an inner collar of quilled petals.

SITE & SOIL: Any well-drained garden soil, but medium or heavy land is preferred. Choose a sunny spot.

PLANT DETAILS: Height 1-2 ft. Spacing 1 ft. Flowering period July–November.

PROPAGATION: Follow the Half Hardy Annual technique (page 82). Tubers may be lifted and overwintered for planting next year.

Dahlia 'Coltness Gem'

D. 'Dandy'

DELPHINIUM Larkspur (HA)

Delphinium ajacis

The Annual Delphinium or Larkspur is a quick-growing plant with varieties suitable for both the back and front of the annual border. The upright flowering spikes bear densely-packed blooms in white, pink, red or blue. The foliage is feathery and the flower-heads are popular for indoor arrangements. Stake tall varieties and remove dead blooms.

VARIETIES: The **D. consolida** group contains the stately **'Giant Imperial'** varieties (4 ft) which produce tall spikes of Stock-like flowers. The **D. ajacis** group produces varieties which are rather shorter and earlier flowering — these so-called Hyacinth-flowering types include **'Tall Rocket'** (2½ ft) and **'Dwarf Rocket'** (1 ft). Remember that the seeds of Delphinium are poisonous.

SITE & SOIL: Any well-drained garden soil will do — thrives in sun or light shade.

PLANT DETAILS: Height 1-4 ft. Spacing 1½ ft. Flowering period June – August.

PROPAGATION: Dislikes root disturbance. For best results sow seeds in September — alternatively sow in March.

D. consolida
'Giant Imperial'

DIANTHUS Sweet William, Indian Pink or Annual Carnation (HHA) or (HB)

Dianthus barbatus

Sweet William, Carnations and Pinks belong to the genus Dianthus, and its list of varieties is as long as its history. The Ancient Greeks called the Carnation the Divine Flower — the Elizabethans of Britain grew a wide variety of fancy gillyflowers (Pinks). In today's garden you will find Dianthus varieties in the rockery, and in beds, borders and window boxes — at the florist you will see the showy blooms of Perpetual Carnations. Dianthus leaves are generally grass-like and often grey- or blue-tinged. Nearly all varieties have a liking for lime but it is not really essential.

VARIETIES: Three species of Dianthus are commonly grown as annuals or biennials. **D. barbatus** is the familiar Sweet William which bears densely-packed, flattened heads of flowers in midsummer. You can buy single-colour or distinctly-eyed varieties. Sweet William is usually grown as a biennial but annual types are available. **D. chinensis** is the Indian or Annual Pink — 1½ in. fragrant flowers in many brilliant colours and combinations; look for **'Baby Doll'** (mixed), **'Snowflake'** (white), **'Queen of Hearts'** (red) and the new bushy **'Telstar'** (mixed). **D. caryophyllus** hybrids are the Annual Carnations — the double flowers are about 2 in. across and these plants make excellent bedding annuals except in the far north. Reliable strains are **'Chabaud'**, **'Knight'** and **'Raoul Martin'**.

SITE & SOIL: Any well-drained garden soil which is not acid will do — choose a sunny spot.

PLANT DETAILS: Height 1-2 ft (Sweet William), 6 in. -1½ ft (Indian Pink), 1½ ft (Annual Carnation). Spacing 9 in. (Sweet William), 6 in. (Indian Pink), 1 ft (Annual Carnation). Flowering period June – July (Sweet William), July – October (Indian Pink and Annual Carnation).

PROPAGATION: Follow the Biennial technique — page 83 (Sweet William). Follow the Half Hardy Annual technique — page 82 or sow seeds outdoors in April (Indian Pink). Follow the Half Hardy Annual technique — page 82 (Annual Carnation).

Dianthus chinensis 'Baby Doll'

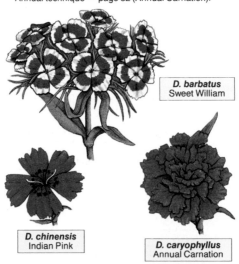

D. barbatus
Sweet William

D. chinensis
Indian Pink

D. caryophyllus
Annual Carnation

Dianthus caryophyllus 'Chabaud'

DIGITALIS   Foxglove
HB

Few annuals and biennials are really happy growing under trees or in other shady places — Foxgloves are notable exceptions. The wild species D. purpurea is sometimes grown in gardens but it is more usual to choose a showy hybrid. Tall spikes bearing bell-like flowers appear above the basal rosette of large downy leaves. It is an easy plant to grow, but you must water copiously in dry weather.

VARIETIES: The best one to pick if you want a tall Foxglove is an **'Excelsior'** hybrid. The blooms are borne almost horizontally all round the flowering spike so that you can clearly see the maroon mottling inside each bell. Flower colours are white, yellow, pink, purple and red. **'Foxy'** is rather similar, but it only reaches 3 ft high and can be grown as a half hardy annual.

SITE & SOIL: The soil should be reasonably rich in humus and the site partially shaded.

PLANT DETAILS: Height 3-5 ft. Spacing 1½ ft. Flowering period June — August.

PROPAGATION: Follow the Biennial technique (page 83).

Digitalis purpurea 'Excelsior'

D. purpurea 'Foxy'

DIMORPHOTHECA   Star of the Veldt
HA

Dimorphotheca is distinctly fussy about its requirements. It needs a well-drained, light soil and as much sun as possible — put it in a shady spot and the flowers will refuse to open. Give it a good home in a rockery, window box or flower bed and the bright, Daisy-like flowers will provide sheets of colour in summer. The flowers are suitable for cutting; remove dead blooms to prolong the display.

VARIETIES: The garden varieties of Dimorphotheca are hybrids of **D. aurantiaca**. Around the dark central disc the petals may be white, yellow, orange or salmon-pink. The largest flowers are borne by **'Goliath'** and **'Orange Glory'** but the popular choice is the compact **'Dwarf Salmon'**. The shining white varieties are eye-catching — pick **'Glistening White'** or **'Pole Star'**.

SITE & SOIL: A well-drained sandy soil in full sun is necessary.

PLANT DETAILS: Height 1 ft. Spacing 9 in. Flowering period June — August.

PROPAGATION: Dislikes root disturbance. Sow seeds in April or May where they are to flower.

Dimorphotheca aurantiaca

D. aurantiaca 'Goliath'

ECHIUM   Annual Borage
HA

If your flower bed is in an open sunny situation and the soil drains freely then this plant is worth considering. It makes a welcome change from the popular range of low-growing annuals, and the flowers which look like upturned bells are fragrant and attractive to bees. The branching stems bear hairy narrow leaves and the long-lasting blooms are borne in dense heads.

VARIETIES: The garden varieties of **E. plantagineum** have been much improved in recent years. No longer need you keep to the original blue — rose, mauve and white are available. But the blue ones are perhaps the best, and **'Blue Bedder'** provides deep blue flowers throughout summer or autumn. For a mixture of colours choose **'Dwarf Hybrids'**.

SITE & SOIL: Any well-drained garden soil, but light or medium land is preferred. Choose a sunny spot.

PLANT DETAILS: Height 1 ft. Spacing 9 in. Flowering period June — October.

PROPAGATION: Sow seeds in August or April where they are to flower. Thin to required spacing.

Echium plantagineum 'Blue Bedder'

E. plantagineum 'Dwarf Hybrids'

ESCHSCHOLZIA Californian Poppy
(HA)

A drift of Californian Poppies in full flower is a colourful sight in summer, but it won't be if your soil is rich and the plants are in partial shade. The flowers are not long-lived but they continue to appear over a long period and the silky petals fluttering in the breeze are part of our garden scenery. After flowering the plants will produce self-sown seedlings — clear them away.

VARIETIES: **E. californica** produces golden yellow flowers in the wild, but there are now hybrids in many colours. For a rainbow mixture grow **'Art Shades'** (frilled petals, semi-double) or **'Ballerina'** (fluted petals, semi-double or double). Some people prefer single colours — choose **'Cherry Ripe'** (cerise), **'Orange King'** (orange) or the dwarf **'Miniature Primrose'** (yellow).

SITE & SOIL: A well-drained soil in full sun is necessary.

PLANT DETAILS: Height 6 in. -1½ ft. Spacing 6 in. Flowering period June–September.

PROPAGATION: Dislikes root disturbance. Sow seeds in September where they are to flower — April sowing is often recommended but is less satisfactory.

Eschscholzia californica

E. californica

GAILLARDIA Annual Gaillardia
(HHA)

The Annual Gaillardia or Blanket Flower is an excellent plant for cutting and garden display but it is not a popular choice. One reason is that there are several other annuals with yellow and red Daisy-like flowers, but the double Gaillardia is a novelty. It is also an untidy plant, but a few twigs will keep it in order. Remove dead blooms to ensure autumn flowering.

VARIETIES: The basic Annual Gaillardia is **G. pulchella** which bears large, yellow-edged red flowers. These blooms are single — a better plan is to choose one of the double-flowering hybrids. The ball-shaped blooms are very colourful and are available in a variety of plant heights. **G. pulchella lorenziana** grows 2 ft high — **'Lollipops'** is a 1 ft dwarf.

SITE & SOIL: Any well-drained garden soil will do — thrives in sun or light shade.

PLANT DETAILS: Height 1-2 ft. Spacing 9 in. -1½ ft. Flowering period June–September.

PROPAGATION: Follow the Half Hardy Annual technique (page 82) or sow outdoors in April in mild districts.

Gaillardia pulchella 'Beauty Mixed'

G. pulchella 'Lollipops'

GAZANIA Gazania
(HHA)

There is perhaps no showier flower than the Gazania for a sunny bed, border or rockery. The plants are low-growing with a tendency to sprawl, the leaves are silvery or grey below and the 3 in. Daisy-like flowers are available in a wide array of colours with contrasting zones. They are perennials but are easily damaged by frosts — it is better to treat them as half hardy annuals. The flowers close in the evening.

VARIETIES: Some nurserymen offer single colours such as **'Mini-Star Yellow'** or **'Red Hybrid'**. You are much more likely to be offered a multi-coloured seed mixture such as **'Harlequin'**, **'Treasure Chest'** or **'Sundance Mixed'**.

SITE & SOIL: Any well-drained garden soil will do — a sunny location is essential. All the Gazanias grow well in seaside areas.

PLANT DETAILS: Height 9-15 in. Spacing 1 ft. Flowering period June–October.

PROPAGATION: Follow the Half Hardy Annual technique (page 82). Plant out when the danger of frost is past.

Gazania 'Sundance Mixed'

G. 'Harlequin'

Godetia grandiflora 'Salmon Princess'

GODETIA   Godetia
HA

Godetias are one of the best loved of all hardy annuals; their gay colours and free-flowering habit have kept them favourites for many years. The funnel-shaped flowers crown the upright leafy spikes which are plentiful enough for both cutting and garden display. The tall varieties require staking and all Godetias need watering when the weather is dry.

VARIETIES: The garden varieties are hybrids of **G. grandiflora**, a native of California. For the middle of the border choose a mixture of tall doubles which grow about 2 ft high. Shorter and bushier are the popular '**Sybil Sherwood**' (pink, edged white) and '**Kelvedon Glory**' (salmon-orange). The Azalea-flowered varieties have wavy-edged double flowers and for the front of the border you can buy seeds of dwarf varieties.

SITE & SOIL: Any well-drained garden soil, but light or medium land is preferred. Choose a sunny spot.

PLANT DETAILS: Height 9 in. -2 ft. Spacing 9 in. -1 ft. Flowering period June – September.

PROPAGATION: Sow seeds in September or April where they are to flower. Thin to required spacing.

G. grandiflora 'Sybil Sherwood'

Flowers for Every Season

JUNE – JULY
(for JANUARY – MAY see page 17)
(for AUGUST – SEPTEMBER see page 35)
(for OCTOBER – DECEMBER see page 33)

The flowering period for nearly all annuals and biennials lies somewhere between the beginning of June and the end of October. However, by careful selection you can have flowers in the annual bed or border almost all year round. For each month there is a list of annuals and biennials which can be expected to be in full bloom — remember that some of these plants may come into flower earlier and can continue to bloom for many weeks afterwards.

JUNE

Ageratum	Heliotropium	Nemesia
Begonia	Iberis	Nemophila
Bellis	Impatiens	Nicotiana
Calendula	Lathyrus	Papaver
Campanula	Limnanthes	Petunia
Delphinium	Linaria	Phlox
Dianthus	Linum	Portulaca
Dimorphotheca	Lobelia	Salpiglossis
Echium	Malcolmia	Tagetes
Eschscholzia	Matricaria	Tropaeolum
Gaillardia	Matthiola	Viola
Godetia	Mimulus	Viscaria

JULY

Ageratum	Digitalis	Matricaria
Agrostemma	Dimorphotheca	Matthiola
Alyssum	Echium	Mimulus
Anchusa	Eschscholzia	Nemesia
Antirrhinum	Gaillardia	Nemophila
Bartonia	Gazania	Nicotiana
Begonia	Godetia	Papaver
Calceolaria	Gypsophila	Petunia
Calendula	Heliotropium	Phacelia
Centaurea	Iberis	Phlox
Chrysanthemum	Impatiens	Portulaca
Cobaea	Lathyrus	Salvia
Convolvulus	Lavatera	Tagetes
Coreopsis	Limnanthes	Tropaeolum
Dahlia	Linaria	Viola
Delphinium	Linum	Viscaria
Dianthus	Lobelia	Zinnia

Gypsophila elegans rosea

GYPSOPHILA   Baby's Breath
HA

Gypsophila is grown to provide material for flower arranging and to provide a welcome contrast to the colourful large blooms in the bed or border. Sprays of small, starry flowers appear above the small, grey-green leaves — the slender plants should be supported with small twiggy branches. Gypsophila thrives best when there is some lime or chalk in the soil.

VARIETIES: One species is grown — **G. elegans**. The white-flowered strains belong to **G. elegans alba**, and the most famous is '**Covent Garden**'. '**Monarch**' is rather smaller (15 in.) and colours other than white are available. Pick **G. elegans rosea** for shell pink flowers or you can buy a multi-coloured mixture — from this you will obtain white, pink, rose and crimson flowers.

SITE & SOIL: Any well-drained, non-acid soil will do — choose a sunny spot.

PLANT DETAILS: Height 1-1½ ft. Spacing 1 ft. Flowering period June – September.

PROPAGATION: Sow seeds in September or April where they are to flower. Thin to required spacing.

G. elegans alba 'Covent Garden'

HELIANTHUS   Sunflower
(HA)

The word 'Sunflower' conjures up a picture of a coarse giant of a plant with yellow plate-like flowers. These mammoths will be grown as long as children and competitions exist, but for general garden display there are these days more compact and attractive varieties. Sow two or three seeds at each planting position — thin to one. For maximum size feed the plants weekly with liquid fertilizer. Stake tall varieties.

VARIETIES: The Annual Sunflowers are varieties of **H. annuus** and you should always check the height in the catalogue or on the packet before buying. The giants, such as **'Russian Giant'** and **'Tall Single'** may reach more than 10 ft with flowers 1 ft across — the dwarf **'Sungold'** reaches only 2 ft with golden double flowers. Between the two is **'Autumn Beauty'** (5 ft) in mixed shades from lemon to dark red.

SITE & SOIL: Any reasonable garden soil in a sunny position will do.

PLANT DETAILS: Height 2–10 ft. Spacing 1–2½ ft. Flowering period July–September.

PROPAGATION: Sow seeds 1 in. deep in April where they are to flower.

Helianthus annuus 'Tall Single'

H. annuus

*H. annuus
'Autumn Beauty'*

HELICHRYSUM   Straw Flower
(HA)

Helichrysum is the most popular of the 'everlasting' flowers which look like double Daisies and bear strawy petals. It is popularly called the Straw Flower or Immortelle, and is prepared for indoor decoration by cutting just before the flowers are fully open. Tie the stems in bunches and hang upside down in a cool place away from sunlight.

VARIETIES: **H. bracteatum** is available as both dwarf and tall varieties in a bewildering array of colours. Amongst the dwarfs the glistening scarlet **'Hot Bikini'** (1 ft) has the brightest flowers. For a mixture of colours for bedding and cutting, choose **'Bright Bikini'**. Buy **'Monstrosum Double Mixed'** if you want large plants — the 2 in. flowers are borne on 3ft stems.

SITE & SOIL: Any well-drained garden soil will do — thrives best in full sun.

PLANT DETAILS: Height 1 or 3 ft. Spacing 1 ft. Flowering period July–September.

PROPAGATION: Sow seeds in April where they are to flower — thin to required spacing. In cold districts treat as a half hardy annual.

Helichrysum bracteatum 'Hot Bikini'

H. bracteatum

HELIOTROPIUM   Heliotrope
(HHA)

Once the Heliotrope or Cherry Pie was a popular summer plant, sharing a place in countless Victorian gardens alongside Fuchsias and Geraniums, but its day is now past. The problem is that each individual bloom is tiny, but the flower-heads are large and the fragrance is very strong. An excellent foil for showy yellow flowers such as Marigolds, but a poor choice for cold and exposed gardens.

VARIETIES: Hybrids of **H. peruvianum** are available in several colours — **'White Lady'** (white), **'Lord Roberts'** (dark blue), **'Vilmorin's Variety'** (purple) and so on. But the range in today's seed catalogue is strictly limited — the only common one is **'Marine'** (1½ ft, royal purple, dark foliage).

SITE & SOIL: Any well-drained garden soil will do — thrives best in full sun.

PLANT DETAILS: Height 1½ ft. Spacing 1 ft. Flowering period June–September.

PROPAGATION: Follow the Half Hardy Annual technique (page 82). Cuttings can be taken from greenhouse plants in spring.

Heliotropium peruvianum

H. 'Marine'

HIBISCUS   Flower of an Hour
(HA)

Unlike its indoor and outdoor perennial relatives, the annual species of Hibiscus is sadly neglected. The flowers have a brief life, a day at the most, but they appear freely and continually on the bushy plants for several months. The short-lived flowers are followed by bladder-like seed pods — an attractive and unusual plant. Keep watch for greenfly — spray if necessary.

VARIETIES: The Annual Hibiscus or Flower of an Hour is **H. trionum**. The flowers are 2 or 3 in. across, the white or pale pastel petals surrounding the central, chocolate brown eye. The leaves are long and toothed, and the modern strains bear flowers which last all day long and not just the brief period indicated by the common name.

SITE & SOIL: Any well-drained garden soil will do — thrives in sun or light shade.

PLANT DETAILS: Height 2 ft. Spacing 1 ft. Flowering period July–September.

PROPAGATION: Sow seeds in April where they are to flower. Thin to required spacing.

Hibiscus trionum

H. trionum

IBERIS   Candytuft
(HA)

Candytuft is one of the most tolerant of all annuals — it thrives in poor soil, smokey air and when sown by tiny fingers. Massed in the front of the border or used as an edging along a pathway, this spreading, quick-growing plant produces clusters of fragrant white, pink or red flowers. The blooms may be numerous enough to completely cover the lance-shaped leaves — dead-head regularly.

VARIETIES: Nearly all types are varieties of **I. umbellata**. You can choose an Annual Candytuft which produces flowers of a single colour — one of the brightest is **'Red Flash'** (1 ft, carmine), but it is more usual to sow **'Fairy Mixture'** (9 in., mixed). For something quite different pick **'Giant Hyacinth-flowered'** (15 in., spikes of white Hyacinth-shaped flowers).

SITE & SOIL: Any well-drained garden soil will do — thrives best in full sun.

PLANT DETAILS: Height 9 in.–1½ ft. Spacing 9 in. Flowering period May–August.

PROPAGATION: Sow seeds in September or March where they are to flower. Thin to required spacing.

Iberis umbellata 'Fairy Mixture'

I. umbellata

IMPATIENS   Busy Lizzie
(HHA)

It is a pity that many gardeners still regard Busy Lizzie solely as a house plant and ignore it as an outdoor plant. The modern F1 hybrids provide low-growing sheets of bright colour in damp and shady places which only the Bedding Begonia can rival amongst the annuals in such a situation. A fine choice for beds, pots and window boxes — the plants can be lifted and kept indoors during winter.

VARIETIES: The **'Imp'** and **'Elfin'** strains grow about 9 in. high, producing large flowers in white, pink, red, orange, mauve and other colours. For edging or the front of the border grow **'Florette'** (6 in.) — in window boxes plant the semi-pendulous **'Futura'**. **'Grand Prix'** bears the largest flowers and the striped blooms of **'Zig-Zag'** are the most eye-catching.

SITE & SOIL: Any well-drained soil will do — thrives in sun or partial shade. Add peat or compost before planting.

PLANT DETAILS: Height 6 in.–1 ft. Spacing 6–9 in. Flowering period June–October.

PROPAGATION: Follow the Half Hardy Annual technique (page 82). Usually bought as bedding plants — do not plant out until early June.

Impatiens 'Imp'

I. 'Grand Prix'

Ipomoea tricolor

IPOMOEA   Morning Glory
(HHA)

The catalogues are correct — Ipomoea is one of our loveliest garden climbers. The wiry stems twine around upright supports — the heart-shaped leaves and large trumpet-like flowers are often seen adorning trellises and pergolas in summer. But the foliage is not plentiful and so Morning Glory does not make an effective screen for hiding an unsightly view. The flowers last for merely a day but they are borne in quick succession.

VARIETIES: I. tricolor (I. rubro-caerulea) bears the largest flowers. This vine will grow 8 ft or more and the blooms are 3–5 in. across **'Heavenly Blue'** is a popular variety — **'Flying Saucers'** is a blue and white striped hybrid. **I. purpurea (Convolvulus major)** may exceed 10 ft — **'Scarlett O'Hara'** is a red hybrid.

SITE & SOIL: Any well-drained garden soil will do, but the site chosen must be sunny and sheltered.

PLANT DETAILS: Height 6–12 ft. Spacing 1½ ft. Flowering period July–September.

PROPAGATION: Follow the Half Hardy Annual technique (page 82). Soak the seeds for 24 hours before sowing into individual pots.

I. 'Heavenly Blue'

Lathyrus odoratus 'Spencer Mixed'

LATHYRUS   Sweet Pea
(HA)

The original Sweet Pea (L. odoratus) came to Britain from Sicily in 1699, but it was not until the Victorian era that the tall garden varieties in a multitude of colours appeared. The range of colours and heights has continued to increase, but some of the old-fashioned fragrance has been lost. The Sweet Pea is an easy plant to grow, producing several dainty flowers on each stem and armfuls of blooms for indoors. There are a few points to remember — prepare the site properly, soak black-seeded varieties overnight before sowing, pinch out the tops when the plants are about 4 in. high, provide support for the tendrils and water thoroughly in dry weather. Regularly remove dead blooms.

VARIETIES: For tall plants and large flowers choose *Spencer* varieties. If you are growing for exhibition, use the cordon method — train a single stem up each cane and remove all unnecessary growth such as tendrils and side-shoots. For garden display choose a highly fragrant variety and grow the plants over a wigwam of canes or against a frame of trellis or plastic netting. First class Spencer varieties include **'Air Warden'** (orange-scarlet), **'Winston Churchill'** (crimson), **'Leamington'** (lavender), **'White Ensign'** (white) and **'Mrs R. Bolton'** (pink). The *Hedge* varieties such as **'Knee-hi'** and **'Jet Set'** are much more compact, growing about 3 ft high and needing little support. The 1 ft high *Dwarf* varieties need no support at all — look for the name **'Bijou'**, **'Snoopea'**, **'Patio'** or **'Little Sweethearts'** on the packet.

SITE & SOIL: Any well-drained garden soil — choose a sunny, open position. For exhibition blooms, deep digging and the incorporation of bulky organic matter are essential.

PLANT DETAILS: Height 1–8 ft. Spacing 6 in.–1 ft. Flowering period June–October.

PROPAGATION: Sow in pots in October and overwinter in a cold frame — plant out in March or April. Alternatively sow outdoors in March or April.

Lathyrus odoratus 'Jet Set Vienna'

L. odoratus 'Leamington'   L. odoratus 'Knee-hi'

Lathyrus odoratus 'Bijou'

LAVATERA
Annual Mallow
(HA)

If you are looking for a bushy plant to provide a temporary hedge or a back-of-the-border specimen covered in bloom during the summer months, the Annual Mallow is a satisfactory answer. The trumpet-shaped flowers are 3 or 4 in. across, large enough to catch attention in the garden and long-lasting enough to serve as excellent cut flowers. The bushes need plenty of space and self-sown seedlings should be removed.

VARIETIES: **L. trimestris** has produced several excellent garden varieties which grow 3–4 ft tall and produce pink flowers — **'Loveliness'** and **'Tanagra'** are popular. The compact varieties grow about 2 ft high and do not require staking — **'Mont Blanc'** bears white flowers and the new **'Silver Cup'** has the brightest of all Mallow blooms.

SITE & SOIL: Any reasonable garden soil will do — thrives in sun or light shade.

PLANT DETAILS: Height 2–4 ft. Spacing 2 ft. Flowering period July–September.

PROPAGATION: Sow seeds in September or March where they are to flower. Thin to required spacing.

Lavatera trimestris 'Loveliness'

L. trimestris 'Silver Cup'

LIMNANTHES
Poached Egg Flower
(HA)

There are several reasons for choosing Limnanthes as an edging plant for the front of the border. It is unusual — a welcome change from the universally-popular Alyssum and Lobelia. It is also very colourful with its two-toned flowers and it is highly attractive to bees. The ferny foliage is pale green and the low-growing, spreading plants make excellent rockery specimens.

VARIETIES: You will only find one type of Limnanthes in the seed catalogues — **L. douglasii**, which came to Britain from California. The yellow petals have a distinct white edge — hence the common name. It is easy to grow and has a long flowering season. The fragrance is sweet but not strong and the blooms are plentiful when grown in a sunny spot.

SITE & SOIL: Any reasonable garden soil will do — thrives best in full sun.

PLANT DETAILS: Height 6 in. Spacing 4 in. Flowering period June–September.

PROPAGATION: Sow seeds in March where they are to flower. September sowing will provide plants which bloom in late spring.

Limnanthes douglasii

L. douglasii

LIMONIUM
Statice
(HHA)

The latin name is Limonium, but to the gardener it is Statice or Sea Lavender. The popular species (L. sinuatum or Statice sinuata) belongs to the 'everlasting' group and is widely grown for indoor decoration. To dry Statice, cut just before the flowers are fully open and tie the stems in bunches. Hang upside down in a cool place away from sunlight.

VARIETIES: The usual practice is to buy a **L. sinuatum Mixture** — the winged stems bear clusters of tiny, papery-petalled flowers in many colours — white, pink, blue, yellow, orange, etc. There are several single-colour varieties available — **'Gold Coast'** (yellow), **'Rose Light'** (pink) and **'Midnight Blue'** (dark blue). An excellent choice for cutting but not for drying is **L. suworowii** — tall, thin spikes clothed in tiny, pink flowers.

SITE & SOIL: Any well-drained garden soil, but light or medium land is preferred. Choose a sunny spot.

PLANT DETAILS: Height 1–2 ft. Spacing 1 ft. Flowering period July–September.

PROPAGATION: Follow the Half Hardy Annual technique (page 82). Plant out when the danger of frost is past.

Limonium sinuatum

L. sinuatum 'Rose Light'

LINARIA Toadflax
(HA)

The way to grow Toadflax is to sow it in small groups in autumn or spring at the front of the border or in the rockery. It is a good plant for children — if the seeds are sown very sparsely then no thinning is required and the compact, bushy plants bear small snapdragons in a wide variety of colours. Trim off the dead flowers once the first flush has faded.

VARIETIES: The varieties of **L. maroccana** are generally low-growing, reaching 1 ft or less. The type which is usually offered is **'Fairy Bouquet'** (½ in. flowers in many colours on 9 in. plants). **'Fairy Lights'** is a similar variety. **L. reticulata** is a much taller plant with larger flowers, but the popular garden variety **'Crimson and Gold'** grows only 1 ft high.

SITE & SOIL: Any well-drained garden soil will do — thrives in sun or light shade.

PLANT DETAILS: Height 9 in. – 1½ ft. Spacing 6 in. Flowering period June – September.

PROPAGATION: Sow seeds in September or April where they are to flower. Thin, if necessary, to required spacing.

Linaria reticulata 'Crimson and Gold'

L. maroccana 'Fairy Bouquet'

Bedding Out

Modern beds have simple outlines — rectangular, oval, circular or informal. Stars and complex outlines are now out of date. Before planting make sure that the ground is weed-free, and rake the earth so that a mound is formed at the centre of the bed. It is necessary to prevent the soil from washing on to the surrounding lawn or pathway — dig a shallow trench at the edge of the bed. You will see examples of the four major types of bedding schemes everywhere, but the carpet bedding scheme beloved by the Victorians has virtually disappeared. Its last stronghold is the floral clock in seaside towns — low-growing foliage plants in many shades, planted so closely together that no earth can be seen.

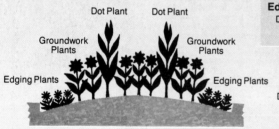

Dot Plant Dot Plant

Groundwork Plants Groundwork Plants

Edging Plants Edging Plants

Edging Plants	Groundwork Plants	Dot Plants
Dwarf plants, up to 8 in.	Medium-height plants, 8 in. – 2 ft	Tall plants, with showy leaves or flowers
Examples:	*Examples:*	*Examples:*
Ageratum	Zinnia	Standard Fuchsia
Alyssum	Petunia	Canna
Lobelia	Bedding Begonia	Kochia (foliage)
Dwarf Phlox	Bedding Dahlia	Indian Corn (foliage)
Viola	Salvia	Abutilon (foliage)
Tagetes	Bedding Geranium	Amaranthus
Verbena	Antirrhinum	Ricinus (foliage)

SINGLE VARIETY BEDDING SCHEME

A single variety such as Begonia semperflorens 'Organdy', Pelargonium 'Paul Crampel' or Petunia hybrida 'Bouquet' is used. Such schemes have been criticised on the grounds of monotony, but the *bedded meadow* effect of a large irregular area treated this way can be spectacular. Increasingly popular in some Continental countries and perhaps the first real breakaway from the Victorian-based schemes.

SINGLE GENUS BEDDING SCHEME

Species or varieties of different size, colour and flower form can be chosen to show the full range of a genus. The introduction of dwarf varieties of several popular annuals has increased the number of plants which lend themselves to this treatment. Sweet Peas, Petunias, Antirrhinums, Begonias, Geraniums and Asters are all excellent examples. A good bedding scheme for the specialist gardener — the Dahlia enthusiast would treat his plants no other way.

STANDARD GARDEN BEDDING SCHEME

Most of the bed is filled with groups or lines of Groundwork Plants — most annuals and biennials belong in this section. Around these specimens are set the low-growing Edging Plants. Styles and species have changed little during the past hundred years, apart from the fall from grace of the once-popular Heliotrope and Calceolaria, but the varieties used have changed greatly.

STANDARD PARK BEDDING SCHEME

The standby of the professional gardener, differing from the Standard Garden scheme by the inclusion of Dot Plants. These tall and colourful bedding plants grow as showy specimens above the Groundwork Plants. They provide focal points — the secret of the attractive park display. Many Dot Plants are rather exotic, such as the variegated Abutilon, decorative Indian Corn and purple-leaved Canna. For something more down to earth plant a small group of tall Antirrhinums or Larkspurs.

Linum grandiflorum 'Rubrum'

LINUM Flax
HA

Linum looks gaunt and spindly as a single plant, but a large group provides an impressive sight in summer. The 2 in. flowers are borne in clusters, fluttering in the breeze above the narrow leaves. Provided there is adequate sunshine each plant will bear a remarkable number of flowers throughout the summer, but they are for garden display only with little value as cut flowers.

VARIETIES: Wild Flax is rarely grown — **L. grandiflorum** provides the garden varieties. The outstanding choice is **L. grandiflorum 'Rubrum'**, the Scarlet Flax. The petals are vivid red and possess a satin-like sheen. There are other colours **'Album'** (white), **'Roseum'** (pink) and **'Blue Flax'** (bright blue).

SITE & SOIL: Any well-drained garden soil will do — thrives best in full sun.

PLANT DETAILS: Height 9 in. –1½ ft. Spacing 6–9 in. Flowering period June–August.

PROPAGATION: Dislikes root disturbance. Sow seeds in September or April where they are to flower. Thin to required spacing.

L. grandiflorum 'Rubrum'

LOBELIA Lobelia
HHA

Lobelia shares the top spot with Alyssum as Britain's favourite edging plant, yet it is more demanding than many less-well-known annuals. To provide an impressive and long-lasting show of flowers it needs humus-enriched soil, occasional feeding and a thorough soaking when the weather is dry. To induce bushiness pinch out the tops when the seedlings are 1 in. high, and transplant as small groups rather than singly.

VARIETIES: You will see the Edging Lobelia (**L. erinus**) everywhere, and the ever-popular deep blue one with a white eye is **'Mrs Clibran Improved'**. Try a different colour for a change — **'Rosamund'** (red), **'White Gem'** (white), **'Cambridge Blue'** (light blue) or **'String of Pearls'** (mixed). In hanging baskets grow the Trailing Lobelia (**L. erinus pendula**) — **'Sapphire'** (deep blue) is a good choice and so is **'Cascade Mixed'**.

SITE & SOIL: Any reasonable garden soil will do, but rich and moist land is preferred. Thrives in sun or light shade.

PLANT DETAILS: Height 4–8 in. Spacing 6 in. Flowering period June–September.

PROPAGATION: Follow the Half Hardy Annual technique (page 82). Plant out when the danger of frost is past.

Lobelia erinus 'Cambridge Blue'

L. erinus 'Mrs Clibran Improved'

LUNARIA Honesty
HB

In late spring and early summer the small flowers appear above the toothed leaves. Purple is the usual colour, but there are varieties with rose or white flowers and the plants are pretty without being particularly noticeable. Honesty earns its place in the garden by producing flat seed pods which look like pearly discs. Cut in August and dry indoors to make a popular component for winter flower arrangements.

VARIETIES: **L. annua** has produced several garden varieties. **'Munstead Purple'** bears fragrant purple flowers and the blooms on **'Alba'** are white. The most unusual form is **'Variegata'**, which has green and cream variegated leaves and rosy purple flowers. All varieties of Lunaria bear 4-petalled flowers in branching sprays — remember not to dead-head if you want to collect the seed pods!

SITE & SOIL: Any well-drained garden soil will do — thrives best in partial shade.

PLANT DETAILS: Height 2–3 ft. Spacing 1 ft. Flowering period April–June.

PROPAGATION: Sow seeds in May or June — follow the Biennial technique (page 83).

Lunaria annua 'Alba'

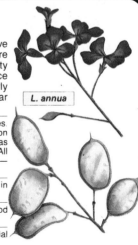
L. annua

Malcolmia maritima

MALCOLMIA
Virginia Stock
(HA)

Poor little Virginia Stock! Many of today's gardeners ventured into horticulture with a packet of radish seed in one hand and Virginia Stock in the other, but many of the textbooks don't even bother to mention it. The cause of this contempt is the ease with which it can be grown. A thin scattering of seeds anywhere — town gardens, semi-shady spots, cracks between paving stones and so on, and a month or two later the plants are in flower.

VARIETIES: M. maritima is usually bought as a packet of mixed seed. It is not usually necessary to thin the seedlings and the slender stems soon bear gay little flowers — white, mauve, pink, red, blue and occasionally yellow. Single-coloured varieties, such as **'Crimson King'**, are available.

SITE & SOIL: Any reasonable garden soil will do, in sun or partial shade.

PLANT DETAILS: Height 6–9 in. Spacing (if necessary) 4 in. Flowering period — In bloom for several weeks 1–2 months after sowing.

PROPAGATION: Sow seeds in spring for summer flowering, summer for late summer flowering or in autumn for blooming in the spring.

M. maritima

Malope trifida grandiflora

MALOPE
Malope
(HA)

Malope is similar to the Annual Mallow (Lavatera trimestris). Both form 3 ft high bushes bearing trumpet-like flowers, 3 or 4 in. across, during the summer months. The Malope colour range is wider, however, and the experts say that Malope is less likely to fail. Blooms are borne abundantly and the plants do not require staking.

VARIETIES: Malope is sold either as **M. trifida** or the large-flowering strain **M. trifida grandiflora**. A good mixture will produce plants bearing white, pink, crimson and purple flowers — a feature of Malope is the prominent veining which occasionally occurs on the petals. The flowers are carried on long, firm stems and are excellent for cutting.

SITE & SOIL: Any well-drained garden soil, but light or medium land is preferred. Choose a sunny spot.

PLANT DETAILS: Height 3 ft. Spacing 15 in. Flowering period July–October.

PROPAGATION: Sow seeds in April where they are to flower. Thin to the required spacing.

M. trifida grandiflora

Matricaria eximia 'Snow Ball'

MATRICARIA
Feverfew
(HHA)

Feverfew may be listed as Matricaria eximia or Chrysanthemum parthenium in the seed catalogues. The compact plant, barely 1 ft high, with its mass of small, cushion-like flowers looks like a miniature Chrysanthemum. The foliage is pungent and the ¾ in. flowers are intensely double. They may be ball-like or there may be an outer ring of short petals. Try it as an unusual summer bedding plant..

VARIETIES: The colour range of Matricaria is distinctly limited — there is just yellow and white. For button-like flowers without an outer ring of guard petals, choose **'Golden Ball'** (yellow) or **'Ball's Double White'** (white). A variation is a cushion-like flower with a frill of short, broad petals — look for **'Snow Puffs'**, **'White Stars'** and **'Snow Ball'**.

SITE & SOIL: Any well-drained garden soil will do — thrives best in full sun.

PLANT DETAILS: Height 8 in.–1 ft. Spacing 1 ft. Flowering period June–August.

PROPAGATION: Follow the Half Hardy Annual technique (page 82).

M. eximia 'Golden Ball'

M. eximia 'Ball's Double White'

MATTHIOLA

Stocks
(HA), (HHA) or (HB)

For hundreds of years Stocks have been a popular feature of beds, borders and cottage gardens. Their soft grey-green foliage and densely-clustered flowering spikes are known to everyone, and the fragrance which hangs in the air around them makes them a delight in any garden. Despite all this popularity they are quite complex — a fair degree of skill is needed to raise them successfully from seed and their classification often leads to confusion.

VARIETIES: There are 4 basic groups. The first one is the *Ten Week Stock* group with **M. incana** as a parent. These plants are treated as half hardy annuals, sown in the spring under glass and then bedded out to flower in the summer about 10 weeks later. Their standard height is 1½ ft, but there are variations ranging from the **Dwarf Ten Week Stock** (1 ft) to the **'Excelsior'** and **'Mammoth'** strains which reach 2½ ft. The earliest to flower is the **'Trysomic Seven Week'**. The second large group consists of the *Brompton Stocks*, grown as biennials by sowing in summer for flowering in the following spring. There is a small third group, the *East Lothian Stock* which can be grown as either a half hardy annual or a biennial, and there is a fourth group which is quite different from the others. This is the *Night-scented Stock* **(M. bicornis)**. It is a hardy annual, sown in spring where it is to flower, and the 1 ft plants bear insignificant flowers which close during the day. But at night . . . ah, that delicious fragrance!

SITE & SOIL: Any well-drained garden soil which is not acid will do — thrives in sun or light shade.

PLANT DETAILS: Height 1–2½ ft. Spacing 9 in.–1 ft. Flowering period June–August (Ten Week Stock Group) or March–May (Brompton Stock Group).

PROPAGATION: Follow the Hardy Annual, Half Hardy Annual or Biennial technique, depending on the variety chosen — see above. If you want double flowers, buy a 'Selectable Variety'. The seedlings with dark green leaves will produce single flowers — discard them at pricking-out time. Seedlings are susceptible to disease — do not overwater and handle by the leaves and not the stem.

Matthiola incana 'Ten Week Stock'

Matthiola incana 'Brompton Stock'

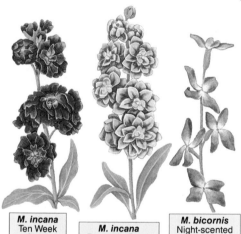

M. incana
Ten Week
Stock

M. incana
Brompton Stock

M. bicornis
Night-scented
Stock

Matthiola incana 'East Lothian Stock'

MESEMBRYANTHEMUM

Livingstone Daisy
(HHA)

In heavy soil, a shady site or a dull summer, the Livingstone Daisy will not be worth the space it occupies. The large Daisy-like flowers of this South African plant open only when the sun is shining and when grown on a shade-free sandy bank it is a strong contender for the Brightest Annual title. The prostrate spreading stems bear glistening succulent leaves and flowers in an astonishing array of gay colours.

VARIETIES: M. criniflorum is the species sold as Livingstone Daisy and it is available as a mixture of bright shades including white, pink, red, orange, yellow and bi-colours. **M. tricolor** bears red and pink flowers but if you want to try something different then grow **M. 'Lunette'**. The yellow petals surround a prominent red disc.

SITE & SOIL: The soil should be well-drained and sandy, and the site must be in full sun.

PLANT DETAILS: Height 4–6 in. Spacing 8 in. Flowering period July–September.

PROPAGATION: Follow the Half Hardy Annual technique (page 82). Plant out when the danger of frost is past.

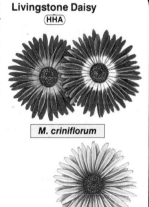

M. criniflorum

M. 'Lunette'

Mesembryanthemum criniflorum

Mimulus 'Royal Velvet'

MIMULUS Monkey Flower
(HHA)

The Monkey Flower, so-called because of an alleged resemblance of the open bloom to the face of a grinning monkey, is a short-lived perennial which is usually grown as a half hardy annual. The plants are low growing and have a special place in the garden — they flourish in damp soil and shady sites where few other annuals can thrive. Use Mimulus for summer bedding in sunless places and in window boxes on the north-facing side of the house.

VARIETIES: The varieties of **M. cupreus** bear trumpet-shaped flowers in orange or red — **'Red Emperor'** (flame-scarlet) is a popular type. **M. luteus** is more colourful, with yellow flowers which are marked with red or purple blotches. The varieties and hybrids of **M. variegatus** are rather similar but are larger — up to 2 in. across. You will find **'Queen's Prize'** and **'Royal Velvet'** in the catalogues.

SITE & SOIL: A moist soil which is not allowed to dry out is essential — some shade is desirable.

PLANT DETAILS: Height 9 in. Spacing 9 in. Flowering period June – September.

PROPAGATION: Follow the Half Hardy Annual technique (page 82). Plant out when the danger of frost is past.

M. variegatus

Molucella laevis

MOLUCELLA Bells of Ireland
(HHA)

A plant which is interesting rather than beautiful and which came to us from Syria and not Ireland, despite its common name. Each flower is white and insignificant but is surrounded by a large, green and bell-like calyx. These floral bells are borne on graceful stems, somewhat colourless in the garden, perhaps, but a joy for the flower arranger.

VARIETIES: There is a single species, **M. laevis**, which is sometimes listed as the Shell Flower. If you want to use it for indoor decoration, cut the stems when the bells are fully open and dry the stems in a cool and airy place away from direct sunlight. These 'everlasting' flowers are most useful for winter flower arrangements.

SITE & SOIL: Any well-drained garden soil will do — thrives in sun or light shade.

PLANT DETAILS: Height 2 ft. Spacing 1½ ft. Flowering period August – September.

PROPAGATION: Follow the Half Hardy Annual technique (page 82). Alternatively in mild areas sow seeds outdoors in April.

M. laevis

Myosotis alpestris 'Blue Ball'

MYOSOTIS Forget-me-not
(HB)

Walk along your street in springtime and you will find Tulips and Wallflowers . . . and Forget-me-nots beneath them. For many of us this blue carpet or edging is indispensable in April, but you can grow a white or pink variety for a change. All of them bear dense clusters of small flowers and are easy to grow. The only requirements are well-drained soil and a watering can if the weather is dry.

VARIETIES: Nearly all garden Forget-me-nots are varieties or hybrids of **M. alpestris**. For traditional blue edging or planting under bulbs choose a compact variety such as **'Ultramarine'** (deep blue) or **'Blue Ball'** (indigo blue). For pink edging grow **'Rose Pink'** or **'Carmine King'**. The tall Forget-me-nots can be grown in a bed of their own — choose from **'Royal Blue'** (bright blue), **'Blue Bouquet'** (deep blue) and **M. sylvatica 'Blue Bird'**.

SITE & SOIL: Any well-drained garden soil will do — thrives best in light shade.

PLANT DETAILS: Height 6 in. – 1 ft. Spacing 8 in. Flowering period April – May.

PROPAGATION: Sow seeds in May or June — follow the Biennial technique (page 83).

M. alpestris

NEMESIA   Nemesia (HHA)

A favourite for three reasons — it is easy to grow, flowers quickly after bedding out and bears blooms which are multicoloured. Grow it in containers and window boxes as well as in beds and borders — any sunny corner can be brightened by these foot-high plants with their clusters of funnel-shaped flowers. Pinch out the tips of seedlings to induce bushiness and water in dry weather. Cut back once the first flush of flowering is over.

VARIETIES: N. strumosa has given rise to many garden varieties and hybrids. You can buy single colours, such as **'Blue Gem'** and **'Fire King'**, but most people buy a mixture. **'Carnival'** and **'Funfair'** are assortments of reds, creams and yellows — **'Sparklers'** is a mixture which contains many bi- and tri-colours.

SITE & SOIL: Any reasonable garden soil will do — thrives best in sun or light shade and lime-free land.

PLANT DETAILS: Height 9 in.–1½ ft. Spacing 6 in. Flowering period June–September.

PROPAGATION: Follow the Half Hardy Annual technique (page 82). Alternatively in mild areas sow seeds outdoors in April.

Nemesia strumosa 'Carnival'

N. strumosa

NEMOPHILA   Baby Blue Eyes (HA)

Nemophila is a low-growing carpeting plant which will flourish at the edge of the border or in the rockery if the conditions are moist and cool. The leaves are feathery and the flowers are shaped like large buttercups. Dryness around its roots is the enemy — dig in organic matter before sowing and water copiously in dry weather. A pretty garden plant but a poor cut flower — the blooms soon fade in water.

VARIETIES: N. menziesii is sometimes listed as **N. insignis** or under its common name of Baby Blue Eyes or Californian Bluebell. The flowers are 1–1½ in. across and the sky blue petals have a prominent white centre. If you search the catalogues you will find one of the more unusual varieties listed — all-white or white with a blue centre.

SITE & SOIL: Any reasonable garden soil will do, but moisture-retaining land is preferred. Thrives in sun or light shade.

PLANT DETAILS: Height 6 in. Spacing 6 in. Flowering period June–September.

PROPAGATION: Dislikes root disturbance. Sow seeds in September or April where they are to flower. Thin to required spacing.

Nemophila menziesii

N. menziesii

NICOTIANA   Tobacco Plant (HHA)

Nicotiana alata (also called N. affinis) has been grown as a garden flower by generations of gardeners who have valued its intense evening fragrance. In the old days it was not particularly decorative — the tall stems needed staking and the flowers closed during the day, but nowadays there are dwarf varieties and with many modern hybrids the long trumpet-like blooms stay open during the daylight hours. Dead-head spent blooms regularly.

VARIETIES: You can still buy **N. alata** with its tall stems, white flowers and evening fragrance. It is a much better plan, however, to buy a more compact variety which opens during the day. There is **'Crimson Rock'** (2 ft), **'Dwarf White Bedder'** (1½ ft) and **'Red Devil'** (1½ ft). Good mixtures include **'Sensation'** (3 ft), **'Nicki Mixed'** (1 ft) and **'Tinkerbelle'** (9 in.). The yellowish **'Lime Green'** is popular.

SITE & SOIL: Any well-drained garden soil will do — thrives in sun or light shade.

PLANT DETAILS: Height 9 in.–3 ft. Spacing 9 in.–1 ft. Flowering period June–October.

PROPAGATION: Follow the Half Hardy Annual technique (page 82). Plant out when the danger of frost is past.

Nicotiana alata 'Sensation'

N. 'Lime Green'

NIGELLA

Love-in-a-mist
(HA)

Love-in-a-mist aptly describes the misty blue flowers which lie half-hidden within the finely-cut foliage. It has been grown in our gardens since Elizabethan times, although nowadays we can grow multicoloured mixtures as well as the traditional cornflower blue. Nigella is easily grown, but for fine bushy plants you should dig compost into the soil before sowing. The dried seed-heads are widely used by flower arrangers.

VARIETIES: The popular species is **N. damascena** and the usual choice is **'Miss Jekyll'** (cornflower blue). Try the pale pink **'Persian Rose'** but **'Persian Jewels'** is the variety which is gaining in popularity — the flowers are pink, blue, mauve and white. There is a dwarf (**'Dwarf Moody Blue'**) which grows 6 in. high and a grey-leaved species — **N. hispanica** (blue flowers, red stamens).

SITE & SOIL: Any well-drained garden soil will do — thrives in sun or light shade.

PLANT DETAILS: Height 1½ ft. Spacing 9 in. Flowering period July – September.

PROPAGATION: Sow seeds in autumn or early spring where they are to flower. Thin to required spacing.

N. damascena 'Miss Jekyll'

Nigella damascena 'Persian Jewels'

PAPAVER

Poppy
(HA) or (HB)

The Poppy is a flower of nostalgia — a reminder of lost childhood and the fallen dead. The buds bow their heads and the delicate petals are short-lived, but modern garden varieties are so gaily coloured that the sad symbolism is lost. The flowers are borne on long stalks — the single varieties are cup-shaped with four wide overlapping petals; the double forms are ball-like with many petals. All Poppies have a dainty appearance but do not need staking. Removing dead blooms, however, is necessary in order to prolong the flowering season.

VARIETIES: The most popular annual Poppies are descended from **P. rhoeas**, the Corn Poppy which grows wild in the countryside. From this wild flower Rev. Wilks evolved the **'Shirley Poppy'** which grows about 2 ft high and is available in both single and double forms. The usual colours are pink, white and red. A rather similar annual is **P. commutatum 'Ladybird'** (1½ ft) which bears black-hearted crimson petals. The showy annual is **P. somniferum**, the Opium Poppy — choose the **'Paeony-flowered Mixture'** for its double blooms. Some Poppies are treated as biennials, sowing in summer and thinning the following spring. **P. nudicaule** (Iceland Poppy) is the favourite one — the tissue-paper petals have the widest colour range of all and they are excellent for cutting if you gather them when the flowers are in bud and sear the cut ends with a match. Typical varieties are **'Champagne Bubbles'**, **'San Remo'** and **'Kelmscott'**. The small **P. alpinum** or Alpine Poppy is also treated as a biennial. White, yellow or orange flowers are borne on hairless stems.

SITE & SOIL: Any reasonable garden soil will do — thrives in sun or light shade.

PLANT DETAILS: Height 6 in. – 3 ft. Spacing 9 in. – 1 ft. Flowering period May – August (P. rhoeas, P. nudicaule and P. alpinum), July – September (P. somniferum).

PROPAGATION: All Poppies dislike being transplanted. With annual varieties sow seeds in April where they are to flower. With biennials sow seeds in August — thin to required spacing in March or April.

Papaver rhoeas 'Shirley Mixed'

P. commutatum 'Ladybird'

P. alpinum

P. rhoeas 'Shirley Poppy'

P. somniferum 'Paeony-flowered Mixture'

P. nudicaule 'Champagne Bubbles'

Papaver nudicaule

PETUNIA

Petunia
(HHA)

P. hybrida
Multiflora

P. hybrida
Grandiflora

Varieties of Petunias get bigger and brighter and bolder. The modern hybrids bear showy, funnel-shaped flowers on top of the sticky stems, a dazzling sight when the sun is shining but a sorry one in prolonged wet weather. An excellent bedding plant, of course, but also very useful for window boxes, containers and hanging baskets. Cut back the stems if they become too straggly — dead-head regularly.

VARIETIES: Buy an F1 hybrid of **P. hybrida** for bedding — there are four groups. The *Multifloras* bear large numbers of 2 in. flowers — **'Resisto'** stands up well to wind and rain. Many colours are available — **'Apple Blossom'**, **'Red Satin'**, **'Starfire'** (red and white stripes), etc. The *Double Multifloras* also bear 2 in. flowers but they have many petals and look like Carnations — **'Cherry Tart'** (rose and white) is a good example. The *Grandifloras* have fewer flowers but the blooms are larger, 3–4 in. across, and they are more susceptible to rain damage. **'Cascade'** is the popular mixture, but there are many single and bi-colour varieties — **'Blue Frost'**, **'Red Cloud'** and the blue-and-white striped **'Telstar'**. The *Double Grandifloras* are the showiest group of all — huge, ruffled blooms in a wide range of colours. Look for **'Bouquet'**, **'Pan American Double'** and **'White Swan'**.

SITE & SOIL: Any reasonable garden soil will do — choose a sunny site.

PLANT DETAILS: Height 6 in.–1½ ft. Spacing 6in.–1 ft. Flowering period June–October.

PROPAGATION: Follow the Half Hardy Annual technique (page 82). Plant out when the danger of frost is past.

P. hybrida
Double
Multiflora

P. hybrida
Double
Grandiflora

Petunia hybrida 'Resisto Rose'

Flowers for Every Season

OCTOBER–DECEMBER
(for JANUARY–MAY see page 17)   (for JUNE–JULY see page 21)
(for AUGUST–SEPTEMBER see page 35)

The flowering period for nearly all annuals and biennials lies somewhere between the beginning of June and the end of October. However, by careful selection you can have flowers in the annual bed or border almost all year round. For each month there is a list of annuals and biennials which can be expected to be in full bloom — remember that some of these plants may come into flower earlier and can continue to bloom for many weeks afterwards.

OCTOBER

Ageratum	Cosmos	Rudbeckia
Amaranthus	Dahlia	Salvia
Antirrhinum	Dianthus	Scabiosa
Calceolaria	Gazania	Tagetes
Calendula	Impatiens	Thunbergia
Callistephus	Lathyrus	Tropaeolum
Clarkia	Nicotiana	Viola
Cobaea	Petunia	Zinnia

NOVEMBER
Viola

DECEMBER
Viola

PHACELIA

Phacelia
(HA)

Most plants have at least one characteristic which sets them apart from the specimens which surround them — with Phacelia it is the intense blue colour of its flowers. The 1 in. upturned bells appear in midsummer above the greyish foliage, the bright yellow stamens clearly standing out against the gentian-coloured petals. Plant Phacelia as an edging or in the rockery.

VARIETIES: The favourite type is **P. campanularia** which grows about 9 in. high. There is a taller hybrid (**P. 'Blue Bonnet'**) which grows twice as tall and has the same bright blue flowers. Other species of Phacelia are available (**P. viscida**, **P. tanacetifolia**) but these tall types have lost the true blue effect.

SITE & SOIL: Any well-drained garden soil, but light land is preferred. Thrives in sun or light shade.

PLANT DETAILS: Height 9 in.–2 ft. Spacing 6 in.–1 ft. Flowering period June–September.

PROPAGATION: Sow seeds in April where they are to flower. Thin to required spacing.

P. campanularia

Phacelia campanularia 'Blue Bonnet'

Phlox drummondii 'Beauty Mixed'

PHLOX
Annual Phlox
(HHA)

One of our basic bedding plants which for generations has done a useful and reliable job in the garden. The stems bear tightly-packed flower-heads which are about 4 in. across. The blooms are available in many colours and the eye is often a different colour. Plant in containers, window boxes, beds or in the rockery, and dead-head regularly. Put down Slug Pellets if ragged holes appear in the leaves.

VARIETIES: There are 2 groups of **P. drummondii**. The *Grandifloras* are tall growing, reaching 1–1½ ft — **'Large-flowered Mix'** is the one to choose. The *Nana Compactas* are dwarfs, 6–9 in. high, and the best of all is **'Beauty Mixed'**. For star-shaped flowers choose **'Twinkle'** or **'Stars'**.

SITE & SOIL: Any well-drained garden soil will do — thrives best in full sun.

PLANT DETAILS: Height 6 in.–1½ ft. Spacing 8 in. Flowering period June–September.

PROPAGATION: Follow the Half Hardy Annual technique (page 82). Alternatively in mild areas sow seeds outdoors in mid April.

P. drummondii

Portulaca grandiflora

PORTULACA
Sun Plant
(HHA)

A sandy bank in full sun is not easy to keep in colour all summer long if the weather is dry — Portulaca is one of the few satisfactory plants for such a site. The semi-prostrate reddish stems bear clusters of long fleshy leaves which in a sunny year can be almost covered by the saucer-shaped flowers. Unfortunately the blooms close once the sun is hidden.

VARIETIES: **P. grandiflora** is the species grown. The 1 in. flowers are brightly coloured — yellow, scarlet, orange, pink, purple and white. **'Double Mixed'** is the usual choice, producing flowers which look like small Shrub Roses — for larger flowers buy **'Sunglo'**. You can try **'Cloudbeater'** — the raisers claim that the flowers do not close on a dull day.

SITE & SOIL: Any well-drained garden soil will do — full sun is essential.

PLANT DETAILS: Height 6 in. Spacing 6 in. Flowering period June–September.

PROPAGATION: Does not like root disturbance. Sow seeds outdoors in April — cover with a cloche until June if necessary.

P. grandiflora 'Double Mixed'

Reseda odorata

RESEDA
Mignonette
(HA)

If you want a colourful annual to brighten up your border then Mignonette would be the wrong plant for you. If on the other hand you want a low-growing inconspicuous plant which can be planted under a window and will fill the room with its fragrance on a warm summer evening, then this old-fashioned, cottage garden plant is for you. Upright at first and then spreading, its tiny yellowish flowers are borne in cone-like trusses.

VARIETIES: There is one species — **R. odorata**. Breeders have improved the flowers over the years — you can buy **'Machet'** (yellow and pink), **'Red Monarch'** (red and green), **'Goliath'** (double red) and so on, but it is better to choose a variety on the basis of the quality of its fragrance rather than the supposed attractiveness of its tiny flowers.

SITE & SOIL: Any reasonable garden soil will do — add lime if it is acid. Choose a sunny spot.

PLANT DETAILS: Height 1 ft. Spacing 9 in. Flowering period July–September.

PROPAGATION: Sow seeds in April where they are to flower. Thin to required spacing.

R. odorata

Rudbeckia 'Gloriosa Daisy'

RUDBECKIA
Rudbeckia
(HHA)

There are several annuals with flowers which look like large yellow or orange Daisies — Rudbeckia is the one with the large and cone-like central disc. It is a fine late-flowering plant which produces masses of large blooms for garden display and indoors — immerse the cut ends in boiling water for about half a minute before arranging. Yellow, orange and deep red are the colours — bi-colours are available.

VARIETIES: R. hirta comes in many varieties and hybrids. For the largest flowers choose the **'Giant Tetraploid Hybrid'** (**'Gloriosa Daisy'**) — the blooms are 7 in. across. **'Marmalade'** (1½ ft) is half the height and the flowers are smaller, but the golden orange shade is most attractive. **'Irish Eyes'** has a green cone instead of the usual dark one and the baby is **'Dwarf Gem'** (1 ft). **'Double Gloriosa Daisies'** have extra petals in place of a central cone.

SITE & SOIL: Any well-drained garden soil will do — thrives in sun or light shade.

PLANT DETAILS: Height 1–3 ft. Spacing 1–2 ft. Flowering period August–October.

PROPAGATION: Follow the Half Hardy Annual technique (page 82). Alternatively in mild areas sow seeds outdoors in mid April.

R. 'Marmalade'

Flowers for Every Season

AUGUST–SEPTEMBER
(for JANUARY–MAY see page 17) (for JUNE–JULY see page 21)
(for OCTOBER–DECEMBER see page 33)

The flowering period for nearly all annuals and biennials lies somewhere between the beginning of June and the end of October. However, by careful selection you can have flowers in the annual bed or border almost all year round. For each month there is a list of annuals and biennials which can be expected to be in full bloom — remember that some of these plants may come into flower earlier and can continue to bloom for many weeks afterwards.

AUGUST

Ageratum	Dianthus	Nemesia
Althaea	Eschscholzia	Nicotiana
Alyssum	Gaillardia	Nigella
Antirrhinum	Gazania	Papaver
Begonia	Godetia	Petunia
Calceolaria	Gypsophila	Phlox
Calendula	Helianthus	Portulaca
Celosia	Helichrysum	Reseda
Centaurea	Heliotropium	Salpiglossis
Chrysanthemum	Hibiscus	Salvia
Clarkia	Impatiens	Scabiosa
Cleome	Ipomoea	Schizanthus
Cobaea	Lathyrus	Tagetes
Convolvulus	Lavatera	Thunbergia
Coreopsis	Limonium	Tropaeolum
Cosmos	Lobelia	Viola
Dahlia	Mesembryanthemum	Zinnia

SEPTEMBER

Ageratum	Cosmos	Mesembryanthemum
Althaea	Dahlia	Molucella
Alyssum	Dianthus	Nemesia
Amaranthus	Eschscholzia	Nicotiana
Antirrhinum	Gaillardia	Nigella
Begonia	Gazania	Papaver
Calceolaria	Godetia	Petunia
Calendula	Gypsophila	Phlox
Callistephus	Helianthus	Rudbeckia
Celosia	Helichrysum	Salpiglossis
Centaurea	Heliotropium	Salvia
Chrysanthemum	Hibiscus	Scabiosa
Clarkia	Impatiens	Tagetes
Cleome	Lathyrus	Thunbergia
Cobaea	Lavatera	Tropaeolum
Convolvulus	Lobelia	Viola
Coreopsis	Malope	Zinnia

Salpiglossis sinuata

SALPIGLOSSIS
Painted Tongue
(HHA)

Eye-catching is the word. The velvety, funnel-shaped flowers are prominently veined — yellow on red, red on yellow, gold on purple, etc, which makes them one of the most exotic of all annuals. Pinch out the tips of young plants to promote bushiness and support with twigs. Salpiglossis is rather tender — do not grow on an exposed site and a warm summer is necessary for it to show its full glory.

VARIETIES: S. sinuata is the garden species and the popular modern hybrid is **'Splash'**. The bushy 1½ ft plants bear a host of flowers in brilliant colours — **'Bolero'** is a rather similar mixture. For the tallest plant and the largest flowers (2 in. across), grow **'Grandiflora'**. The upright, non-branching variety is **'Monarch'**.

SITE & SOIL: Any well-drained garden soil will do — choose a sunny and sheltered spot.

PLANT DETAILS: Height 1½–2½ ft. Spacing 1 ft. Flowering period July–September.

PROPAGATION: Follow the Half Hardy Annual technique (page 82). Plant out when the danger of frost is past.

S. sinuata

SALVIA

Sage
HA, HHA or HB

The popular Salvia is the Scarlet Sage (S. splendens), which can be seen in any street or park in summer — neat rows of plants about 1 ft high with erect spikes of brilliant red flowers. Pinch out the tips of seedlings to induce bushiness and remember to feed and water when necessary. Red is not the only colour — pink and purple are available.

VARIETIES: There are many red varieties of the half hardy annual **S. splendens** — favourite ones include **'Blaze of Fire'**, **'Flarepath'** and **'Caribinière'**. For a change try **'Royal Purple'** or the red, pink and purple mixture **'Dress Parade'**. Another half hardy annual is the dark blue **S. farinacea** and the hardy annual **S. horminum** is grown for its brightly-coloured bracts. For the back of the border there is the biennial Clary (**S. sclarea**) — a cottage garden plant with tall spikes of pale flowers.

SITE & SOIL: Any reasonable garden soil will do — thrives best in full sun.

PLANT DETAILS: Height 9 in. – 1½ ft. Spacing 1 ft. Flowering period June – October.

PROPAGATION: Follow the Hardy Annual, Half Hardy Annual or Biennial technique depending on the variety chosen.

Salvia splendens 'Blaze of Fire'

S. splendens

S. horminum

SCABIOSA

Sweet Scabious
HA

Sweet Scabious has never become a popular plant like its perennial cousin, although it has been grown in our gardens for hundreds of years. Once it was only available in dull crimson but there are now varieties in white, blue, pink and purple. The domed fragrant heads are borne on wiry stems and are excellent for cutting. Dead-head spent blooms or dry indoors for flower arranging.

VARIETIES: The most popular tall variety (3 ft) of **S. atropurpurea** is **'Blue Moon'** (pale blue). A pink form (**'Rose Cockade'**) is available but the usual choice is a mixture — **'Monarch Cockade'**..This mixture produces large, double blooms in various colours — similar colours can be obtained with **'Tom Thumb'** or **'Dwarf Double Mixed'** which grow only 1½ ft high.

SITE & SOIL: Any well-drained soil will do — add lime if the soil is acid. Choose a sunny spot.

PLANT DETAILS: Height 1½ or 3 ft. Spacing 1 ft. Flowering period July – October.

PROPAGATION: Sow seeds in September or March where they are to flower. Thin to required spacing.

Scabiosa atropurpurea 'Blue Moon'

S. atropurpurea

SCHIZANTHUS

Poor Man's Orchid
HHA

The Poor Man's Orchid or Butterfly Flower is a popular pot plant which can be used as a summer bedder outdoors. There are both tall and dwarf varieties which bear miniature orchid-like flowers above the ferny leaves. The petals are streaked and spotted in a wide variety of colours and patterns — a truly exotic plant for British gardens. Pinch out the tips of young plants to induce bushiness and support the stems with twigs.

VARIETIES: There are several named varieties of **S. pinnatus** and its hybrid **S. wisetonensis**. The best of the tall ones (3 ft) are the **'Magnum Hybrids'** but the dwarf types are usually preferred. **'Hit Parade'** (1 ft) is the one you are most likely to find but there is now an even more compact one — **'Star Parade'** (6 in.).

SITE & SOIL: Any well-drained garden soil will do — thrives best in full sun.

PLANT DETAILS: Height 6 in. – 3 ft. Spacing 9 in. – 1½ ft. Flowering period July – August.

PROPAGATION: Follow the Half Hardy Annual technique (page 82). Alternatively in mild areas sow seeds outdoors in late April.

Schizanthus 'Monarch Strain'

S. 'Hit Parade'

TAGETES

African Marigold, French Marigold, Tagetes
(HHA)

The ever-popular French and African Marigolds, ranging from a few inches to several feet tall, are mis-named — they both originated in Mexico. Some experts feel that we rely too much on the numerous varieties of Tagetes for summer bedding, but these plants continue to be the main source of yellow, orange and brown in the small flower bed. Staking is rarely necessary but dead-heading is required to prolong the floral display. The foliage is pungent when crushed and the flowers may be single or double.

VARIETIES: Tagetes are divided into three major groups. The *African Marigolds* (**T. erecta**) are the tallest and the flowers by far the largest, reaching a diameter of several inches. The blooms are double and ball-shaped in colours ranging from pale yellow to deep orange. Some are dwarfs, like **'Golden Age'** (1 ft) — others such as **'Doubloon'** are 3 ft high with 5 in. blooms. The *French Marigolds* (**T. patula**) are shorter and the flowers are smaller, but there is an immense variety of colours and colour blends. This is the really popular group and seed catalogues offer many, many varieties — look for **'Naughty Marietta'** (1 ft, single, yellow and maroon), **'Petite'** (6 in., double, mixed colours), **'Tiger Eyes'** (10 in., double, red with yellow centre) and **'Yellow Jacket'** (6 in., double, yellow). The third major group is made up of the dainty *Tagetes* varieties (**T. signata**) which are widely used for edging. The plants are compact and the flowers are small and single. **'Lemon Gem'** (9 in.) is popular — the new novelty is the yellow, orange and brown combination **'Starfire'** (6 in.). The dividing lines between the groups are no longer clear-cut — there are Afro-French varieties such as **'Sunrise'** (1 ft, double, orange and red).

SITE & SOIL: Any reasonable garden soil will do — thrives best in full sun.

PLANT DETAILS: Height 1–3 ft (African Marigolds), 6 in.–1 ft (French Marigolds) or 6–9 in. (Tagetes). Spacing 1–1½ ft (African Marigolds) or 6–9 in. (French Marigolds and Tagetes). Flowering period June–October.

PROPAGATION: Follow the Half Hardy Annual technique (page 82). Alternatively in mild areas sow seeds outdoors in May.

Tagetes patula 'Yellow Jacket'

T. patula 'Naughty Marietta'
French Marigold

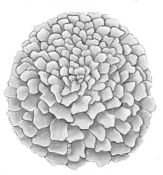

T. erecta 'Doubloon'
African Marigold

T. patula 'Tiger Eyes'
French Marigold

T. 'Sunrise'
Afro-French Marigold

T. signata 'Lemon Gem'
Tagetes

Tagetes erecta 'Yellow Climax'

THUNBERGIA

Black-eyed Susan
(HHA)

Many of the annuals described in this book will grow anywhere, but Thunbergia is not one of them. It needs a sunny and sheltered spot and is only really reliable in the south and west. Its twining stems grow quickly, requiring trellis-work, netting or canes for support — alternatively you can grow it in a hanging basket and let the stems trail downwards.

VARIETIES: A packet of **T. alata** seeds produces plants with heart-shaped leaves and funnel-shaped flowers which are about 2 in. across. The petals are cream, yellow, pale brown or orange and the throat is dark purple, giving a black eye effect. It is a vigorous climber growing up to 10 ft, but the variety usually on offer is **'Susie'**. This grows about 4–6 ft and some of the flowers have the black eyes missing.

SITE & SOIL: Any well-drained garden soil will do — full sun is essential.

PLANT DETAILS: Height 4–10 ft. Spacing 2 ft. Flowering period July–October.

PROPAGATION: Follow the Half Hardy Annual technique (page 82). Plant out when the danger of frost is past.

Thunbergia alata

T. alata

TROPAEOLUM Nasturtium
(HA)

There are varieties of Nasturtium (T. majus) for all sorts of purposes — climbers for clothing walls and fences or covering banks, semi-trailers for window boxes and dwarfs for bedding and edging. For a blaze of red, yellow or orange plant in poor, free-draining soil and do not feed. Spray, if necessary, against blackfly. Canary Creeper (T. peregrinum) is suitable for richer soil — a vigorous climber with small, yellow flowers and lobed leaves.

VARIETIES: Nasturtiums are grouped according to size — the *Climbers* grow up to 6 ft (look for **'Tall Mixed'** or **'Climbing Mixed'**) and the *Semi-trailers* reach about 1 ft. This latter group is dominated by the fragrant semi-double Gleam varieties — **'Golden Gleam'** (yellow) and **'Scarlet Gleam'** (red). There are also the compact *Dwarfs* which grow 6–9 in. high — popular varieties include **'Red Roulette'** (orange-red), **'Empress of India'** (dark red), **'Whirlybird'** (mixed) and **'Tom Thumb'** (mixed).

SITE & SOIL: Thrives in poor sandy soil in either full sun or partial shade.

PLANT DETAILS: Height 6 in. – 6 ft. Spacing 6 in. –1½ ft. Flowering period June–October.

PROPAGATION: Sow seeds in compost under glass in February or in April where they are to flower.

Tropaeolum majus 'Whirlybird Gold'

T. majus

T. peregrinum

URSINIA Ursinia
(HHA)

Ursinia is a colourful South African daisy which will brighten up a sunny bed or border in midsummer. It has not achieved the popularity of some other Daisy-like plants such as Rudbeckia and Mesembryanthemum, but the flowers are large (about 2 in. across) and attractively zoned. Unfortunately the colour range is limited and the flowering period is rather short.

VARIETIES: Catalogues offer the species **U. anethoides** or a mixture of **'Special Hybrids'**. The plants are bushy and the pale green leaves are finely divided. The petals are generally orange but yellow strains do exist. At the base of each petal there is a red or maroon band and the central disc turns purple as the flower matures.

SITE & SOIL: Thrives in light, well-drained soil — full sun is essential.

PLANT DETAILS: Height 1–1½ ft. Spacing 9 in. Flowering period July–August.

PROPAGATION: Follow the Half Hardy Annual technique (page 82). Alternatively sow seeds outdoors in May.

Ursinia anethoides

U. anethoides

VENIDIUM Monarch of the Veldt
(HHA)

You will have to search through the catalogues to find this one. It certainly deserves to be better known. The Sunflower-like blooms are 4 in. across and they are quite distinctive — at the base of each inner petal is a purple-black blotch, providing a rayed effect around the rim of the prominent black disc. The blooms on their long stems make excellent cut flowers.

VARIETIES: V. fastuosum grows about 2 ft high. The deeply-lobed foliage is silvery and the flowers are orange. The stems usually require staking. **'Dwarf Hybrids'** require no support — the plants do not exceed 1 ft and the flower colours range from pale cream to deep orange. A good choice for tubs in a sunny situation.

SITE & SOIL: Thrives in light, well-drained soil — full sun is essential.

PLANT DETAILS: Height 1 or 2 ft. Spacing 1 ft. Flowering period June–October.

PROPAGATION: Follow the Half Hardy Annual technique (page 82). Alternatively sow seeds outdoors in May.

V. fastuosum

Venidium fastuosum

VERBENA

Verbena
(HHA)

A favourite for many years in small beds and window boxes. Verbena is a low-growing plant which bears small, Primrose-like flowers in clusters on top of the stems. The blooms are usually fragrant and white-eyed, and the stems can be pegged down to provide a floral carpet. Add organic matter to the soil before sowing, pinch out the tips of young plants, dead-head regularly and water in dry weather.

VARIETIES: **V. hybrida** varieties are available in many colours — white, pink, purple, red and blue. For a bright splash of a single colour, pick **'Blaze'** (scarlet), **'Delight'** (pink), **'Amethyst'** (blue), **'Lawrence Johnston'** (cherry red) or **'Sparkle'** (scarlet, prominent white eye). Many people prefer a mixture of colours — for them there is **'Royal Bouquet'**, **'Showtime'** and **'Sparkle Mixed'**.

SITE & SOIL: Any well-drained garden soil will do — thrives best in full sun.

PLANT DETAILS: Height 6 in.–1 ft. Spacing 1 ft. Flowering period July–September.

PROPAGATION: Follow the Half Hardy Annual technique (page 82). Plant out when the danger of frost is past.

V. hybrida

Verbena hybrida 'Showtime'

VIOLA

Pansy, Viola
(HA) or (HB)

Pansies may have an old-fashioned look but they are in fact a 19th century creation, developed from the wild flower V. tricoior. In mid-Victorian times the varieties with large multi-coloured 'faces' were popular and have remained so ever since. In the 1860s V. cornuta was crossed with the Garden Pansy and the result was the Viola (V. hybrida). The dividing line between the Pansy and the Viola is not a clear one, although you will often find them on different pages in the catalogue. In general the Viola is more compact and not as easy to grow and the flowers are smaller and often single-coloured. Both Pansies and Violas are short-lived perennials which are usually grown as annuals or biennials. The plants are used for bedding, edging and window boxes, and the flowers are cut for use indoors. Dead-head regularly, protect from slugs and greenfly, and water in dry weather.

VARIETIES: There is a multitude of Pansy varieties. The *Winter-flowering* group blooms in late autumn onwards if sown in late spring — varieties include **'Floral Dance'**, **'Celestial Queen'** and **'Helios'**, but it is more usual to buy a mixture. The *Large-flowered* group includes the **'Roggli (Swiss) Giants'**, **'Azure Blue'**, **'Majestic Giants'**, **'Queen of the Planets'**, **'Sunny Boy'**, and **'Jumbo'**. The range of Viola varieties is smaller — a few well-known ones are **'Arkwright Beauty'** (red), **'Yellow Bedder'** (golden yellow), **'Chantreyland'** (orange), **'Blue Heaven'** (sky blue) and **'Avalanche'** (white). For small flowers with 'whiskers' on the face, choose **'Bambini'**.

SITE & SOIL: Any reasonable garden soil in sun or partial shade.

PLANT DETAILS: Height 6–9 in. Spacing 9 in.–1 ft. Flowering period January–December, depending on the variety chosen.

PROPAGATION: The Biennial technique (page 83) is usually recommended for the best results, but Pansies and Violas can be grown as annuals, using either the Hardy Annual (page 83) or Half Hardy Annual technique (page 82).

Viola tricolor 'Floral Dance'

V. tricolor 'Roggli Giant' Pansy

V. hybrida 'Chantreyland' Viola

Viola tricolor 'Sunny Boy'

Viola hybrida 'Blue Heaven'

Viscaria oculata 'Brilliant Mixed'

VISCARIA
Viscaria
(HA)

What a welter of latin names have been given to the lowly Viscaria — Viscaria oculata, Silene coeli-rosa and Lychnis coeli-rosa. All refer to the easy-to-grow annual which is thin and weedy when seen as a single plant but *en masse* produces a gay kaleidoscope of colour. The cup-shaped flowers measure about 1 in. across and are recommended for cutting.

VARIETIES: You can buy single-colour varieties of Viscaria — the two you are most likely to find are **'Blue Angel'** (azure blue) and **'Love'** (rose-pink). The usual choice is a mixture, such as **'Treasure Island'** or **'Brilliant Mixed'** — sow a large patch and masses of white, pink, lavender, red, purple and blue flowers will appear all summer. The **'Tom Thumb'** hybrids (6 in.) are in the textbooks but in very few catalogues.

SITE & SOIL: Any well-drained garden soil will do — thrives in sun or partial shade.

PLANT DETAILS: Height 6 in. or 1 ft. Spacing 6 in. Flowering period June–August.

PROPAGATION: Sow seeds in September or April where they are to flower. Thin to required spacing.

V. oculata

Xeranthemum annuum

XERANTHEMUM
Common Immortelle
(HA)

The Common Immortelle grows wild in Southern Europe and the Near East — in Britain it is a garden plant grown for its 'everlasting' flowers. The petals of the Daisy-like blooms are strawy and crisp with an outstanding reputation for keeping their colour after drying. Support the plants with small twigs. The blooms appear in midsummer on the top of wiry stems.

VARIETIES: The wild **X. annuum** is purple, but mixtures of varieties are available for garden use. Planting such a mixture produces single, semi-double and double blooms in white, pink, purple and lilac. It is prepared for indoor decoration by cutting just before the flowers are fully open. Tie the stems in bunches and hang upside down in a cool place away from sunlight.

SITE & SOIL: Any well-drained garden soil will do — full sun is essential.

PLANT DETAILS: Height 2 ft. Spacing 1½ ft. Flowering period July–September.

PROPAGATION: Sow seeds in September or March where they are to flower. Thin to required spacing.

X. annuum

Zinnia 'Envy'

ZINNIA
Youth and Old Age
(HHA)

Few annuals look as appealing as Zinnia in the seed catalogue, but to get similar results you will need fertile soil and a fine summer. The Daisy-like flowers may be single, semi-double or double, and the largest are 6 in. across. The tall, strong stems do not require staking and the cut blooms last well in water.

VARIETIES: Zinnias are available in many colours — there is even an attractive green one (**'Envy'**). The whites, reds, purples and yellows are varieties of **Z. elegans** — the small browns and yellows, such as **'Persian Carpet'** are derived from **Z. angustifolia**. The smallest of all is **'Thumbelina'** (6 in.) and the largest is the Dahlia-flowered **'State Fair'** (2½ ft). Between them you will find Scabious-, Chrysanthemum-, cactus- and Gaillardia-flowered types . . . a truly dazzling array.

SITE & SOIL: Any compost-enriched garden soil will do — thrives best in full sun.

PLANT DETAILS: Height 6 in.–2½ ft. Spacing 6 in.–1 ft. Flowering period July–October.

PROPAGATION: Follow the Half Hardy Annual technique (page 82). Plant out when the danger of frost is past.

Z. 'Ruffles'

Z. 'Chippendale'

CHAPTER 3

BORDER PERENNIALS

As the textbooks will tell you, herbaceous perennials are plants which die down every winter and produce new stems and foliage each spring. This standard definition does indeed apply to most of the herbaceous perennials we grow in the garden, but you can find exceptions to both halves of this over-simple description.

First of all, not all herbaceous perennials die down in winter. From tiny Saxifrages hugging the earth to the large arching leaves of Pampas Grass you will find evergreens in a variety of shapes and sizes – Brunnera, Helleborus, Heuchera, Nepeta, Stachys and Tiarella are examples. Your border should contain some of these evergreen types if you wish to avoid a completely bare look during the depths of winter.

Secondly, the statement that they pop up afresh every spring is also not always true. Some types are not completely hardy and so are liable to die in severe winters, and several others which are completely hardy are not long-lived even when the growing conditions are ideal. Aquilegia, Anchusa and Perennial Flax are well-known examples of plants with a strictly limited life span. Nearly all of the rest will go on year after year, but many require lifting and dividing every few years to prevent deterioration. There is just a small group of plants to which the word 'perennial' *really* applies – plants like Acanthus, Helleborus and Paeonies which should be left alone so that they can continue to flourish without disturbance for decades.

An enormous number of plants are classified as herbaceous perennials, and the ones which grow to a foot or more are termed border perennials, because the herbaceous and the mixed borders are their traditional homes. To see border perennials at their classical best, look at a herbaceous border in midsummer.

Towards the end of the nineteenth century there was a violent swing away from the regimented rows of bedding plants in the flower beds of the mid Victorians. Under the influence of William Robinson and Gertrude Jekyll the herbaceous border was born, and all sorts of rules were developed. A backdrop of a hedge (preferably Yew) or weathered brick was essential and border perennials were planted in groups, carefully tiered with the tallest specimens at the back and the low-growing perennials at the front to divide the border from the lawn. Plans were carefully drawn before planting took place – colour clashes were avoided like the plague, neighbouring plants had to bloom in sequence, contrasting flower forms were put next to each other to add interest, and so on. The length had to be impressive and the width no less than 9 ft – in its de-luxe form two parallel borders faced each other and were separated by a broad path of closely-mown turf.

The herbaceous border is a thing to see – you will find splendid examples at Wisley, Hampton Court, Gt. Dixter and many other grand gardens in Britain. It is a thing to see but not to make these days. It requires a great deal of space and attention, and it can be seen from only one side. The screening hedge cuts down both light and air circulation so that the back row leans forward unless it is carefully and constantly staked, and even with loving and skilful care the best of borders have a barren look for part of the year.

If you want to have an area just for border perennials then make an island bed instead (see page 5). Here the plants can be seen from all sides and there is no shading effect from surrounding walls or hedges. The tallest plants are set in the middle and the not-so-strict rule is that their height should be no more than half the width of the bed. You can see excellent examples at Bressingham Gardens in Norfolk – the birthplace of the island bed.

For the average-sized garden the mixed border is the answer. This owes as much to the idea of the old cottage garden as it does to the principles of herbaceous and shrub borders. The basic concept is to have some colour all year round – choose from where you will amongst the complete range of garden plants. Roses with evergreen and flowering shrubs provide a woody and colourful framework – within this setting the border perennials are planted in groups of three or five – avoid the spotty effect resulting from growing single isolated specimens. Plant annuals and bulbs to fill the bare spots close to the front of the border. The annuals will provide a summer-long floral display and bulbs will bring the border to life in late winter or early spring. There are a few rules to ensure success – get rid of perennial weeds before planting a mixed border and choose the smaller and sturdier modern varieties of border perennials so as to reduce the need for staking. Above all, check in the A-Z guides that the plants you have picked are suitable for the conditions.

ACANTHUS Bear's Breeches

The Acanthus leaf is the motif found on the columns in Ancient Greece — deeply-divided arching foliage around the tall spires of tubular purple and white flowers which appear in midsummer. This perennial needs plenty of space and dislikes disturbance — grow it as a specimen plant. The handsome leaves should be cut back to near ground level once the flowering season is over. A long-lived plant, but not if your soil is heavy and poorly drained.

VARIETIES: **A. spinosus** is the one which is usually selected. The purple hooded flowers have white lips and both the leaves and bracts bear spines. No staking is necessary and the flower-heads can be used indoors, both fresh and dried. Height 4 ft. Spacing 2½ ft. Flowering period July – September. **A. mollis latifolius** is quite similar, but its leaves and bracts are spineless.

SITE & SOIL: Any well-drained garden soil will do — light land is preferred. Thrives in sun or light shade.

PROPAGATION: Sow seeds under glass in spring. When the plants are large and overcrowded, divide the clumps in early autumn.

Acanthus spinosus

A. spinosus

ACHILLEA Yarrow, Milfoil

There are several Yarrows for the back or middle of the border. All are easy to grow with no special soil requirements and the pungent, ferny foliage is crowned in midsummer with flat heads or loose clusters of tiny flowers. It is excellent for cutting — the flower-heads can be dried for winter decoration. Yarrow will withstand dry conditions but may need staking on an exposed site. Cut down to ground level in autumn.

VARIETIES: **A. filipendulina 'Gold Plate'** is a popular variety. It grows 4½ ft high and bears flat-topped 6 in. yellow heads — like other herbaceous border Yarrows it should be planted at 2 ft intervals and the flowers appear between June and September. **'Coronation Gold'** is smaller (3 ft) and the golden heads are more compact — the silvery-leaved **'Moonshine'** (2 ft) is even shorter. **A. ptarmica** is quite different — **'Perry's White'** and **'The Pearl'** (2½ ft) bear loose clusters of ball-shaped white flowers. Still another variant is **A. millefolium 'Cerise Queen'** (oval heads of deep pink flowers).

SITE & SOIL: Any well-drained garden soil will do — thrives best in full sun.

PROPAGATION: Sow seeds in the open in late spring or divide clumps in autumn or spring.

Achillea filipendulina 'Gold Plate'

A. filipendulina 'Coronation Gold'

ACONITUM Monkshood

Monkshood has flourished in British gardens for many hundreds of years, and will flourish in yours if the soil is rich in organic matter and there is some shade — an ideal plant for growing under trees at the back of the border. The leaves are deeply cut and the curiously helmeted flowers are borne on tall spikes. It is sometimes recommended as a cut flower, but all parts of the plant are poisonous.

VARIETIES: The best species for the garden is **A. napellus.** The flower colour is usually blue or violet and its statistics are height 3½ ft, spacing 2 ft, flowering period June – August. The most popular variety is **'Bressingham Spire'** (violet) — others include **'Bicolor'** (blue and white), **'Newry Blue'** (deep blue) and the tall **'Spark's Variety'** (4½ ft). For a rose-coloured one choose **A. napellus roseum** and for maximum height you will have to grow **A. wilsonii 'Barker's Variety'** which grows 5 ft or more and flowers until October.

SITE & SOIL: Any moisture-holding garden soil will do — thrives best in partial shade.

PROPAGATION: Divide clumps in autumn or spring.

Aconitum napellus 'Bicolor'

A. 'Spark's Variety'

AGAPANTHUS   African Lily

From the basal rosette of strap-like leaves a series of long stems appear, on top of which the flowers are clustered. Each trumpet-shaped bloom is about 2 in. long and is nearly always blue in colour. The African Lily is not for everyone — it is only reliably hardy in the southern and western counties, and even there the crowns should be covered with sand or bracken in winter. Mulch the plants in May and water in dry weather. An excellent perennial for cutting and planting in tubs.

VARIETIES: The African Lily you are most likely to see is a hybrid of **A. africanus (A. umbellatus)**. One of the hardiest is **'Headbourne Hybrid'** — height 2½ ft, spacing 2 ft and a flowering period from July to September. The smaller **A. campanulatus** is generally regarded as the best to grow in unfavourable situations — **'Isis'** produces large heads of lavender flowers and **'Albus'** bears white blooms. Seed heads of all varieties can be cut and dried for winter decoration.

SITE & SOIL: A well-drained soil containing adequate organic matter is required — thrives only in full sun.

PROPAGATION: Divide clumps in April or May.

Agapanthus campanulatus 'Isis'

A. 'Headbourne Hybrid'

Flowers for Every Season

JANUARY – MAY
(for JUNE – JULY see page 48) (for AUGUST – SEPTEMBER see page 53)
(for OCTOBER – DECEMBER see page 57)

By careful selection you can ensure that your border will be in bloom during every month of the year. For each month there is a list of perennials which can be expected to be in full flower — remember that some of these plants may come into bloom earlier and can continue to flower for many weeks afterwards.

JANUARY
Helleborus niger   Iris stylosa

FEBRUARY
Helleborus niger   Iris stylosa
Helleborus orientalis   Viola odorata

MARCH
Bergenia cordifolia   Primula variabilis
Helleborus niger   Primula vulgaris
Helleborus orientalis   Ranunculus ficaria
Primula japonica   Viola odorata

APRIL
Bergenia cordifolia   Paeonia mlokosewitschii
Brunnera macrophylla   Primula japonica
Caltha palustris   Primula variabilis
Doronicum plantagineum   Primula vulgaris
Epimedium spp.   Pulmonaria officinalis
Euphorbia polychroma   Ranunculus ficaria
Iris (Dwarf Bearded)   Viola odorata

MAY
Ajuga reptans   Nepeta mussinii
Aquilegia vulgaris   Omphalodes cappadocica
Dicentra spectabilis   Paeonia officinalis
Doronicum plantagineum   Papaver orientale
Epimedium spp.   Polygonatum hybridum
Euphorbia polychroma   Pyrethrum roseum
Incarvillea delavayi   Tiarella cordifolia
Iris (Intermediate Bearded)   Trollius hybridus
Iris pseudacorus   Veronica gentianoides

AJUGA   Bugle

Bugle is an undemanding and unspectacular plant — it spreads and creeps between bulbs or under tall plants. A low-growing perennial for moist and shady places — almost evergreen in most parts of the country. The blue flowers are borne in short spikes and are quite pretty but the main colour is derived from the leaves — both multicoloured and variegated forms are available. Not all varieties of Ajuga are carpeters — the non-creeping A. pyramidalis grows upright but reaches only 4 in.

VARIETIES: The creeping varieties of Bugle have been evolved from the wild flower **A. reptans**. The basic plant details are height 4–6 in., spacing 15 in., flowering period May–August. Leaf colour separates the different types — **'Variegata'** (leaves grey-green and cream), **'Multicolor'** (leaves mottled bronze and red), **'Atropurpurea'** (leaves reddish purple) and **'Burgundy Glow'** (leaves metallic bronze). A white-flowered form (**'Alba'**) is available.

SITE & SOIL: Any reasonable garden soil will do — thrives in sun and partial shade.

PROPAGATION: Divide clumps in autumn or spring.

Ajuga reptans 'Burgundy Glow'

A. reptans 'Multicolor'

Alchemilla mollis

ALCHEMILLA   Lady's Mantle

A delightful old-fashioned perennial, seen at its best when the leaves are sparkling with dewdrops. Alchemilla grows as a flat-topped clump of foliage, each pale green leaf being lobed and serrated with a fine, hairy covering. It is a useful ground cover plant in light shade, bearing fluffy branching sprays of tiny flowers in summer. Both leaves and floral sprays are widely used in flower arrangements. Once flowering has finished, cut the plants back to just above ground level and in October cover the crowns with coarse sand, peat or bracken.

VARIETIES: The species grown in the herbaceous border is **A. mollis.** Basic details are height 1½ ft, spacing 1½ ft and a flowering period from June to August. The flowers are greenish yellow and about ⅛ in. across. A much more compact species (**A. alpina,** 6 in.) is grown in rockeries.

SITE & SOIL: Any well-drained garden soil will do — thrives in sun or light shade.

PROPAGATION: Easily raised from seed sown in spring. Divide clumps in April or May.

A. mollis

Alstroemeria 'Ligtu Hybrids'

ALSTROEMERIA   Peruvian Lily

A pretty flower to grow — lily-like trumpets about 2 in. across borne in loose clusters on top of leafy stems. It is, however, quite a challenge because it is so temperamental — Alstroemeria sometimes does not grow at all in the first year after planting and it may take three years before it is fully established. To ensure success, buy the specimen in a pot or container and plant carefully in deep, sandy soil which has been enriched with compost. Cut blooms are long-lasting in water.

VARIETIES: **A. aurantiaca** bears yellow or orange flowers in which the two upper petals are attractively streaked in red. Height 3 ft, spacing 1½ ft, flowering period June – August. There are several named varieties, such as **'Lutea'** (yellow), **'Orange King'** (orange) and **'Dover Orange'** (orange-red). **A. 'Ligtu Hybrids'** are shorter growing (2 ft) and offer a wider range of colours — white, pink and red as well as yellow and orange.

SITE & SOIL: Thrives in fertile sandy soil — requires a sunny sheltered spot.

PROPAGATION: Sow seeds under glass in spring. Only divide up clumps when they have outgrown their allotted space.

A. aurantiaca

Anaphalis triplinervis

ANAPHALIS   Pearl Everlasting

The illustration on the right shows the features for which this plant is grown. The leaves are covered with white hairs which gives them an attractive silvery appearance, and in late summer there are clusters of small starry flowers. These white or ivory flower-heads provide material for arranging indoors and they can be cut and dried — the colour and texture is retained. Anaphalis will succeed in nearly all situations although it dislikes heavy, poorly-drained soils. The only problem is that it is liable to spread quite quickly and grow beyond its allotted area.

VARIETIES: The various species of Anaphalis should be planted 1½ ft apart and the flowering period is August and September. **A. triplinervis** (1½ ft) is the one you are most likely to find at the garden centre — the leaves are large and the flowers off-white. **A. margaritacea** is similar in size but the leaves are smaller — the largest type is **A. yedoensis** (2½ ft) which also has the densest flower-heads.

SITE & SOIL: Any well-drained garden soil will do — thrives in sun or light shade.

PROPAGATION: Plant cuttings in a cold frame in spring or divide clumps in autumn or spring.

A. triplinervis

ANCHUSA   Alkanet

Few perennials can match the vivid blue of Anchusa in full bloom, but the straggly, branching flower-stems need staking and the plants are short-lived. For maximum display and longevity, plant in the spring and put a mulch around the stems in May. Dead-head faded blooms and at the end of the flowering season cut the stems down to ground level. A fine plant for the middle or back of the border — the large, rough leaves are described in one of its common names — Ox Tongue. Its one major hate is waterlogged soil.

VARIETIES: The favourite variety of **A. azurea** (**A. italica**) is **'Loddon Royalist'.** It flowers between June and August and like all Anchusas should be planted about 1½ ft apart. The average height is 3 ft — **'Royal Blue'** reaches the same height. You can go higher or lower. **'Opal'** (pale blue) reaches 4 ft and both the white-eyed **'Morning Glory'** and the deep blue **'Dropmore'** grow 5 ft high. At the other end of the scale **'Little John'** grows only 1½ ft tall.

SITE & SOIL: Any well-drained garden soil will do — thrives best in full sun.

PROPAGATION: Divide clumps in March or take root cuttings in winter.

A. azurea 'Loddon Royalist'

Anchusa azurea

ANEMONE   Japanese Anemone

Don't confuse the low-growing, brightly flowered Anemones raised from small corms with the Japanese Anemones which are found in the herbaceous border. A. japonica is a tall plant — 2 to 4 ft high, with saucer-shaped flowers and deeply-lobed leaves. The 2 in. blooms appear from August until the first frosts of October — white- or pink-petalled with a central boss of golden stamens. It is slow to establish and hardiness can be a problem in a severe winter — do not remove the dead stems until spring as they provide some protection.

VARIETIES: Several named varieties of **A. japonica** (**A. hybrida**) are available — leave 1 ft (shorter types) or 1½ ft (tall types) between the plants. In the short-growing group are **'Bressingham Glow'** (rose-red) and **'September Charm'** (pink), reaching about 2 ft, and the popular semi-double pink variety **'Queen Charlotte'** grows about 2½ ft high. There are several whites in the tall group (3–4ft) — **'White Giant', 'Louise Uhink'** and **'Honorine Jobert'.**

SITE & SOIL: Any well-drained garden soil will do — thrives in sun or partial shade.

PROPAGATION: Clumps can be divided in spring but Anemones do not like disturbance. Take root cuttings in winter.

A. japonica 'Queen Charlotte'

Anemone japonica 'September Charm'

AQUILEGIA   Columbine

The Columbine is at home in the cottage garden and the herbaceous border. It is a dainty plant, bearing grey-green ferny leaves and attractively coloured flowers early in the season. Unfortunately Columbines are not long-lived, but they are very easily raised by sowing seed in the spring. For best results place a mulch around the stems in late spring and dead-head the spent blooms. Water copiously during periods of drought and spray with a systemic insecticide if greenfly are a nuisance. Cut down the stems once flowering is over.

VARIETIES: The old-fashioned Columbine in cottage gardens is **A. vulgaris**, a 2–3 ft plant bearing short-spurred flowers in blue or white during May and June. It is much better to grow **A. hybrida** these days — the flowers are much more colourful and the spurs are longer. You can buy named varieties such as **'Crimson Star'** (2 ft, red with white centres) and **'Snow Queen'** (1½ ft, pure white) but the best choice is undoubtedly a selection of **'McKana Hybrids'** (2–3 ft, mixed colours). Plant 1 ft apart.

SITE & SOIL: Any well-drained garden soil will do — thrives best in partial shade.

PROPAGATION: Sow seeds outdoors in April or divide clumps in autumn or spring.

A. 'McKana Hybrids'

Aquilegia hybrida

ARUNCUS Goat's Beard

Aruncus needs four things — a partially shaded site, moist soil containing adequate humus, plenty of water in dry weather and plenty of space at all times. It is an imposing perennial for the back of the border, poolside, wild garden or on its own as a specimen plant. For a few weeks in June or July the tall stems are crowned with large fluffy flower spikes. Each one is about 8 in. long and bears a multitude of tiny white flowers. Watch out for caterpillars in spring — spray immediately. Cut the stems down to an inch or two above ground level in late autumn.

VARIETIES: There is a single species — **A. sylvester,** formerly known as **Spiraea aruncus.** It may take a year or two to become properly established, but given the right conditions Aruncus will reach 6 ft or more. Set the plants 2½ ft apart. A. sylvester is too large for most gardens — choose the variety **'Kneiffii'** (2 ft) where space is limited.

SITE & SOIL: Any reasonable garden soil will do — add organic matter before planting. Choose a spot which receives some shade during the day.

PROPAGATION: Divide clumps in autumn — mature plants are difficult to split.

Aruncus sylvester

A. sylvester

ASTER Michaelmas Daisy

Michaelmas Daisies are regarded by some gardeners as plants which can be left to look after themselves, bearing pink or lavender flowers each autumn on 3 ft stems. Such views are either wrong or incomplete. The Aster is certainly not a trouble-free plant — powdery mildew and other diseases can be a serious problem and the staking of tall varieties will be necessary. All types apart from A. amellus need lifting every other year and the centre of the clump discarded — only the healthy outer sections should be replanted. Pink and lavender may be the popular colours but they are certainly not the only ones, and there are giants and dwarfs as well as the favourite 3 and 4 ft varieties. General care consists of mulching in May, watering in dry weather, dead-heading regularly and cutting down the stems once flowering is over.

VARIETIES: The true Michaelmas Daisy is **A. novi-belgii** and the most popular varieties belong here. The height range is 2–4 ft and the planting distance is 1½ ft. Flowering occurs in September and October. The stems are smooth and the branched flower-heads bear many blooms. Well-known varieties include **'Ada Ballard'** (3 ft, lavender-blue), **'Crimson Brocade'** (3 ft, double, red), **'Marie Ballard'** (3 ft, double, blue), **'Royal Velvet'** (2 ft, violet-blue) and **'Winston S. Churchill'** (2½ ft, rich ruby). There are also dwarf varieties for the front of the border — look for **'Snowsprite'** (1 ft, white), **'Jenny'** (1 ft, red) and **'Audrey'** (1½ ft, mauve). **A. novae-angliae** varieties are another large group — taller and stiffer than the A. novi-belgii ones. The stems are hairy and the flower-heads wide spreading — **'Harrington's Pink'** (5 ft, pink) is the one you are most likely to see. There are a number of interesting Asters which are not true Michaelmas Daisies. **A. amellus** grows about 2 ft high and bears its large flowers in August and September. The favourite is the violet-blue **'King George'** — pink **'Lady Hindlip'** is also recommended. **A. frikartii** (2½ ft) blooms even earlier, in July, and so does the grey-leaved **A. thomsonii 'Nana'** (1½ ft).

SITE & SOIL: Any well-drained garden soil will do — thrives best in full sun.

PROPAGATION: Divide clumps in autumn or spring.

Aster novi-belgii 'Winston S. Churchill'

A. amellus 'Lady Hindlip'

A. novi-belgii 'Snowsprite'

A. novi-belgii 'Crimson Brocade'

A. frikartii 'Wonder of Stafa'

A. thomsonii 'Nana'

A. novae-angliae 'Harrington's Pink'

Aster novae-angliae 'September Ruby'

ASTILBE   Astilbe

Some perennials will grow almost anywhere in the garden, but not Astilbe. This attractive plant, sometimes called False Spiraea, will only thrive if the soil is moist and peaty — it can be used in boggy land where little else would succeed. The foliage is deeply cut and often coppery in spring, and the flowers are tiny. What the blooms lack in size they make up for in quantity — between June and August large feathery plumes appear which are clothed with a multitude of flowers. Water freely in dry weather.

VARIETIES: The popular varieties belong to **A. arendsii**—height 2–3 ft, spacing 1½ ft. The upright spikes are available in many colours — **'Bressingham Beauty'** (pink), **'Fire'** (red), **'Deutschland'** (white). The deep red **'Fanal'**, the rose-coloured **'Federsee'** and the white **'Irrlicht'** are also widely available. The plumes are not always erect — **'Ostrich Plume'** (pink) bears pendent flower-heads. For dwarf plants grow **A. simplicifolia 'Sprite'** (1 ft, pink).

SITE & SOIL: Soil must be moist and rich in humus — thrives best in light shade.

PROPAGATION: Divide clumps every 2 or 3 years in spring.

Astilbe arendsii 'Fanal'

A. arendsii 'Bressingham Beauty'

ASTRANTIA   Masterwort

Any review of flowering perennials must list a large range of the showy modern hybrids which are available in garden centres, but it would be sad if the unspectacular and no longer popular cottage garden plants were omitted. Masterwort is one of our oldest garden flowers and would certainly not win a prize in a beauty contest — the round flowers are usually white or pinkish in colour, about 1 in. across, with a frill of papery bracts. The stems are slender and the leaves deeply divided; the blooms are excellent for cutting. Stake in exposed situations, keep watch for slugs and water freely in dry weather.

VARIETIES: The most popular species is **A. major** — height 2 ft, spacing 1½ ft, flowering period June–July. The flowers are pinkish green and not at all eye-catching. There are brighter species available — **A. maxima** bears shell pink flowers and **A. carniolica 'Rubra'** (1½ ft) produces dark red blooms.

SITE & SOIL: Any moisture-retentive garden soil will do — thrives best in partial shade.

PROPAGATION: Sow seeds under glass in spring. When plants are large and overcrowded, divide the clumps in autumn or spring.

Astrantia maxima

A. major

BERGENIA   Large-leaved Saxifrage

Bergenia is a splendid ground cover for a herbaceous or mixed border. It thrives under shrubs and trees, spreads rapidly when the conditions are favourable and provides colour nearly all year round. The large and leathery leaves are bright green, turning red in autumn. Above them rise the flower-heads in spring, Hyacinth-like spikes bearing white, pink, red or purple bell-shaped flowers. It will grow in all types of soils, including wet peats and dry chalks.

VARIETIES: The basic species is **B. cordifolia** — height 1½ ft, spacing 1½ ft, flowering period March–April. The deep pink flowers are borne in drooping sprays — the variety **purpurea** has pale purple flowers. **B. crassifolia**, a similar species, bears upright flower-heads. Nowadays a number of named hybrids are available — make your choice from this group. Amongst the best are **B. 'Ballawley'** (rose-red), **B. 'Silberlicht'** (white, tinged pink) and **B. 'Sunningdale'** (deep lilac).

SITE & SOIL: Any well-drained garden soil will do — thrives in sun or partial shade.

PROPAGATION: When plants are large and overcrowded, divide the clumps in autumn.

Bergenia 'Ballawley'

B. cordifolia

Brunnera macrophylla

BRUNNERA   Perennial Forget-me-not

A ground cover plant which will grow quite happily in the shade under leafy trees. The large, branching sprays of small, star-shaped flowers in pale blue give the impression of a giant Forget-me-not, but the leaves show that it is more closely related to Anchusa than to Forget-me-not (Myosotis). These heart-shaped leaves are large and rough to the touch, producing dense clumps of foliage by the end of the season. Water during dry spells and cut off the flowering stems when the blooms have faded. An easy plant for difficult situations.

VARIETIES: A single species is grown in gardens — **B. macrophylla**, which used to be called **Anchusa myosotidiflora.** Its statistics are height 1½ ft, spacing 1½ ft, flowering period April–June with a second flush in autumn. The flowers are about ¼ in. across. The popular choice is the variegated variety **B. macrophylla 'Variegata'.** Its leaf edges are cream — a shady site is essential for the development of this variegation.

SITE & SOIL: Any well-drained garden soil will do — thrives best in shade.

PROPAGATION: Divide clumps in autumn or spring, or take root cuttings in winter.

B. macrophylla

Flowers for Every Season

JUNE–JULY
(for JANUARY–MAY see page 43) (for AUGUST–SEPTEMBER see page 53)
(for OCTOBER–DECEMBER see page 57)

By careful selection you can ensure that your border will be in bloom during every month of the year. For each month there is a list of perennials which can be expected to be in full flower — remember that some of these plants may come into bloom earlier and can continue to flower for many weeks afterwards.

JUNE

Ajuga reptans
Anchusa azurea
Aquilegia vulgaris
Astrantia major
Centaurea dealbata
Chrysanthemum maximum
Delphinium hybrids
Dianthus plumarius
Eremurus robustus
Filipendula hexapetala
Geranium 'Johnson's Blue'
Geum chiloense

Iris (Tall Bearded)
Iris kaempferi
Lupinus hybrids
Meconopsis betonicifolia
Nepeta mussinii
Paeonia lactiflora
Primula florindae
Prunella grandiflora
Ranunculus aconitifolius
Saxifraga umbrosa
Stachys macrantha
Veronica incana

JULY

Achillea filipendulina
Aconitum napellus
Alchemilla mollis
Alstroemeria aurantiaca
Anchusa azurea
Astilbe arendsii
Campanula spp.
Catananche caerulea
Centranthus ruber
Coreopsis grandiflora
Delphinium hybrids
Dianthus allwoodii
Dictamnus albus
Erigeron speciosus
Gaillardia aristata
Gypsophila paniculata
Hemerocallis hybrids

Heuchera hybrids
Linum narbonense
Lychnis chalcedonica
Lythrum salicaria
Meconopsis cambrica
Monarda didyma
Nepeta mussinii
Penstemon gloxinioides
Platycodon grandiflorum
Polemonium caeruleum
Potentilla hybrids
Scabiosa caucasica
Sidalcea malvaeflora
Thalictrum dipterocarpum
Tradescantia virginiana
Trollius ledebouri
Verbascum hybridum

Caltha palustris

CALTHA   Kingcup, Marsh Marigold

Caltha is a water lover, and so it is only suitable for marshy or boggy ground. Plant it by the poolside or in shallow water, but never in a herbaceous border which dries out in summer. The dark green heart-shaped leaves have serrated edges and in spring the flowers appear. These golden heads, 1 to 2 in. across, are carried on branching stems above the leaves. They are free-flowering, providing a splash of bright colour for many weeks. If the planting site is above water level it will be necessary to ensure that the ground is kept constantly moist.

VARIETIES: The basic species, **C. palustris,** grows wild as an aquatic plant in Britain. Its details are height 1 ft, spacing 1 ft and flowering period April–June. The single flowers are golden yellow and there is a white variety **'Alba'** which may be more unusual but is also more unreliable and less free-flowering. Best of all is the double-flowering form **'Plena'** or **'Flore Pleno'.**

SITE & SOIL: An organic-rich, moist soil is essential — thrives in sun or partial shade.

PROPAGATION: Divide clumps immediately after flowering has finished.

C. palustris 'Plena'

CAMPANULA Bellflower

Campanulas are one of the mainstays of the British garden and they appear in several sections of this book — as biennials (page 13), rockery plants (page 91) and on this page as perennials for the mixed and herbaceous border. The large flowers are either star-shaped or bell-shaped, and the usual colours are blue and lavender. The stems are upright and the flowers appear between June and August. The arrangement of the flowers on the stem gives a clue to the species, and all varieties are excellent for cutting. Keep watch for slugs, stake tall plants and dead-head to prolong the floral display.

VARIETIES: Nearly all border Campanulas belong to one or other of 4 species. **C. persicifolia** is the most popular, growing 2 or 3 ft high. The cup-shaped flowers are borne along the wiry main stems which rise up above a basal rosette of evergreen leaves. **'Telham Beauty'** (light blue) is the established favourite — for a change try **'Snowdrift'** (white) or the double-flowered **'Bernice'** (blue). Set the plants about 1 ft apart. **C. latifolia** (4–5 ft) is a taller species than persicifolia, and the large flowers are shaped like long bells. They are borne on tall spikes and there are several recommended varieties — **'Alba'** (white), **'Brantwood'** (violet) and **'Gloaming'** (lilac). **C. lactiflora** (3–5 ft) is another tall-growing species, but here the open-bell flowers are borne in branching heads. **'Loddon Anna'** (pink) is a popular choice, so is **'Pritchard's Variety'** (lavender-blue). The fourth species is **C. glomerata** (2 ft), represented in the catalogues by the violet-blue **'Superba'**. In this species the small, bell-like flowers are borne in spherical clusters.

SITE & SOIL: Any well-drained garden soil will do — thrives in sun or partial shade.

PROPAGATION: Plant cuttings in a cold frame in spring or divide clumps in autumn or spring.

Campanula glomerata 'Superba'

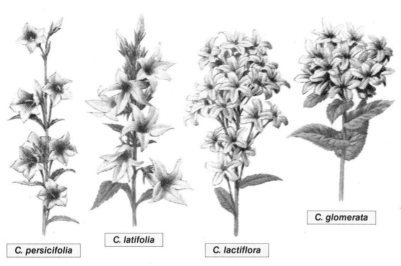

C. persicifolia

C. latifolia

C. lactiflora

C. glomerata

Campanula latifolia 'Alba'

CATANANCHE Cupid's Dart

Catananche will thrive in dry, sandy soil where moisture-loving perennials would undoubtedly fail. The wiry flower stems rise above the greyish grassy leaves in early summer and the silvery buds are eye-catching. The flowering season is a long one, the buds opening to produce papery flowers which are about 1½ in. across. The ends of the petals are blunt and serrated — a useful key to recognition. Support the stems with twigs and cut the flowers for indoors — they can be used fresh or dried for winter decoration. Cut back the stems once flowering is over.

VARIETIES: There is one species — **C. caerulea**. Basic details are height 2 ft, spacing 1 ft, flowering period June–September. The flowers are somewhat similar to Cornflowers and the plants are relatively short-lived. The best variety to grow is **'Major'** — the lavender-coloured blooms are large. For white flowers grow **'Alba'** or **'Perry's White'** — for blue-centred flowers with white edges buy the variety **'Bicolor'**.

SITE & SOIL: Any well-drained garden soil will do — thrives best in light land. A sunny spot is essential.

PROPAGATION: Sow seeds under glass in spring. Alternatively take root cuttings in winter.

Catananche caerulea

C. caerulea

Centaurea montana

CENTAUREA Cornflower, Knapweed

Annual Cornflowers are listed on page 14 — below you will find the perennial varieties suited to the herbaceous border. All bear thistle-like flowers which are excellent for cutting, producing their main flush of blooms in summer with a second flush in autumn. Under good growing conditions the Perennial Cornflower spreads rapidly and should be lifted and divided every three years. Stake tall-growing types and dead-head to prolong the flowering display. Cut the stems down to ground level in late autumn.

VARIETIES: C. dealbata has 2 fine varieties which grow about 2 ft tall and bloom in June and July. Space the plants 1½ ft apart. **'Steenbergii'** bears large crimson flowers with white centres and the yellow-centred pink flowers of **'John Coutts'** are even larger. Less popular but equally attractive is the taller **C. macrocephala** (3–4 ft) which produces yellow globular blooms on thick stems. **C. montana** (1½ ft, flowering period May–July) produces large numbers of feathery flowers in white, pink or purple.

SITE & SOIL: Any well-drained garden soil will do — thrives in sun or light shade.

PROPAGATION: Divide clumps in autumn or spring.

C. dealbata
'Steenbergii'

Centranthus ruber

CENTRANTHUS Red Valerian

A fine cottage garden plant which will thrive in any soil that does not become waterlogged in winter. It will grow readily from self-sown seed as the clumps colonising old walls clearly demonstrate. Another outstanding feature of Centranthus is its long flowering season from early summer to late autumn, although the plants are unfortunately short-lived. The small flowers are borne in clusters above the shiny, lance-shaped leaves; in autumn cut down the stems to ground level. An undemanding plant which anyone can grow.

VARIETIES: The basic species is **C. ruber**, pink-flowered, 1½ ft high and in bloom from June to October. It is much better to buy one of the varieties. **'Coccineus' ('Atrococcineus')** is taller (2½ ft) with bright crimson flowers. Set the plants about 2 ft apart. Another good variety is **'Albiflorus' ('Albus')**, similar in size and shape to 'Coccineus' but bearing snow white flowers. The varieties 'Coccineus' and 'Albiflorus' are sometimes planted together.

SITE & SOIL: Any well-drained soil will do — thrives best in full sun.

PROPAGATION: Sow seeds under glass in April or plant cuttings in a cold frame in spring.

C. ruber
'Coccineus'

Chrysanthemum maximum 'Esther Read'

CHRYSANTHEMUM Shasta Daisy

The hardy perennial Chrysanthemum which is so often seen in herbaceous borders is the Shasta Daisy (C. maximum). The flowers are large, 2½–4 in. across, and may be single, semi-double or double. The petals are white and at the centre of each single variety is a prominent yellow eye. It is an excellent plant for garden display and cutting, but it should be given some care and attention. Divide the clumps about every 3 years and mulch around the plants in May. Dead-head spent blooms and cut down the stems to ground level in autumn.

VARIETIES: There are many named varieties of **C. maximum** (height 2½–3 ft, spacing 1½ ft, flowering period June–August). The most popular one is the double-flowered **'Esther Read'** but a better choice is **'Wirral Supreme'** which bears larger flowers. There are several reliable single varieties, such as **'Everest'** and **'H. Seibert'**. More difficult to find is the low-growing **C. rubellum** (1½ ft). It flowers from August to October, just when the popular ones are finishing, and the petals are pink or yellow rather than plain white.

SITE & SOIL: Any well-drained soil will do — add lime if it is acid. Thrives best in full sun.

PROPAGATION: Plant cuttings in a cold frame in March or divide clumps in spring.

C. maximum
'Wirral Supreme'

CIMICIFUGA   Bugbane, Snakeroot

Many of the plants in this section are known to nearly all gardeners, but Cimicifuga may well be new to you. It is a tall woodland plant belonging to the Buttercup family, producing white, plume-like flowering spikes in late summer or autumn. It will not succeed unless you provide the necessary conditions — humus-rich soil below and partial shade above. It also needs space, so it is a perennial for the middle or back of a large herbaceous border which is shaded by a wall or trees. Mulch around the stems in May and provide support. Cut down to ground level in November.

VARIETIES: C. foetida grows 4–6 ft high with a planting distance of 2 ft. The flowering spikes are erect and branched with the unusual property of deterring insects, but the unpleasant smell may also deter you. The variety to grow is **'White Pearl'**, blooming in September and October. **C. cordifolia (C. americana)** is a smaller species (2–4 ft). **C. racemosa** (5–7 ft) produces flowers in July and August which are slightly fragrant rather than evil smelling.

SITE & SOIL: Thrives in moist soil and light shade.

PROPAGATION: Divide clumps in autumn or spring.

Cimicifuga racemosa

C. foetida 'White Pearl'

CLEMATIS   Clematis

The popular varieties of Clematis are climbers, but there are a few herbaceous perennial species which grow no more than 4 ft high and are suitable for the border. They are not difficult to grow, but they are difficult to find unless you go to a supplier of unusual plants. Before planting in the herbaceous border add compost to the soil — if the ground is badly drained it would be foolhardy to grow this out-of-the-ordinary plant. Support the stems with twigs, apply a mulch in May and refrain from hoeing close to the plants.

VARIETIES: C. heracleifolia is the species you are most likely to find. Basic details are height 3–4 ft, spacing 1½–2 ft, flowering period August–September. The fragrant 1 in. blossoms have light blue, curled-back petals. **C. recta** grows to the same height but the flowers are quite different — large clusters of white fragrant blooms in June and July. **C. integrifolia** is a smaller plant (1½–2 ft) blooming from June to August. The blue bell-shaped flowers, about 1½ in. across, are borne singly on top of the stems.

SITE & SOIL: Any well-drained moist soil will do. Add lime if the soil is acid. Thrives in sun or light shade.

PROPAGATION: Plant cuttings in a cold frame in April or divide clumps in autumn or spring.

Clematis heracleifolia

C. heracleifolia

COREOPSIS   Tickseed

Coreopsis is a familiar sight in the herbaceous border — bright yellow Daisy-like flowers borne freely on slender stems. The blooms are usually large and they are excellent for cutting. The most popular species is C. grandiflora, a plant with the annoying habit of dying after a few years. Provided you have not planted it in heavy soil it will not be your fault if it dies — it is basically shorter-lived than the other species of garden Coreopsis. With all types provide support for the wiry stems and water when the weather is dry. Cut the shoots down to ground level in late autumn.

VARIETIES: The basic details of **C. grandiflora** are height 1½ ft, spacing 1½ ft, flowering period June–September, bloom diameter 2 in. Some named varieties are taller than the parent — **'Badengold'** (3 ft), **'Sunburst'** (2½ ft), **'Mayfield Giant'** (2½ ft) etc, but one is a dwarf — **'Goldfink'** (9 in.). **C. verticillata** bears yellow star-shaped flowers and ferny foliage. A compact bushy plant, 1½–2 ft high — grow the variety **grandiflora**.

SITE & SOIL: Any well-drained garden soil will do — thrives in sun or light shade.

PROPAGATION: Sow seeds under glass or outdoors in March. Alternatively divide clumps in autumn or spring.

Coreopsis 'Goldfink'

C. grandiflora

C. verticillata

CORTADERIA Pampas Grass

Decorative grasses have no place in a book on garden flowers, but one of these grasses produces a flowering spike which is so spectacular and so popular that it deserves a place here. The silvery silky plumes of Pampas Grass are about 1½ ft long and their tips are up to 10 ft above the ground. Female plants produce the best plumes and the display is always at its best after a hot summer. Plant in April as a single specimen in the lawn or against a background of dark evergreen foliage. The bluish green leaves are narrow and arching — wear gloves when handling them. In late autumn cut off the flowering stems and in early spring cut away or burn the dead leaves.

VARIETIES: C. selloana (C. argentea) grows about 7 ft high, bearing showy plumes on stiff stems. The tallest plants and the largest plumes are produced by the variety **'Sunningdale Silver'** — the plumes are more spreading than those of other varieties. The dwarf is **pumila**, growing about 4 ft high and the decorative-leaved form is **'Gold Band'** (6 ft), bearing yellow-and-green striped foliage.

SITE & SOIL: Any well-drained garden soil will do — thrives in sun or partial shade.

PROPAGATION: Clumps can be divided in April but it is better to buy new plants.

C. selloana

Cortaderia selloana 'Sunningdale Silver'

DELPHINIUM Delphinium

Many people have resolved to grow Delphiniums after seeing a group of well-grown giants towering over their heads in a border owned by an experienced gardener. Spikes clothed with large flowers in white, blue, pink, mauve or purple — hardly any other border plant can catch the eye in quite the same way. You can, of course, achieve the same sort of results if you have the space, but tall Delphiniums are not easy plants to grow to perfection. You will need to ensure that the soil is fertile and well drained and planting should take place in spring. Strong canes will have to be inserted at an early stage and you must keep careful watch for slugs and powdery mildew. Water in dry weather. When the main flowering period during June and July has passed, cut back the flowering stems to induce another flush of flowers in autumn. In late autumn cut the stems down to ground level. The plants will slowly deteriorate with age and there is nothing you can do about it. The answer is to lift the clumps in spring every few years and divide them, replanting only the most vigorous sections.

VARIETIES: The popular garden varieties have been derived from **D. elatum** and are placed in 3 groups. The *Elatum* group have the classical Delphinium shape and flower form, growing up to 8 ft tall with upright spikes bearing large flat flowers which may be semi-double or double. The tall ones (height 5–8 ft, spacing 2½ ft) include **'Vespers'** (blue-mauve), **'Butterball'** (cream) and **'Mullion'** (blue). Amongst the dwarfs (height 3–4½ ft, spacing 1½ ft) can be found **'Mighty Atom'** (lilac), **'Cinderella'** (purple) and **'Blue Tit'** (dark blue). The second major section of Delphiniums is the *Belladonna* group — height 3–4 ft, spacing 1½ ft. These slender plants produce branching flower-heads which bear cupped (not flat) blooms. Compared with the Elatum group, the flowers are smaller and more widespread — the popular varieties are **'Pink Sensation'** (pink) and **'Blue Bees'** (pale blue). The third section is the *Pacific Giants* group — tall and large flowered, they can be raised from seed but unfortunately live only for a few years. Buy a mixture or a named variety, such as **'Galahad'** (white) or **'King Arthur'** (purple).

SITE & SOIL: Well-drained and fertile soil is necessary — thrives best in a sunny and sheltered situation.

PROPAGATION: Plant cuttings in April or divide clumps in spring. Sow Pacific Giants seeds under glass in early spring.

Delphinium 'Butterball'

D. elatum
Elatum group

D. elatum
Pacific Giants group

D. elatum
Belladonna group

Delphinium 'Pink Sensation'

DIANTHUS   Border Carnation, Pinks

Dianthus is found in several parts of the garden. In the rockery you will see the Alpine Pinks and in the flower beds both Sweet William and the Annual Carnations are popular. This section deals with the hardy perennial varieties — the Border Carnations, the Old-fashioned Pinks and the Modern Pinks. All form tufts of grassy grey-green leaves with flowers borne on upright stems. Perfume is an important feature and all will flourish in chalky soil and urban smoke. The Border Carnations produce stout stems and the blooms are large. Staking is essential. A typical Carnation is quite different from a typical Pink, but the dividing line is not clear cut. Pinks have more delicate stems, narrower leaves, smaller flowers and a more dainty appearance.

Dianthus caryophyllus 'Mixed Hybrids'

VARIETIES: The basic details of *Border Carnations* are height 2–3 ft, spacing 1½ ft, flowering period July (southern counties), August (northern counties). After a few seasons the plants deteriorate and will need to be replaced. The petals are smooth-edged (unlike the serrated petals of the Florist Carnation) and there are selfs (single colour), fancies (2 or more colours) and picotees (pale colour with a darker edging). The list of varieties is enormous — you will find names like **'Edenside Fairy'**, **'Consul'**, **'Fiery Cross'** and **'Perfect Clove'**. *Old-fashioned Pinks* grow about 1 ft high and should be planted 1 ft apart. There is a single flush of flowers in June and they are slow growing, but there is still a place for **'Mrs Sinkins'** and **'White Ladies'** (white), **'Excelsior'** (carmine) and **'Emil Paré'** (pink). The *Modern Pinks* (hybrids of **D. allwoodii**) are steadily taking over because they are quicker growing and have a 'perpetual-flowering' habit, blooming in June and July and again in autumn. Choose your Pinks from this Modern group — there are **'Doris'** (salmon-pink), **'Show Pearl'** (white), **'Robin'** (scarlet) and many others.

SITE & SOIL: Any well-drained garden soil which is not acid will do — choose a sunny spot.

PROPAGATION: Sow seeds under glass in April or plant cuttings in a cold frame in July. Alternatively layer side shoots in August.

Dianthus plumarius 'Mrs Sinkins'

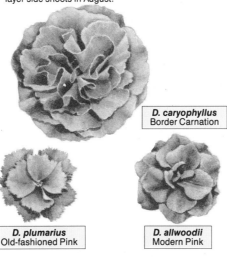
D. caryophyllus Border Carnation

D. plumarius Old-fashioned Pink

D. allwoodii Modern Pink

Dianthus allwoodii 'Doris'

Flowers for Every Season

AUGUST–SEPTEMBER

(for JANUARY–MAY see page 43) (for JUNE–JULY see page 48)
(for OCTOBER–DECEMBER see page 57)

By careful selection you can ensure that your border will be in bloom during every month of the year. For each month there is a list of perennials which can be expected to be in full flower — remember that some of these plants may come into bloom earlier and can continue to flower for many weeks afterwards.

AUGUST

Acanthus spinosus	Lysimachia clethroides
Achillea filipendulina	Macleaya cordata
Agapanthus africanus	Oenothera missouriensis
Anchusa azurea	Phlox spp.
Campanula spp.	Physostegia virginiana
Dianthus caryophyllus	Polygonum affine
Echinacea purpurea	Potentilla hybrids
Echinops ritro	Rudbeckia fulgida
Eryngium spp.	Salvia superba
Gaillardia aristata	Saponaria officinalis
Helenium autumnale	Sidalcea malvaeflora
Helianthus decapetalus	Solidago hybrida
Heliopsis scabra	Stachys lanata
Hosta spp.	Stokesia laevis
Kniphofia uvaria	Thalictrum dipterocarpum
Ligularia dentata	Tradescantia virginiana
Limonium latifolium	Verbascum hybridum

SEPTEMBER

Acanthus spinosus	Lysimachia clethroides
Achillea filipendulina	Lythrum salicaria
Agapanthus africanus	Oenothera missouriensis
Anaphalis spp.	Phlox spp.
Anemone japonica	Physalis franchetii
Aster novi-belgii	Physostegia virginiana
Chrysanthemum rubellum	Polygonum affine
Cimicifuga foetida	Potentilla hybrids
Clematis heracleifolia	Rudbeckia fulgida
Cortaderia selloana	Salvia superba
Echinacea purpurea	Saponaria officinalis
Eryngium spp.	Schizostylis coccinea
Inula hookeri	Sedum spectabile
Kniphofia uvaria	Solidago hybrida
Liatris spicata	Stokesia laevis
Ligularia dentata	Tradescantia virginiana
Liriope muscari	Viola odorata

Dicentra spectabilis

DICENTRA   Bleeding Heart

Dicentra has collected many common names during its long history as a cottage garden plant. It flourishes in humus-rich soil under tall shrubs and trees, the arching stems above the ferny leaves bearing curiously-shaped flowers which give rise to the popular names such as Dutchman's Breeches and Lady in the Bath. Choose a sheltered spot at the front of the border or plant them to provide ground cover in a woodland garden. Applying a mulch each May is the only treatment required by this easy-to-grow old favourite.

VARIETIES: The most popular Dicentra is the largest — **D. spectabilis**. The basic details are height 2–3 ft, spacing 1½ ft, flowering period May–June. The rosy red, locket-like flowers bear protruding white petals and hang from the arching stems. This species is not always the best choice — it dies down after flowering and can be damaged by spring frosts. These faults are not shared by the smaller feathery-leaved species — **D. formosa** (1–1½ ft) and **D. eximia** (1½ ft).

SITE & SOIL: Any well-drained garden soil will do — thrives best in light shade.

PROPAGATION: Divide clumps in autumn or spring — be careful not to break the brittle roots.

D. spectabilis

Dictamnus albus

DICTAMNUS   Burning Bush

The popular Burning Bush is Kochia, an annual grown for its foliage which turns red in the autumn. Dictamnus, however, is the *true* Burning Bush — strike a match close to the flower-heads once the blooms have faded and on a warm still day the volatile oils will ignite. A blue flame will surround the upper part of the bush but the plant will not be damaged. It is more than a novelty to amuse the children — Dictamnus produces fragrant spidery flowers above deeply-cut, lemon-scented leaves in midsummer. It will take a couple of years to become established but after that the plant is reliable and long-lived.

VARIETIES: The basic details of **D. albus (D. fraxinella)** are height 2 ft, spacing 1½ ft, flowering period June–August. The tall spikes bear white or pale purple flowers which measure 1½ in. in diameter. For even larger flowers grow the variety **caucasicus** and the brightest blooms are borne by **'Purpureus'**, a pink-flowered variety with red stripes.

SITE & SOIL: Any well-drained soil which is not acid will do — thrives in sun or light shade.

PROPAGATION: Do not divide the clumps. Buy a container-grown plant or sow seeds under glass in spring if you are willing to wait 3 years for the plants to reach flowering size.

D. albus 'Purpureus'

Doronicum caucasicum 'Spring Beauty'

DORONICUM   Leopard's Bane

If you want to fill a patch of your bed or border with large and yellow Daisy-like flowers, a glance through this book will reveal a wide choice. Doronicum is the one to select when you also want earliness — in many herbaceous borders it is this plant which provides the first splash of bright colour amongst the herbaceous perennials. It involves no particular problems — provide some support for the stems and dead-head the spent blooms. Keep watch for slug damage and cut the stems down to ground level in the autumn. Divide the clumps and replant every three years.

VARIETIES: D. plantagineum bears 3 in. flowers — its basic details are height 2–3 ft, spacing 1½ ft and flowering period April–June. There are 2 outstanding varieties — **'Miss Mason'** (2 ft) and **'Harpur Crewe'** (3 ft). **D. caucasicum** is a smaller species (1–1½ ft) with 2 in. flowers — it has produced the fully double variety **'Spring Beauty'**. The smallest Doronicum of all is also the first to flower — **D. 'Gold Dwarf'** (6 in.).

SITE & SOIL: Any reasonable garden soil will do — thrives in sun or partial shade.

PROPAGATION: Divide clumps in autumn or spring.

D. plantagineum 'Harpur Crewe'

Echinacea purpurea 'Bressingham Hybrid'

ECHINACEA   Purple Coneflower

Echinacea is a reliable late-flowering perennial which is closely related to Rudbeckia. The kinship is clearly seen at the centre of each large Daisy-like flower — there is a prominent cone-like central disc. The difference lies in the colour of the petals — yellow or orange is the basic colour of Rudbeckia but it is rose or purple in Echinacea. An easy plant to grow but a hungry one — add compost to the soil before planting and feed in summer. Dead-head faded blooms and cut the stems down to ground level at the end of the season.

VARIETIES: **E. purpurea** is the species grown in the garden. Basic details are height 3–4 ft, spacing 2 ft, flowering period July–October. The toothed leaves are rough to the touch and the flowers are excellent for cutting. The usual variety is **'The King'** — 4 ft tall with drooping, dull pink petals around the central cone. **'Bressingham Hybrid'** (3 ft) is brighter and there is also a white-petalled variety with a yellow cone — **'White Lustre'**.

SITE & SOIL: Any well-drained garden soil will do — thrives best in full sun.

PROPAGATION: Divide clumps in spring.

E. purpurea
'The King'

ECHINOPS   Globe Thistle

A fine erect-growing plant for the back of the border — stout stems bearing grey-green deeply lobed leaves, long and thistle-like, with globular flower-heads in summer. These blue heads are 2 to 3 in. across and if the stems are cut before the blooms are fully open they can be dried for winter decoration. It is an undemanding plant, thriving in dry as well as chalky soils, but it is unhappy in shade or shallow soil. Wear gloves when handling the stems and leaves — some people develop a rash when pricked by the spines which occur in some varieties.

VARIETIES: The most popular species is **E. ritro** — height 3–4 ft, spacing 2 ft, flowering period July–September. The flowers are steely blue and the leaves are downy underneath. **E. humilis** (5 ft) is a taller plant with smaller flowers — the recognition feature is the cobwebby cover on the foliage. The named varieties offer a range of heights — the short one is **E. 'Veitch's Blue'** (3 ft, dark blue); a tall Echinops is **E. 'Taplow Blue'** (5 ft, light blue).

SITE & SOIL: Any well-drained garden soil will do — thrives best in full sun.

PROPAGATION: Divide clumps in autumn or spring.

Echinops 'Veitch's Blue'

E. ritro

EPIMEDIUM   Barrenwort, Bishop's Hat

This ground cover perennial which flourishes in the light shade under shrubs or trees only just qualifies for a place in a book on flowers. It is grown primarily for its foliage — leathery, heart-shaped leaves borne on wiry stems and changing colour as the season progresses, pink-veined in spring and overall bronze in autumn. The flowers are small and somewhat insignificant, but they appear before the new leaves — pink, red, yellow, purple or white blooms on long stalks. Do not remove the foliage in autumn; it will remain on the plants over winter.

VARIETIES: Several species of Barrenwort are available — the basic details are height 9 in., spacing 1 ft, flowering period April–May. **E. warleyense** bears coppery flowers, **E. perralderianum** produces sprays of yellow blooms in June. **E. versicolor 'Sulphureum'** is another yellow-flowering variety and the largest-flowering type is **E. grandiflorum** (1 in. blooms). The brightest Epimedium is probably **E. pinnatum colchicum** (bright yellow flowers, red autumn foliage).

SITE & SOIL: Any reasonable garden soil will do — thrives best in partial shade.

PROPAGATION: Divide clumps in autumn or spring.

E. grandiflorum

Epimedium versicolor 'Sulphureum'

Eremurus robustus

EREMURUS Foxtail Lily

The Foxtail Lily rivals the Delphinium in stateliness — colourful and massive upright spikes rising well above head-height. Their appearance, however, is quite unlike the Delphinium — Eremurus spikes are made up of countless starry flowers in white, pink or yellow. It is not an adaptable plant and you will have to choose its site carefully. Both full sun and protection from cold winds are necessary, and copious watering is required during dry weather in spring. Prolonged hard frost in winter can be fatal — protect the crowns with bracken or peat in late autumn.

VARIETIES: A typical giant Eremurus is **E. robustus**, height 8–10 ft, spacing 3 ft, flowering period May–June, flower colour peach. **E. elwesii** (7–10 ft, fragrant pink flowers) is another stately species with a white variety **'Albus'**. The favourite variety for the smaller garden is the yellow-flowered **E. bungei (E. stenophyllus)** which grows about 3 ft high.

SITE & SOIL: Well-drained soil with full sun in the afternoon and evening are essential.

PROPAGATION: Divide clumps in autumn or spring.

E. bungei

Erigeron speciosus

ERIGERON Fleabane

At first glance this popular front-of-the-border plant can be mistaken for a small Michaelmas Daisy. The petals, however, are more numerous and it blooms earlier. The disc is always yellow and the flowers are single or semi-double. Erigeron is easy to grow — provide some support for the stems and dead-head faded blooms. Take some of the flowers indoors for arranging and in the autumn cut the stems down to ground level.

VARIETIES: Fleabanes have been grown in cottage gardens for hundreds of years. Several types were grown and the most widely planted was the purple narrow-petalled **E. speciosus**. The blooms of this species tend to droop and these days hybrids of E. speciosus have taken over — the flowers are larger, brighter and hold their heads up. The basic details of the varieties are height 1–2 ft, spacing 1 ft, flowering period June–August. Typical hybrids are **'Prosperity'** (light blue), **'Foerster's Liebling'** (pink), **'Darkest of All'** (violet) and **'Dignity'** (lilac).

SITE & SOIL: Any well-drained garden soil will do — thrives in sun or light shade.

PROPAGATION: Divide clumps in spring.

E. 'Foerster's Liebling'

E. 'Dignity'

Eryngium bourgatii

ERYNGIUM Sea Holly

The Sea Holly in bloom is quite unmistakeable. The rosette of thistle-like leaves and the branching stems usually have a bluish tinge, and each thimble-shaped blue flower-head has an intricately spined ruff. It is happiest in the dry, sandy soil of its native seaside home, but it will flourish in any well-drained, non-acid soil. At the end of the season cut the stems down to ground level — to increase your stock each mature clump can be divided, but it is better to buy new plants.

VARIETIES: Sea Hollies should be planted 1–1½ ft apart — the flowering period is July–September. Height depends on the species chosen — two low-growing ones are **E. variifolium** (2 ft, evergreen, white-veined leaves) and **E. alpinum** (2 ft, metallic blue flowers). A popular and taller species is **E. oliverianum** (3 ft, pale purple flowers), and **E. tripartitum** (3 ft) bears attractive grey-blue flowers. The most compact type is **E. bourgatii** (1½ ft) with its silvery blue leaves and flowers.

SITE & SOIL: Any well-drained garden soil will do — thrives best in full sun.

PROPAGATION: Clumps can be divided in spring, but Eryngium does not like root disturbance.

E. oliverianum

EUPHORBIA   Spurge

Hardy Spurges are the poor relations of the showy Poinsettias which brighten homes at Christmas time. The outdoor varieties serve as border, rockery and ground cover plants, succeeding in sun and shade, in rich and poor soils, and requiring little attention. There are evergreen types bearing bluish green foliage throughout the year and all bear insignificant flowers surrounded by bracts. Unfortunately these bracts are small and with a single exception are either yellow or green. No show-piece then, but a useful workhorse in the herbaceous border.

E. polychroma

VARIETIES: E. polychroma (E. epithymoides) grows 1½ ft high, producing sulphur yellow flowers in April and May. **E. robbiae** bears yellow flowers at the same time of the year and should be planted 1½ ft apart. In addition to these ground cover plants there is the tiny and evergreen **E. myrsinites** (6 in., yellowish green flowers in May). At the other end of the scale **E. wulfenii** grows 4 ft tall and for colour grow **E. griffithii 'Fireglow'** which bears flame-coloured bracts in May and June.

SITE & SOIL: Any well-drained soil will do — thrives in sun or partial shade.

PROPAGATION: Plant cuttings in a cold frame in spring or divide clumps in autumn or spring.

Euphorbia griffithii 'Fireglow'

Flowers for Every Season

OCTOBER–DECEMBER
(for JANUARY–MAY see page 43)
(for JUNE–JULY see page 48)
(for AUGUST–SEPTEMBER see page 53)

By careful selection you can ensure that your border will be in bloom during every month of the year. For each month there is a list of perennials which can be expected to be in full flower — remember that some of these plants may come into bloom earlier and can continue to flower for many weeks afterwards.

OCTOBER

Anemone japonica
Aster novi-belgii
Centranthus ruber
Chrysanthemum rubellum
Cimicifuga foetida
Cortaderia selloana
Echinacea purpurea
Liriope muscari

Phlox paniculata
Physalis franchetii
Polygonum affine
Saxifraga fortunei
Scabiosa caucasica
Schizostylis coccinea
Sedum spectabile
Viola odorata

NOVEMBER

Iris stylosa
Liriope muscari

Saxifraga fortunei
Viola odorata

DECEMBER

Iris stylosa

FILIPENDULA   Dropwort

A small group of old-fashioned plants which used to be included with Spiraea. The leaves are often fern-like and the stems bear terminal clusters of small flowers. With some varieties the foliage is the main attraction and the flowers are removed — with others the blooms are attractive enough for garden display and indoor decoration. Filipendula offers no particular problems — add organic matter to the soil before planting, apply a mulch in May, water in dry weather and cut down the stems in autumn.

F. hexapetala 'Flore Pleno'

VARIETIES: F. ulmaria 'Aurea' (Golden Meadow Sweet) is grown for its yellowish foliage — remove flowers as they form. **F. hexapetala** (Dropwort) is grown for its pink-tinged flowers as well as its ferny foliage — basic details are height 2½ ft, spacing 2 ft, flowering period June–July. The small blooms are borne on branching sprays — grow the double-flowered form **'Flore Pleno'**. In the woodland garden grow the pink **F. rubra** (4–6 ft).

SITE & SOIL: Any moist garden soil will do — thrives best in light shade.

PROPAGATION: Divide clumps in autumn or spring.

Filipendula hexapetala

GAILLARDIA Blanket Flower

A familiar sight in herbaceous borders everywhere — large Daisy-like flowers, measuring 2 to 4 in. across, with red or orange petals tipped with yellow or gold. The blooms continue to appear from early summer until autumn and cut blooms are long-lasting in water, but the Blanket Flower has one major problem. In badly-drained soil it will die out in winter and even when given an ideal environment of sandy, well-drained soil and full sun, deterioration takes place in just a few years. To prolong its life, remember to cut the stems down to ground level in September and to divide the clumps every three years.

G. aristata
'Wirral Flame'

VARIETIES: The species grown is **G. aristata (G. grandiflora)** — height 1½ – 2½ ft, spacing 1½ ft, flowering period June – September. The stems require support. Popular varieties include **'Dazzler'** (red centre, orange outside), **'Wirral Flame'** (dark red, tipped yellow), **'Croftway Yellow'** (all yellow) and the red and yellow **'Mandarin'**. A few dwarfs are available — the most famous is **'Goblin'** (9 in., flame red, tipped yellow).

G. aristata
'Goblin'

SITE & SOIL: Any well-drained garden soil will do — light land is preferred. Choose a sunny spot.

PROPAGATION: Sow seeds under glass or outdoors in spring. Divide clumps in March or take root cuttings in early spring.

Gaillardia aristata 'Dazzler'

GERANIUM Crane's-bill

The Geranium or Crane's-bill should not be confused with the half hardy Pelargonium (see page 144) which is popularly referred to as 'Geranium'. The Geranium of the herbaceous border is a hardy perennial which is grown as a ground cover, its mounds of dense and deeply divided leaves serving to suppress weed growth. The 1 to 2 in. saucer-shaped flowers are white, pink, blue or red and should be removed once they have faded. Keep watch for slugs in spring and cut back the stems to ground level in autumn.

G. psilostemon

VARIETIES: There are numerous species and varieties — making a choice is not easy. If you are new to Geraniums, pick one of the reliable favourites. There are **G. 'Johnson's Blue'** (1½ ft, spacing 1½ ft, flowering period May – August), **G. endressii 'Wargrave Pink'** (1½ ft) and the violet-blue **G. platypetalum** (2 ft) which blooms in July and August. The low-growing **G. macrorrhizum 'Walter Ingwersen'** (1 ft, pink flowers) is popular — so is **G. psilostemon** (2½ ft) with its magenta flowers. There are dwarf varieties for the rock garden — see page 94.

G. platypetalum

SITE & SOIL: Any well-drained soil will do — thrives in sun or light shade.

PROPAGATION: Sow seeds of species (not named varieties) under glass in spring. Divide clumps in autumn or spring.

Geranium endressii 'Wargrave Pink'

GEUM Avens

Geum forms dense, weed-smothering clumps at the front of the border, and in early summer wiry stems appear which bear the bright, bowl-shaped flowers. These blooms are about 1½ in. across — single, semi-double or double and in shades of yellow, orange and red. It is an easy plant to grow, but will benefit greatly if you enrich the soil with compost or peat before planting, provide support for the stems and cut back to ground level once the flowering season is over. The popular varieties are short-lived — divide the clumps every few years.

G. chiloense
'Fire Opal'

VARIETIES: The popular species is **G. chiloense** (height 1–2 ft, spacing 1½ ft, flowering period May – September). You will find a number of named varieties in catalogues and garden centres but two have remained strong favourites for many years — **'Mrs Bradshaw'** (double scarlet) and **'Lady Stratheden'** (double yellow). For a change try **'Fire Opal'** (flame), **'Prince of Orange'** (orange) or **'Golden West'** (yellow). **G. borisii** (1 ft, orange) is useful for the front of the border — **G. rivale** (1 ft) is at home in boggy land.

G. chiloense
'Lady Stratheden'

SITE & SOIL: Any well-drained garden soil will do — thrives in sun or light shade.

PROPAGATION: Sow seeds under glass in spring or divide clumps in autumn or spring.

Geum chiloense 'Mrs Bradshaw'

GYPSOPHILA   Baby's Breath

Gypsophila provides a welcome relief from the large-flowering colourful varieties in the herbaceous border — from the untidy collection of thin stems and greyish green grassy leaves arise the loose clusters of small flowers. White or pale pink, these blooms form a billowy cloud — hence the common name. Alkaline soil is necessary; add lime if your land is acid. Deep soil is another requirement and Gypsophila should not be divided or transplanted once it is established. Provide support for the lax stems and cut some of the flowers for indoor decoration. Cut the shoots down to ground level in autumn.

VARIETIES: **G. paniculata** is the border species and the standard choice is **'Bristol Fairy'** — height 3 ft, spacing 3 ft, blooming period June–August. Its flowers are white and double, but white is not the only Gypsophila colour. **'Rosy Veil'** is widely available — a compact 1 ft variety which produces double blooms, white at first but turning pink with maturity.

SITE & SOIL: Any well-drained non-acid garden soil will do — thrives in sun or light shade.

PROPAGATION: Buy 'Bristol Fairy' from your local shop or nursery — seed sown in spring under glass will not all breed true. Plant cuttings in a cold frame in summer.

Gypsophila paniculata

G. paniculata 'Bristol Fairy'

HELENIUM   Sneezewort

Erect and easy-to-grow perennials for the middle and back of the border, regarded by many as an indispensable source of yellows and reds in late summer. Each of the large Daisy-like flowers has a prominent central disc and the blooms are excellent for indoor decoration. Mulch around the stems in spring and water in dry weather. Provide support for the stems if the site is exposed and dead-head spent blooms. The quality of the flowers steadily deteriorates — to avoid this, lift the clumps every few years and divide them, retaining only the vigorous outer sections.

VARIETIES: By far the most popular variety of **H. autumnale** is **'Moerheim Beauty'** — bronze red and an example of the average-sized Helenium: height 3 ft, spacing 2 ft and flowering period July–September. Others in this range include **'Butterpat'** (golden yellow) and **'Coppelia'** (orange and red). There are also late-flowering giants, such as **'Chipperfield Orange'** (4½ ft, August–October) and early dwarfs, such as **'Crimson Beauty'** (2 ft, June).

SITE & SOIL: Any well-drained garden soil will do — thrives in sun or light shade.

PROPAGATION: Divide clumps in autumn or spring.

Helenium autumnale 'Coppelia'

H. autumnale 'Butterpat'

H. autumnale 'Moerheim Beauty'

HELIANTHUS   Sunflower

The giant Sunflower is the annual variety (see page 22). The perennial types grow 4 to 6 ft tall with flowers measuring 2 or 3 in. across — a far cry from the dinner-plate blooms of H. annuus. The perennial Sunflower is suited to the back of the border, its strong stems bearing yellow or golden blooms in late summer and early autumn. It is a sun lover but there are no special soil requirements — the only problem is that the plants deteriorate with age. Lift the clumps every 3 years and divide to prevent exhaustion.

VARIETIES: **H. decapetalus** has single, semi-double and double varieties, all of which are suitable for flower arranging. The best of the singles is the large-flowered **'Maximus'** (6 ft), but the perennial Sunflower which is most often recommended is the double **'Loddon Gold'** (height 5 ft, spacing 2 ft, flowering period July–September). Other recommended types are the semi-double **'Triomphe de Gand'** and **'Soleil d'Or'**.

SITE & SOIL: Any well-drained garden soil will do — thrives best in full sun.

PROPAGATION: Sow seeds under glass or outdoors in April or divide clumps in autumn or spring.

Helianthus decapetalus 'Soleil d'Or'

H. decapetalus 'Loddon Gold'

Heliopsis scabra 'Golden Plume'

HELIOPSIS Heliopsis

Yet another summer-flowering yellow Daisy for the middle of the border. This group of flower types is an overcrowded one, but Heliopsis has at least three points in its favour. The 3 ft high plants are compact and bushy, they do not have to be lifted and divided every few years, and the blooms are unusually long-lasting. It will grow in almost any type of soil and very little attention is needed. The 3 in. flowers are yellow or golden, and may be single, semi-double or double. At the end of the season cut the stems down to ground level.

VARIETIES: H. scabra has provided the garden varieties — height 3–4 ft, spacing 2 ft, flowering period July–August. The single-flowered types are **'Gigantea'** (4 ft) and **patula** (3 ft). The popular choice is the double-flowered **'Golden Plume'** (3½ ft) — well-formed Sunflower-like blooms which are excellent for cutting. **'Incomparabilis'** (3 ft) has Zinnia-like blooms and the novelty is **'Goldgreenheart'** with lime-centred flowers.

SITE & SOIL: Any reasonable garden soil will do — thrives best in full sun.

PROPAGATION: Divide clumps in autumn or spring.

H. scabra 'Golden Plume'

Helleborus niger

HELLEBORUS Christmas Rose, Lenten Rose

The ideal place for Helleborus is close to the front of the shrub border where nearby evergreens will protect it from the worst of the winter winds and where the welcome early flowers will be in full view. The large saucer-shaped blooms may be white, pink or purple, depending on the variety, and the time of flowering ranges from mid winter to late spring. The deeply lobed leaves provide good ground cover and the flowers last well in water. A much-loved plant which needs very little attention — dig in compost, leaf mould or peat before planting, watch for slugs in spring and water in dry weather.

VARIETIES: H. niger is the Christmas Rose — height 1–1½ ft, spacing 1½ ft, flowering period January (despite the popular name) to March. The flowers are white with a central boss of golden stamens — the largest flowers are borne by **'Potter's Wheel'**. The Lenten Rose (**H. orientalis**) blooms later, between February and April, and the petals may be white, pink or purple. **H. foetidus** (1½ ft, February–April) bears purple-rimmed yellow flowers.

SITE & SOIL: Requires well-drained moist soil — thrives best in partial shade.

PROPAGATION: Buy young plants from your garden shop or nursery. If clumps are overcrowded divide in spring.

H. niger

H. orientalis

Hemerocallis 'Golden Chimes'

HEMEROCALLIS Day Lily

Day Lilies such as H. fulva have been grown in Britain for hundreds of years, but only recently have they become widely popular. No longer is the gardener restricted to the dull yellow and orange shades — modern hybrids are available in a vast range of colours from palest yellow to richest red, the Lily-like trumpets measuring up to 7 in. across and both 1½ ft dwarfs and 4 ft giants are available. The great virtue of the Day Lily is its ease of cultivation — give it a moisture-retentive soil and it will grow almost anywhere. Clumps of strap-like leaves give rise to branching flower stalks in summer, each flower lasting a single day but new buds appearing continually during the flowering season. Water thoroughly in dry weather.

VARIETIES: Basic details for the Hemerocallis Hybrids are height 3 ft, spacing 2 ft, flowering period June–August. Choose from **'Pink Damask'** (pure pink), **'Stafford'** (yellow-eyed red), **'Black Magic'** (yellow-eyed dark red), **'Golden Orchid'** (orange), **'Golden Chimes'** (2 ft, yellow) . . . but there are scores of others.

SITE & SOIL: Any reasonable garden soil will do — thrives in sun or light shade.

PROPAGATION: Divide clumps when overcrowded in autumn or spring.

H. 'Stafford'

HEUCHERA   Coral Flower

Heuchera has been used for many years as ground cover in herbaceous or mixed borders and for edging along pathways. The evergreen rounded leaves form neat mounds and in early summer the slender stems appear, bearing dense clusters of tiny bell-shaped flowers. These blooms are suitable for cutting but until the modern hybrids were developed the colour range was strictly limited. Mulch around the plants in spring and cut down the stems after flowering. After a few years the crown of the plant tends to push out of the ground — lift the clump in autumn or spring, divide and then replant.

VARIETIES: Numerous hybrids have been developed from **H. sanguinea** and **H. brizoides**. Basic details are height 1½ – 2½ ft, spacing 1½ ft, flowering period June – August. Brightest of all is **'Red Spangles'** with its crimson flowers — at the other extreme is **'Pearl Drops'** with its pure white blooms. There are several pinks — **'Hyperion'**, **'Scintillation'**, **'Jubilee'**, etc, and a greenish yellow one (**'Greenfinch'**). Some nurseries offer a small, pretty-leaved hybrid of Heuchera and its relative Tiarella — **Heucherella tiarelloides**.

SITE & SOIL: Any well-drained garden soil will do — thrives in sun or light shade.

PROPAGATION: Divide clumps in autumn or spring.

Heuchera 'Red Spangles'

H. sanguinea

HOSTA   Plaintain Lily

Hosta is a dual-purpose plant, grown for its spikes of trumpet-shaped flowers as well as its attractive broad leaves, often variegated or distinctly coloured. It thrives in the partial shade beneath shrubs and trees and as a ground cover plant it effectively suppresses weeds. Its drawbacks in this situation are the deciduous nature of its leaves and the attractiveness of the young spring foliage to slugs. Add compost or peat to the soil before planting and mulch around the plants in spring. Dead-head the faded blooms.

VARIETIES: Many catalogues and garden centres offer a large selection of Hostas, ranging from near-blue to almost pure yellow foliage. The basic details are height 1½ – 3 ft, spacing 2 ft, flowering period July – August. For deep shade choose the green-leaved, white-flowered **H. 'Royal Standard'** which blooms until October. For partial shade there is **H. fortunei 'Albopicta'** (green-edged cream leaves), **H. sieboldiana 'Elegans'** (large bluish green leaves, purple-tinged white flowers), **H. ventricosa** (dark green leaves, 3 ft spikes of lilac flowers), **H. 'Thomas Hogg'** (white-edged green leaves) and **H. undulata** (wavy-edged leaves).

SITE & SOIL: Any reasonable soil will do — thrives best in partial shade.

PROPAGATION: Divide clumps in spring.

Hosta sieboldiana 'Elegans'

H. ventricosa

INCARVILLEA   Chinese Trumpet Flower

Despite its odd growth habit and conservatory-plant appearance, there is nothing difficult about Incarvillea. In early May the flower stalks push through the ground and in early summer the Gloxinia-like flowers open. Several of these 3 in. trumpets are borne on each stalk, and the plant's peculiar feature is the appearance of the leaves *after* flowering has taken place. Add compost to the soil before planting and mark the plant's position with a stick in autumn — all growth disappears in winter and it is so easy to cut off the emerging flowers when hoeing in spring!

VARIETIES: I. delavayi is the basic species — height 2 ft, spacing 1 ft, flowering period May – June. The dark green leaves are fern-like and the flowers deep pink. A pale pink variety (**'Bees Pink'**) is available. Less easy to find but more colourful is the smaller variety **I. grandiflora**. The stems grow about 1 ft tall, the leaves are not ferny and the rose-red flowers have yellow throats.

SITE & SOIL: Well-drained soil and full sun are essential.

PROPAGATION: Sow seeds outdoors in spring. Division of clumps in autumn is possible but difficult.

I. delavayi

Incarvillea delavayi

INULA Inula

There are many yellow Daisy-like perennials — some well-known and others unusual like this one. It is a better choice than its popular colleagues when your soil is heavy, the site is partially shaded and you prefer finely-rayed flowers to those with broad petals. It is long-lived and free-flowering, but the clumps should be lifted every 3 years, divided, and then replanted. Apply a mulch in spring and water during dry spells. Cut the stems down to ground level once the flowers have faded.

VARIETIES: There are several varieties in the catalogues but you may have to search to find one at the garden centre. **I. hookeri** (height 2 ft, spacing 1½ ft, flowering period August–September) has 3 in. finely-rayed flowers — the equally large flowers of **I. orientalis** also have very slender petals. The giant **I. magnifica** (6 ft) is more suited to a woodland garden than a herbaceous border — its leaves may be over 3 ft long. Where space is limited grow **I. ensifolia** — 2 in. blooms on 1 ft high plants.

SITE & SOIL: Any reasonable garden soil will do — thrives in sun or partial shade.

PROPAGATION: Divide clumps in autumn or spring.

Inula orientalis

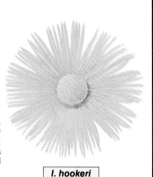

I. hookeri

IRIS Iris

Irises are a vast group of plants ranging from bold-flowering specimens with 4 ft stems to tiny alpines peeping above the earth. Classification is complex, but getting a working knowledge of the main types is not difficult. There are two basic groups — the *Bulb* group (see page 118) and the *Rhizome* group described below, which spread by means of a thickened underground stem which creeps along horizontally. This latter group contains the most popular ones and they are dominated by the Bearded Irises (see the illustration for recognition details). The thick rhizomes bear a fan of flat, broad leaves at the tips and should be planted soon after the flowers have faded, choosing a day between midsummer and early autumn when the soil is moist. Set the rhizomes about 1 ft apart — leave the top half uncovered but if the soil is sandy completely cover the rhizome. Trim the tops off the leaves. Most gardeners look no further than the Bearded Irises but as listed below there is a wide range of interesting Beardless Irises.

VARIETIES: The Bearded Irises have been given many true and false names — Flag Iris, German Iris, **I. germanica** and June Iris. The 3 sections are based on height and are derived from several species. The *Tall* section (2½ ft or over, June flowering) includes thousands of hybrids — a few names are **'Party Dress'** (flamingo pink), **'Jane Phillips'** (pale blue), **'Frost and Flame'** (white, red beard), **'Top Flight'** (apricot) and **'Staten Island'** (gold standards, red falls). The *Intermediate* section (9 in.–2½ ft, May flowering) also has many named hybrids — such as **'Golden Fair'** (yellow) and **'Piona'** (purple). The *Dwarf* section (under 9 in., April flowering) are for the front of the border or the rockery. These Irises are much less popular than the taller ones — look for **'Blue Doll'** or **'Bright White'**. A bearded novelty is the evergreen Gladwyn Iris (**I. foetidissima**), grown for its decorative orange seeds. The Beardless Irises are separated into several sections — some of the popular ones include the *Sibiricas* (**I. sibirica 'Perry's Blue'**, 3 ft, June–July, moisture-loving), *Winter-flowering Irises* (**I. stylosa**, 1 ft, November–February, sun-loving), *Water Irises* (**I. pseudacorus**, 2½ ft, May–June, water-loving) and *Bog Irises* (**I. kaempferi**, 2½ ft, June–July, wet soil-loving).

SITE & SOIL: Bearded Irises require well-drained soil and full sun.

PROPAGATION: Divide rhizomes in late summer every few years. Discard old and damaged portions.

Iris 'Jane Phillips'

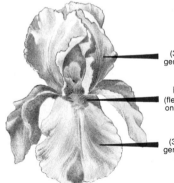

Standards
(3 inner petals, generally standing erect)

Beard
(fleshy hairs on the falls)

Falls
(3 inner petals, generally hanging downwards)

Bearded Iris

Iris sibirica

Iris stylosa

KNIPHOFIA   Red Hot Poker

Over the years this plant has changed its latin name from Tritoma to Kniphofia, and the hybridists have also extended its colour range. A word of caution — you can buy a Red Hot Poker and it may be all-red, yellow or even white, so choose with care if you want the traditional red-tipped variety. Whatever the flower colour, all produce clumps of grass-like foliage and spikes bearing long tubular flowers. Mulch in late spring and water in dry weather. Cold winters can be a problem. In autumn remove the flower spikes, tie the leaves together and cover with peat.

VARIETIES: The popular choice is a variety or hybrid of **K. uvaria** — height 2½ – 5 ft, spacing 3 ft, flowering period July – September. For a 'true' poker — red or orange at the top and yellow at the base, choose **'Royal Standard'**, **'The Rocket'**, **'Springtime'** or **'H.C. Mills'**. For single colours, pick **'Alcazar'** (orange), **'Maid of Orleans'** (white) or **'Bees Lemon'** (yellow). The giant is **'Samuel's Sensation'** (5–6 ft, red). There is a dainty orange dwarf — **K. galpinii**.

SITE & SOIL: Any well-drained garden soil will do — thrives best in full sun.

PROPAGATION: Divide overcrowded clumps in spring.

Kniphofia uvaria 'Springtime'

K. uvaria 'Royal Standard'

LIATRIS   Gayfeather

In late summer or early autumn the erect spikes appear, densely clothed with small fluffy flowers coloured pink or pale purple. Look at the spike closely to spot the unusual feature — the blooms open from the top downwards. The foliage is grass-like and the plants will live for many years provided the soil is not waterlogged in winter. Add peat or well-rotted compost before planting and mulch in the spring. Water when the weather is dry and remove the spikes when the flowers have faded. Mark the position of the plant with a small stick as all traces of the clump will disappear in winter and new growth can be damaged when hoeing in spring before the new leaves appear.

VARIETIES: L. spicata is the species you are most likely to find — height 1½ ft, spacing 1½ ft, flowering period August – September. The popular variety is **'Kobold'** (mauve; broader spikes than the species). **'Silver Tips'** (3 ft) is taller and the flowers are lavender. **L. callilepis** is also a tall-growing plant, producing 2–3 ft spikes of carmine flowers.

SITE & SOIL: L. spicata flourishes in moist soil but good drainage in winter is essential — thrives in sun or light shade.

PROPAGATION: Divide clumps in autumn or spring.

Liatris spicata 'Kobold'

L. spicata

LIGULARIA   Ligularia

Do not grow Ligularia unless you have moisture-retentive soil, a large space to fill and some shade overhead. The large, deeply incised leaves cover the ground and effectively smother weeds, and in summer the flower-heads appear. Each individual bloom is a yellow or orange Daisy, but its size and arrangement on the plant will depend on the variety. Mulch around the plants in May, water copiously if there is a prolonged dry spell and cut back the stems when flowering is over. Lift the clumps every 3 years, divide and then replant.

VARIETIES: L. dentata (L. clivorum) is a popular species — you might find it and other Ligularias listed under 'Senecio' in the catalogues. Its basic features are height 3–4 ft, spacing 2½ ft, flowering period July – September. The flowers are borne in large, spreading heads and the heart-shaped leaves are up to 1 ft across, purplish **('Desdemona')** or red underneath **('Othello')**. The small yellow flowers of **L. przewalskii 'The Rocket'** (5 ft) are borne on erect spikes.

SITE & SOIL: Moist soil and a partially shaded site are essential.

PROPAGATION: Divide clumps in autumn or spring.

Ligularia przewalskii 'The Rocket'

L. dentata

Plants for Flower Arranging

Acanthus spinosus
Achillea spp.
Agapanthus africanus
Alchemilla mollis
Alstroemeria hybrids
Anaphalis triplinervis
Aruncus sylvester
Astrantia spp.
Campanula spp.
Catananche caerulea
Centaurea spp.
Chrysanthemum maximum
Delphinium spp.
Dianthus spp.
Dicentra spectabilis
Doronicum plantagineum

Echinops spp.
Eremurus spp.
Erigeron hybrids
Eryngium spp.
Gaillardia aristata
Geum chiloense
Gypsophila paniculata
Helenium autumnale
Heliopsis 'Golden Plume'
Heuchera hybrids
Iris hybrids
Kniphofia uvaria
Liatris spicata
Limonium latifolium
Lychnis chalcedonica
Macleaya spp.

Oenothera spp.
Paeonia spp.
Papaver orientale
Penstemon hybrids
Phlox spp.
Physalis franchetii
Polygonatum hybridum
Polygonum bistorta
Pyrethrum roseum
Ranunculus spp.
Rudbeckia spp.
Scabiosa caucasica
Schizostylis coccinea
Solidago hybrids
Stokesia laevis
Thalictrum dipterocarpum

Limonium latifolium 'Blue Cloud'

LIMONIUM   Sea Lavender, Statice

Limonium is a dual-purpose plant — grow it to produce a summer-long display of frothy clouds of tiny blooms in beds and borders, and also cut it to provide a supply of 'everlasting flowers' for indoor decoration. For drying, cut the stems just before the flowers are open and tie in bunches. Hang upside down in a cool place away from sunlight. Limonium (more commonly known as Statice) is often grown as an annual, but the perennial varieties are taller and bear masses of pink or lavender flowers year after year. It will grow in poor and stony soils, requiring little attention apart from the need to be cut down to ground level in autumn. The rootstock is woody and the plant takes some time to become established — do not propagate by dividing old plants.

VARIETIES: L. latifolium (Statice latifolia) is the basic species — height 2½ ft, spacing 1½ ft, flowering period July–September. The spreading flower panicles appear above the rosettes of oval leaves — good varieties are **'Blue Cloud'** (large, lavender flowers), **'Collyers Pink'** (pink flowers) and **'Violetta'** (violet-blue flowers).

SITE & SOIL: Any well-drained garden soil will do — thrives best in full sun.

PROPAGATION: Sow seeds under glass in spring or take root cuttings in winter.

L. latifolium

Linum narbonense

LINUM   Perennial Flax

Compared to the leafy stems and long-lasting flowers of many herbaceous border plants, Perennial Flax has a fleeting delicacy. The wiry stems with their narrow leaves bear 5-petalled blooms which open and then begin to fade within a day. But during the summer months there are always more buds to open — a pretty blue picture which is seen at its best in sandy soil and hot weather. Mulch in spring and water during dry spells in summer, but no matter how careful you are the plants will be short-lived. Fortunately, fresh stock can be raised easily from seed or cuttings.

VARIETIES: L. narbonense produces 1 in. flowers with rich blue petals and white centres. The basic details are height 1–2 ft, spacing 1 ft, flowering period June–August. **'Six Hills'** is a popular variety — the shortest is **'Heavenly Blue'** (1 ft). **L. perenne** produces paler flowers — a delightful sky blue. This type is perhaps the best one to grow. At large nurseries you might find its white, pink or red varieties.

SITE & SOIL: Any well-drained garden soil will do — thrives best in full sun.

PROPAGATION: Sow seeds under glass in spring or plant cuttings in a cold frame in May.

L. perenne

LIRIOPE   Lily Turf

It is strange that Liriope has remained so uncommon. It will not thrive in chalky soils, but if your land is lime-free then this tufted plant will remain evergreen in most areas and produce spikes of tiny bell-shaped flowers throughout the autumn. It will withstand both shade and drought, and can be used for the front of the border or as ground cover under taller plants. If you don't want it to spread, lift and divide the clumps every few years. Cut off faded flower stems in autumn and trim back old leaves in spring.

VARIETIES: The basic species is **L. muscari (L. platyphylla)** — height 1–1½ ft, spacing 1 ft, flowering period September–November. The flowers which appear above the grassy leaves are similar to Grape Hyacinth in shape — the usual colour is mauve or violet, but a white variety is available and there is also a yellow variegated form. **L. spicata** (Creeping Lily Turf) has narrower leaves than the more popular L. muscari.

SITE & SOIL: Any lime-free garden soil will do — thrives in sun or partial shade.

PROPAGATION: Divide clumps in spring.

Liriope muscari

L. muscari

LUPINUS   Lupin

Before the 1930s Lupins were nothing special, but the introduction of the Russell Hybrids changed all that. They are now amongst the most popular of all perennials, their large pea-like flowers crowded on to stately spires in a vast range of colours. They are accommodating plants — quick-growing, tolerant of light shade and town conditions, but they are also short-lived. Add peat (not compost) before planting and cover the crowns in winter if your garden is in a frost pocket. Lupins unfortunately have a number of enemies — virus (mottled leaves and brown stems), slugs and mildew.

VARIETIES: The usual practice is to buy a mixture of Russell Hybrids of **L. polyphyllus** which have been raised from seed. The basic details are height 3–4 ft, spacing 2 ft, flowering period June–July (and September if the first flush is removed when blooms have faded). Named varieties are available — some are a single colour, such as **'Lady Fayre'** (pink) and **'Lilac Time'** (lilac), and others are bi-colours, like **'Blue Jacket'** (blue/white) and **'Mrs Micklethwaite'** (pink/gold).

SITE & SOIL: Any well-drained garden soil will do — acid land is preferred. Thrives in sun or light shade.

PROPAGATION: Sow seeds under glass in spring or plant basal cuttings (with a few roots attached) in March.

Lupinus 'Monarch'

L. polyphyllus 'Russell Hybrid'

LYCHNIS   Campion

The Campions are sun-lovers bearing flowers which are generally red or pink . . . and there is hardly any other common feature which links together the various species grown as garden perennials. Although differing markedly in appearance, they do have similar cultural requirements. Stake the stems on exposed sites and water copiously in dry weather. Dead-head to prolong the flowering display and cut down the stems to ground level in autumn.

VARIETIES: The best Campion to grow is **L. chalcedonica** (Jerusalem Cross) — height 3 ft, spacing 1½ ft, flowering period June–August. Large heads of bright red flowers are borne on long leafy stems. The flowers of **L. coronaria** (Rose Campion) are borne in loose sprays above the grey foliage — it grows about 1½ ft high and both magenta and white varieties are available. **L. flos-jovis** (Flower of Jove) produces rose-coloured flowers above the silvery foliage in June and July; **L. viscaria 'Splendens Plena'** (1½ ft) bears clusters of double pink flowers above the sticky leaves in early summer.

SITE & SOIL: Any well-drained garden soil will do — thrives best in full sun.

PROPAGATION: Sow seeds under glass in spring or divide clumps in autumn.

Lychnis chalcedonica

L. chalcedonica

L. coronaria

Lysimachia clethroides

LYSIMACHIA   Loosestrife

Lysimachia is a useful plant for a damp site in partial shade. The erect stems bear white or yellow flowers, depending on which of the two species you grow, and you would never guess that they were related. Dig plenty of compost into the soil before planting and remember that these plants can spread rapidly. To prevent them from crowding other plants, dig up the clumps, divide and then replant every three years. Creeping Jenny (L. nummularia) is an old favourite in rockeries — see page 98.

VARIETIES: **L. clethroides** (Chinese Loosestrife) bears curved spikes about 5 in. long of tiny white flowers — the lance-shaped leaves and flower spikes give it the appearance of a small Buddleia bush. Basic details are height 3 ft, spacing 2 ft, flowering period July – September. **L. punctata** (Yellow Loosestrife) is rather smaller (2½ ft) and blooms earlier (June – August). Its leafy stems bear whorls of yellow, starry flowers which have a reddish tinge at the base of the petals.

SITE & SOIL: Any moisture-retentive garden soil will do — thrives in sun or partial shade.

PROPAGATION: Divide clumps in autumn or spring.

L. punctata

Lythrum salicaria 'Firecandle'

LYTHRUM   Purple Loosestrife

This water-loving plant is at its best in boggy ground by the poolside or in the wild garden, but it will grow quite happily in humus-rich soil in the herbaceous border. The leaves are dark green and elongated — above them rise the narrow flower spikes, densely packed with pink or red starry blooms. These spikes are colourful, prolific and long-lasting — Lythrum is a good choice if you have moist soil. Mulch in spring, water copiously if the ground is dry and cut the stems down to ground level in autumn.

VARIETIES: The basic species is **L. salicaria** — it can reach 5 or 6 ft, but the named varieties are shorter and generally more attractive — height 2½ – 4 ft, spacing 1½ ft, flowering period June – September. One of the brightest is **'The Beacon'** (3 ft, crimson) — other popular types are **'Lady Sackville'** (4 ft, rose-pink) and **'Firecandle'** (3 ft, rose-red). For the middle of the border choose **'Robert'** (2½ ft, pink). **L. virgatum** is a smaller species with daintier spikes — named varieties include **'Rose Queen'** (2 ft, rose-pink) and **'The Rocket'** (2 ft, deep pink).

SITE & SOIL: Any moisture-retentive garden soil will do — thrives in sun or partial shade.

PROPAGATION: Divide mature clumps in autumn or spring. Alternatively plant basal cuttings in a cold frame in April.

L. salicaria

Macleaya microcarpa 'Coral Plume'

MACLEAYA   Plume Poppy

This one is not for you if your garden is small. Macleaya (still referred to by its old name Bocconia by many gardeners) is a glutton for space. Not only does it grow more than head-high but its underground suckers are invasive, spreading out in all directions. But for the back of an extensive herbaceous border or as a specimen plant in a large lawn it is an excellent choice. The deeply-cut leaves are greyish or bronze-coloured above and hoary white below, attractive for much of the year but only in midsummer does the full beauty of the plant occur. Large plume-like panicles of tiny flowers provide a white or pinkish haze above the foliage. Cut down the stems in autumn.

VARIETIES: The basic details of **M. cordata** are height 6 – 8 ft, spacing 3 ft, flowering period July – August. The 3 ft plumes bear pearly white flowers — the plant which produces buff-coloured flowers with a distinct pinkish tinge is often sold as 'M. cordata' but is really **M. microcarpa 'Coral Plume'**. Its bronzy flowers are very small but in all other ways it is similar to M. cordata.

SITE & SOIL: Any reasonable soil will do — thrives in sun or partial shade.

PROPAGATION: Divide clumps in autumn or spring. Alternatively plant basal cuttings in a cold frame in April.

M. cordata

MECONOPSIS   Meconopsis

There are numerous species of this Poppy-like perennial for the collector of unusual plants, but for the ordinary gardener there are just two — the Himalayan Blue Poppy and the Welsh Poppy. Both need humus-rich soil which must be kept moist in summer — add compost or peat at planting time and water copiously in dry weather. Provide some support if the site is exposed and don't try to grow these plants if your ground becomes waterlogged in winter. The blooms of Meconopsis are short-lived and unfortunately so are the plants. Your stock will have to be regularly replenished from seed.

VARIETIES: The Himalayan Blue Poppy, once called **M. baileyi** but now referred to as **M. betonicifolia**, has been much admired since its introduction in the 1930s. The basic details are height 3 ft, spacing 1½ ft, flowering period June–July. The sky blue flowers are 3 in. across but must not be allowed to appear too early — remove all buds which appear during the first year. The Welsh Poppy **M. cambrica** is smaller and less demanding — height 1 ft, spacing 9 in., flowering period June–September. The blooms are yellow or orange.

SITE & SOIL: Requires lime-free, well-drained soil in light shade.

PROPAGATION: Sow seeds under glass in spring.

Meconopsis cambrica

M. betonicifolia

MONARDA   Bergamot

The wild Bergamots grow close to water or in damp woodland — the garden hybrids are at home in the herbaceous border but they do need moist soil. If your ground is short of humus, add plenty of compost or peat at planting time. Mulch the plants in spring and water copiously if the summer is hot and dry. The clumps of stems bear hairy, Mint-like leaves which are strongly aromatic — pick and dry quickly to provide an ingredient for pot-pourri. The flower-heads, made up of whorls of tubular flowers, are borne on top of upright stems. To keep the plants vigorous lift, divide and then replant the clumps every three years. Cut back the stems to ground level in autumn.

VARIETIES: The hybrids have been derived from **M. didyma** — basic details are height 2–3 ft, spacing 2 ft, flowering period June–September. The two popular varieties are **'Croftway Pink'** (rose-pink) and **'Cambridge Scarlet'** (red) — other types include **'Prairie Night'** (purple), **'Snow Maiden'** (white) and **'Adam'** (rose-red).

SITE & SOIL: Any moisture-retentive garden soil will do — thrives in sun or light shade.

PROPAGATION: Divide clumps in autumn or spring.

Monarda didyma 'Cambridge Scarlet'

M. didyma 'Croftway Pink'

NEPETA   Catmint

Catmint is popular with gardeners for use as an edging plant — it is even more popular with cats who love to roll amongst its aromatic grey-green leaves. It will flourish in sandy, stony and chalky soils but will die out rapidly in heavy or shallow soils which remain sodden in winter. The small tubular flowers are borne on upright spikes — dead-heading will encourage further flushes and the bushy plants will stay in flower from late spring until early autumn. Do not cut down the stems in autumn — remove the old growth when new shoots start to appear in the spring. An easy-to-grow plant which deserves its popularity — lift, divide and replant the clumps every three years.

VARIETIES: The basic species is **N. mussinii (N. faassenii)** — height 1 ft, spacing 1½ ft, flowering period May–September. The flowers are pale purple. Taller varieties are available — **'Superba'** (2–3 ft) produces lavender flowers and **'Six Hills Giant'** (2 ft) has blooms which are violet. These taller Catmints require staking.

SITE & SOIL: Any well-drained garden soil will do — thrives best in full sun.

PROPAGATION: Divide clumps in spring (not autumn).

Nepeta mussinii

N. mussinii

Plants suitable for Shady Sites

Dry sites

Alchemilla mollis
Anaphalis spp.
Anemone japonica
Bergenia spp.
Brunnera macrophylla
Cortaderia selloana
Doronicum plantagineum
Epimedium spp.
Euphorbia spp.
Iris foetidissima
Liriope muscari
Physalis franchetii
Pulmonaria spp.
Salvia superba

Moist sites

Aconitum napellus
Ajuga spp.
Alchemilla mollis
Aquilegia hybrids
Astilbe arendsii
Astrantia major
Bergenia spp.
Caltha palustris
Cimicifuga foetida
Dicentra spectabilis
Filipendula spp.
Helleborus spp.
Hosta spp.
Ligularia spp.

Lysimachia clethroides
Lythrum salicaria
Monarda hybrids
Omphalodes spp.
Physostegia virginiana
Polygonum affine
Ranunculus spp.
Rodgersia spp.
Saxifraga umbrosa
Thalictrum spp.
Tiarella cordifolia
Tradescantia virginiana
Trollius hybridus
Viola spp.

OENOTHERA Evening Primrose

Oenothera tetragona 'Fireworks'

The buds of these attractive flowers usually open in the evening — hence the common name. The blooms are large, saucer-shaped and silky — somewhat similar to Poppies, perhaps, but nothing like Primroses. They love sun and sand — choose something else if your soil is heavy and poorly drained. For best results mulch around the stems in spring, water during dry spells in summer and cut the stems down to ground level in late autumn. The blooms are excellent for indoor arrangements.

VARIETIES: The largest blooms, 3–4 in. across, are borne by the low-growing **O. missouriensis**. The basic details are height 6–9 in., spacing 1½ ft, flowering period July–September. The yellow, bowl-shaped flowers are borne above the sprawling stems. **O. tetragona** is a taller plant — height 1½ ft, spacing 1 ft, flowering period June–August. The flower stems arise from a basal rosette of leaves — the most colourful variety is **'Fireworks'** (purplish leaves, red buds and yellow flowers). Another reliable and popular Evening Primrose is **O. fruticosa 'Yellow River'** (1½ ft, yellow flowers).

SITE & SOIL: Any light or loamy well-drained garden soil — thrives best in full sun.

PROPAGATION: Divide clumps in spring. O. missouriensis is an exception — sow seeds under glass in spring.

O. missouriensis

OMPHALODES Navelwort, Blue-eyed Mary

Omphalodes cappadocica

The range of reliable carpeting plants which will flourish and flower in the shade under trees and shrubs is quite limited — Navelwort is worth searching for. The blue flowers are borne early in the season in loose sprays above the foliage which remains green almost all year round. The roots require humus — add peat, compost or leaf mould when planting and mulch around the stems in spring. Dead-heading will prolong the floral display.

VARIETIES: O. cappadocica produces all-blue flowers, about ½ in. across, in graceful sprays. Basic details are height 9 in., spacing 1 ft, flowering period May–June. The variety **'Anthea Bloom'** bears pale blue flowers. A variation in flower colour is found in **O. verna** — each blue bloom has a prominent white centre. It is rather lower-growing than O. cappadocica and there are other differences — it is earlier flowering (March–May) and quicker growing. Choose O. verna if you want to cover a patch of ground with Omphalodes in the shortest possible time.

SITE & SOIL: Any moisture-retentive garden soil will do — thrives best in shade.

PROPAGATION: Divide clumps in autumn.

O. cappadocica 'Anthea Bloom'

PAEONIA Paeony, Peony

Paeonies are the aristocrats of the herbaceous perennial world. The flower stalks rise up above the attractive foliage and each one bears several blooms — blooms which make most other garden flowers blush with shame. Vast bowls of petals up to 7 in. across — single, semi-double, double or Anemone-flowered in a wide array of colours. When making your choice, remember that doubles last longer than singles and the species determines the month when the plants can be expected to bloom (see below). Regard Paeonies as a long-term investment and learn the rules before you start planting. Choose an open, sunny spot but try to avoid a situation where early morning sun will shine on the plants. Early autumn is the best time for planting and the soil should be deeply dug and enriched with compost or leaf mould. Set the crown of the plant no lower than 1 in. below the soil surface. The main thing you then have to remember is to leave the plant alone — it may not flower in the first season and will not be properly established for three years. Avoid transplanting at all costs and do not try to divide clumps to increase your stock. The cultural rules are quite straightforward — mulch in spring, stake the stems, water when the weather is dry, dead-head faded blooms, feed with a general fertilizer in late summer and cut down the stems to ground level in autumn.

VARIETIES: The *Common* or *May-flowering Paeony* **(P. officinalis)** grows wild in many parts of Europe and is an old cottage garden favourite — height 2 ft, spacing 1½ ft, flowering period May – June. The 5 in. blooms are red in the wild species but you can now buy double varieties in several shades — **'Alba Plena'** (white), **'Rosea Plena'** (pink), etc. The most popular Paeonies are the varieties of the *Chinese* or *June-flowering Paeony* **(P. lactiflora)** — height 2½ – 3 ft, spacing 2 ft, flowering period June – July. The blooms are up to 7 in. across and the range of colour and flower shapes is extensive. There are fine doubles like **'Sarah Bernhardt'** (pink), **'Festiva Maxima'** (white) and **'M Jules Elie'** (silvery rose). There are singles such as **'William Cranfield'** (red) and the beautiful Anemone-flowered **'Bowl of Beauty'** (pink; cream centre). For an early display grow the *April-flowering Paeony* **(P. mlokosewitschii)** — height 1½ ft, spacing 1½ ft, flowering period April – May. The 4 in. single flowers are yellow and the leaves have a bronzy tinge.

SITE & SOIL: Any well-drained cultivated soil will do — thrives best in full sun.

PROPAGATION: Buy a named variety from a nursery or garden centre — do not divide clumps.

Paeonia 'Bowl of Beauty'

P. 'Sarah Bernhardt'
Chinese Paeony

P. officinalis 'Rubra Plena'
Common Paeony

P. mlokosewitschii
April-flowering Paeony

Paeonia officinalis

PAPAVER Oriental Poppy

When in full flower the Oriental Poppy often overpowers the smaller and more subtle blooms which surround it. The bowl-shaped flowers are up to 6 in. across — colourful and usually black-based petals enclosing a boss of black anthers. Unfortunately it loses this competitive nature when flowering is over — large leafless gaps are left in the border until the bristly, deeply-cut leaves reappear. Papaver is easy to grow and sure to please if you avoid heavy and badly-drained land and remember to stake the flower stems. Cut the plants down to ground level once the flowering season is over. Lift and divide the plants every three years.

VARIETIES: The basic details of **P. orientale** are height 3 ft, spacing 1½ ft, flowering period May – June. Many named varieties are available, ranging in colour from pure white to deep red. Pick from **'Perry's White'** (white), **'Mrs Perry'** (pink), **'Marcus Perry'** (orange-scarlet), **'Salmon Glow'** (double, salmon-orange) and **'Goliath'** (red).

SITE & SOIL: Any well-drained soil will do — thrives best in full sun.

PROPAGATION: Divide clumps in spring or take root cuttings in winter.

Papaver orientale 'Goliath'

P. orientale 'Mrs Perry'

PENSTEMON   Beard Tongue

The catalogue may sing the praises of this perennial — glossy leaves, attractive tubular flowers clustered on erect spikes all summer long, etc, but it is only reliable in sheltered areas with a better than average climate. It is killed by severe winter frosts, especially if the ground is not free-draining, and even in mild regions its life span is usually less than five years. Of course, this challenge may encourage you to grow it — then water copiously in dry weather, dead-head faded blooms, cut down the stems in autumn and cover the crowns with peat in winter. If you don't like to gamble then grow Penstemon from cuttings as a summer-flowering bedding plant.

VARIETIES: The popular hybrids are grouped under **P. gloxinioides (P. hartwegii)** and red is the favourite colour. Basic details are height 1½–2 ft, spacing 1 ft, flowering period June–September. **'Firebird'** is the red variety which is usually offered, but **'Garnet'** is hardier. **'Sour Grapes'** bears slate-blue flowers. Many garden centres offer **P. barbatus** which flowers at the same time as the hybrids but is taller — height 3 ft, spacing 1½ ft, flower colours white, pink and red.

SITE & SOIL: A well-drained soil is essential — thrives best in full sun.

PROPAGATION: Plant cuttings in a cold frame in late summer.

Penstemon gloxinioides 'Garnet'

P. gloxinioides 'Firebird'

PHLOX   Phlox

Phlox is one of the mainstays of the herbaceous border — in late summer it provides waist-high sheets of colour and scent. Each flat-faced flower measures about 1 in. across, nothing very special as individuals but most impressive when seen in large trusses above the narrow, pointed leaves. Prolific flowering is the hallmark of this garden favourite and these days you can buy almost any shade from white to deep purple. It is not a particularly fussy plant — it likes a moist soil (add compost or peat when planting) and the flower colours are at their best when it is grown in light shade. Mulch in spring and water in summer if the weather is dry. Some form of support should be provided if the site is exposed and the stems require to be cut down to a couple of inches above ground level in late autumn when flowering is over. No cultural difficulties, but there is one hidden enemy which can cause havoc. The microscopic phlox eelworm shrivels leaves and distorts the stems. Young shoots are killed and older ones are stunted — look for the tell-tale narrow, strap-like foliage. There is nothing you can do but dig up and burn the plants — do not replant with Phlox, Gypsophila nor Primula for at least three years.

VARIETIES: The popular Garden Phlox is **P. paniculata (P. decussata)** — height 2–4 ft, spacing 1½ ft, flowering period July–October. Large garden centres and comprehensive catalogues offer an abundance of varieties; you will find some or all of the following — **'Brigadier'** (orange-red), **'Balmoral'** (rose-lavender), **'The King'** (violet-purple), **'White Admiral'** (white), **'Starfire'** (deep red), **'Fairy's Petticoat'** (mauve) and **'Endurance'** (salmon-orange). For extra brightness you can plant the purple-flowered **'Harlequin'** which has variegated leaves or you can grow varieties with mirror-imaged blooms — **'Graf Zeppelin'** (red-eyed white flowers) and **'Sweetheart'** (white-eyed red flowers). All these varieties of P. paniculata bear their blooms in rounded clusters — for a different arrangement grow the much less common **P. maculata** which bears its blooms in long columns. Its basic details are height 2–3 ft, spacing 1½ ft, flowering period July–September — the best-known variety is **'Alpha'** (pink).

SITE & SOIL: Any moisture-retentive garden soil will do — thrives in sun or light shade.

PROPAGATION: Divide clumps in autumn or spring; take root cuttings in winter.

Phlox paniculata 'Harlequin'

Phlox paniculata 'Starfire'

P. paniculata   P. maculata

Phlox maculata

Physalis franchetii

PHYSALIS   Chinese Lantern

The sight of Physalis in full bloom would certainly not justify its place in the garden nor its inclusion in this book. The small and nondescript white flowers have little decorative value, but the picture changes when autumn arrives and the leaves start to turn yellow. Large papery structures expand around the fruits, producing golden or flame-coloured Chinese Lanterns hanging from the stems. A novelty in the garden but much more useful as dried plant material for winter flower arrangements. Cut the stems in September and tie in small bunches — hang upside down in a cool and airy place away from direct sunlight. Any soil will do and it will grow in sun or shade.

P. franchetii

VARIETIES: The best species to grow is **P. franchetii** — height 2 ft, spacing 3 ft, flowering period July–August, fruiting period September–October. The 2 in. long 'lanterns' are decorative in the border, but Physalis is best grown in an odd corner away from other plants. Its problem is the invasive nature of its underground stems — if surrounded by other plants it is a good idea to cut around the crown with a spade each autumn.

SITE & SOIL: Any reasonable garden soil will do — thrives in sun or partial shade.

PROPAGATION: Divide clumps in autumn or spring.

Physostegia virginiana 'Summer Snow'

PHYSOSTEGIA   Obedient Plant

An odd name like Obedient Plant needs some explanation. It arises from the peculiar property of the tubular flowers on the upright spikes when moved away from their natural position. Instead of breaking off or springing back like blooms of other plants, they stay in the position to which they have been pushed. Obedient, indeed! It is an easy plant to grow — all that is necessary is to add some compost or peat to the planting hole if your soil lacks humus, water when the weather is dry and cut down the stems in autumn. The taller varieties may require staking on an exposed site.

P. virginiana 'Vivid'

VARIETIES: There is just one species — **P. virginiana**. The basic details are height 2–3 ft, spacing 1½ ft, flowering period July–September. The white, pink or purple flowers are borne in vertical rows on each spike. It can spread and get out of hand — lift, divide and replant every 3 years. The most popular variety is the late-flowering **'Vivid'** (2 ft, rose-pink) — others are **'Summer Snow'** (3 ft, white) and **'Summer Spire'** (3 ft, deep pink).

SITE & SOIL: Any well-drained garden soil will do — thrives in sun or partial shade.

PROPAGATION: Divide clumps in spring.

PLATYCODON   Chinese Bellflower, Balloon Flower

The buds swell into large, angular balloons before opening out to produce saucer-shaped flowers. These blooms are about 2 in. across and long-lasting — Platycodon is an interesting and attractive flower which should be more widely grown. Finding a suitable spot should not be difficult — it has no special soil requirements and will tolerate light shade. Mulch around the young shoots in early summer and cut back the stems in autumn. It does have one problem — all the top-growth disappears in winter and the new shoots do not appear until late spring. It is therefore easy to dig up when cultivating the border and a plant label next to the clump will warn you to steer clear.

P. grandiflorum 'Mariesii'

VARIETIES: The basic details of **P. grandiflorum** are height 1–2 ft, spacing 1 ft, flowering period June–September. White and pink varieties are available but the favourite one is the compact pale blue **'Mariesii'** (1 ft). **'Snowflakes'** is a semi-double white and the pink variety is **'Mother of Pearl'**.

SITE & SOIL: Any well-drained garden soil will do — thrives in sun or light shade.

PROPAGATION: Do not divide the clumps. Sow seeds under glass in spring or buy a named variety from a garden centre or nursery.

Platycodon grandiflorum 'Mariesii'

POLEMONIUM   Jacob's Ladder

Polemonium foliosissimum

P. caeruleum

Jacob's Ladder has been grown in our gardens for many hundreds of years — it has also lived on our hillsides as a wild flower for many thousands of years. Its long history should not deter you from using it in a modern herbaceous border. The bright blue flowers studded with golden stamens first appear in late May or June and then continue throughout the summer. The leaves are deeply-divided into a series of rung-like leaflets — hence the common name. There are no problems about cultivation — add peat or compost at planting time, provide some form of support, dead-head regularly to prolong the flowering season and cut down the stems in autumn.

VARIETIES: The old cottage garden plant is **P. caeruleum** — height 2 ft, spacing 1 ft, flowering period June – August. The ½ in. flowers are blue, but a white form is available. One of the problems with this species is its short-lived nature — choose instead the larger and longer-lived **P. foliosissimum** (height 3 ft, spacing 1½ ft, flowering period June – September). If space is limited there are 2 excellent hybrids — **P. 'Blue Pearl'** (1 ft, deep blue) and **P. 'Sapphire'** (1½ ft, sky blue).

SITE & SOIL: Any well-drained soil will do — thrives in sun or partial shade.

PROPAGATION: Sow seeds under glass in April or divide clumps in autumn or spring.

POLYGONATUM   Solomon's Seal

Polygonatum hybridum

P. hybridum

A shade-loving plant which will thrive in the shadow of trees and shrubs in a mixed border or in the semi-wild garden. The oval leaves clasp the arching stems, providing a graceful and decorative effect even before the bell-like flowers appear in early summer. The green-tipped white blooms are about 1 in. long — small pendent clusters lining the upper part of the stems. The flowering stems are popular with flower arrangers for indoor decoration. Add compost or peat to the soil at planting time, mulch in spring, water during dry spells and cut down the stems in autumn. When growing close to other plants, lift and divide every three years. Watch for sawfly caterpillars in summer — if left unchecked they can skeletonise the foliage in a few days.

VARIETIES: The one listed in the catalogues is **P. hybridum**, usually described as **P. multiflorum** — height 2 – 3 ft, spacing 2 ft, flowering period May – June. For something different try **P. japonicum 'Variegatum'** (2 ft) which bears green and white striped leaves.

SITE & SOIL: Any reasonable garden soil will do — thrives best in shade.

PROPAGATION: Divide clumps in autumn or spring.

POLYGONUM   Knotweed

Polygonum bistorta 'Superbum'

P. affine 'Donald Lowndes'

A large and varied group containing both weeds and garden plants. The tiny flowers are borne on long spikes which appear over a prolonged period stretching from midsummer until autumn. The garden varieties are mainly vigorous ground covers which can spread and become a nuisance if not kept in check. The leaves are sometimes red-tinted and all flourish in moisture-retentive soil. Water during dry spells.

VARIETIES: The most useful Polygonum is **P. affine** — height 1 ft, spacing 2 ft, flowering period June – October. The leaves of this evergreen ground carpeter turn yellow and bronze in autumn as the pink flower spikes begin to fade. The two varieties are **'Darjeeling Red'** (deep pink) and **'Donald Lowndes'** (rose-red). **P. bistorta 'Superbum'** (2 ft) produces tall pokers of pink flowers between July and September, and **P. amplexicaule** bears red pokers above its heart-shaped leaves. It is taller than the others, reaching 3 – 4 ft, and popular varieties are **'Firetail'**, **'Speciosum'** and **'Atrosanguineum'**. The prettiest Polygonum is the non-invasive **P. campanulatum** (3 ft) which bears its pink flowers in loose sprays.

SITE & SOIL: Any reasonable garden soil will do — thrives in sun or partial shade.

PROPAGATION: Divide clumps in autumn or spring.

POTENTILLA   Cinquefoil

Woody Potentillas are popular plants for the shrub border. These small-leaved compact bushes bear bright flowers all summer long — a property shared with the herbaceous Potentillas grown in the flower border. The herbaceous varieties, however, do not form neat clumps like their woody relatives — they have weak sprawling stems and strawberry-like leaves. Grow them close to the front of the border, mulch around the shoots in spring, and provide support for the stems. Water in dry weather and your reward will be a continual display of bright saucer-shaped flowers. Cut down the stems in autumn; lift and replant every three years.

VARIETIES: The named garden hybrids have been developed from **P. nepalensis**, **P. atrosanguinea** and **P. argophylla** — basic details of these hybrids are height 1–2 ft, spacing 1½ ft, flowering period June–September. The popular trio are **'Miss Willmott'** (red), **'Gibson's Scarlet'** (red) and **'William Rollisson'** (semi-double, deep orange, yellow reverse). The most colourful variety is **'Firedance'** — red-centred and yellow-fringed blooms borne in great profusion.

P. 'Gibson's Scarlet'

SITE & SOIL: Any well-drained soil will do — thrives best in full sun.

PROPAGATION: Divide clumps in autumn or spring.

Potentilla 'Firedance'

PRIMULA   Primrose

A vast genus of garden plants — there are tender Primulas for indoors, water-loving varieties for the bog garden, compact and miniature types for the rockery and several sorts, described below, which are excellent for use in the herbaceous border. The dividing line between these groups is not clear-cut — some so-called alpine varieties are suitable for the small border, and some bog Primulas are quite at home in a peaty flower bed. As a general rule all the Primulas thrive best in partial shade and soil which is rich in humus. The species (but not the named varieties) can be grown from seed but all the Primulas tend to be short-lived. Mulch in spring, water in summer and dead-head faded blooms.

Primula variabilis 'Pacific Strain'

VARIETIES: The Common Primrose (**P. vulgaris**) has a place in the cottage garden, its yellow flowers appearing on 6 in. stems in March and April. The great favourite, however, is the Polyanthus (**P. variabilis**) — a hybrid of the Common Primrose and the Cowslip (**P. veris**). The Polyanthus is much bigger and brighter than the ordinary Common Primrose — its basic details are height 1 ft, spacing 1 ft, flowering period March–May. Its 1–1½ in. flowers are borne in large trusses on stout stems. The **'Pacific Strain'** has a wide range of colours — the **'Goldlace Strain'** has yellow-edged petals. In **P. denticulata** the yellow-eyed lavender flowers are small and crowded on 3 in. wide globular heads — hence the common name Drumstick Primrose. **P. florindae** (height 2 ft, spacing 2 ft, flowering period June–July) is the Giant Yellow Cowslip, each tall stem bearing a loose head of pendent, fragrant flowers. It needs constantly moist soil and is ideal for a poorly-drained site. A large group of Primulas produce 'candelabra' flower-heads — the blooms are borne as a series of whorls up the stem. **P. japonica** (height 1½ ft, spacing 1 ft, flowering period March–May) is a good example — so is the larger and later-flowering **P. pulverulenta**. Other candelabra types include the orange-flowered **P. bulleyana** (2–3 ft), the lilac-coloured **P. beesiana** (2 ft) and the red **'Chungensis Hybrids'** (2 ft).

SITE & SOIL: Any reasonable garden soil containing adequate organic matter will do — thrives best in partial shade.

PROPAGATION: Sow seeds under glass in March or divide clumps of named varieties in spring.

| **P. variabilis** Polyanthus | **P. denticulata** Drumstick Primrose | **P. florindae** Giant Yellow Cowslip | **P. japonica** Candelabra Primrose |

Primula bulleyana

Prunella webbiana 'Pink Loveliness'

PRUNELLA   Self-heal

Self-heal is a mat-forming ground cover for the front of the border or the rockery — not often seen but most useful for keeping down weeds. The foliage is dark green and in midsummer the flower spikes appear, each one bearing a cluster of tubular hooded flowers. There are no problems involved in its cultivation — mulch in spring, water during dry spells, dead-head faded blooms and cut the stems down to ground level in autumn. Lift, divide and replant the clumps every two or three years.

P. grandiflora

VARIETIES: P. grandiflora bears pale purple flowers — basic details are height 9 in., spacing 1½ ft, flowering period June–July. **P. webbiana** is quite similar, but the leaves are broader and the tubular 1 in. flowers are available in several colours. The favourite variety is **'Pink Loveliness'** (clear pink) — others to choose from are **'Alba'** (white), **'Loveliness'** (mauve) and **'Rosea'** (rose-pink).

SITE & SOIL: Any reasonable garden soil will do — thrives in sun or light shade.

PROPAGATION: Divide clumps in autumn or spring.

Pulmonaria saccharata

PULMONARIA   Lungwort

Lungwort is an old favourite, with white-spotted leaves and bearing flowers which change from pink to blue as they open. But not all Lungworts follow this pattern — the brightest-flowered ones possess all-green foliage and some varieties produce blooms in other colours. The role of this plant in the garden is to provide ground cover under trees and shrubs — it revels in shade and spreads rapidly. If space is limited you will have to lift the clumps every few years, divide them and then replant. Water copiously in dry weather and cut back the stems in autumn.

P. angustifolia

VARIETIES: The cottage garden Lungwort is **P. officinalis** — height 1 ft, spacing 1 ft, flowering period April–May. The oval leaves are white-spotted and the clusters of tubular flowers are purplish blue when fully open. The silver markings on the foliage of **P. saccharata** (Bethlehem Sage) are much more eye-catching — choose **'Pink Dawn'** (pink) or **'Mrs Moon'** (rose). If you don't care for spotted leaves choose the all-green **P. angustifolia (P. azurea)**. The bright blue flowers open in April — **'Munstead Blue'** and **'Mawson's Variety'** bear the richest-coloured blooms.

SITE & SOIL: Any reasonable soil will do — thrives best in partial shade.

PROPAGATION: Divide clumps in autumn or spring.

Pyrethrum roseum 'Brenda'

PYRETHRUM   Feverfew

A border plant beloved by flower arrangers — the large Daisy-like flowers are borne singly on long stalks above the attractive feathery foliage. Pink and red are the dominant colours — the single blooms, measuring 2 in. or more in diameter, bear a prominent central disc and the doubles, which usually are smaller and less vigorous in growth habit, have a mass of miniature petals within an outer ring of large ones. Pyrethrum is happiest in light sandy soil and the most important rule is to remove the flower stems once the blooms have faded — in this way the flowering season will be prolonged. Provide support for the stems in spring and water when the weather is dry.

P. roseum
'E. M. Robinson'

P. roseum
'Vanessa'

VARIETIES: The garden varieties are hybrids of **P. roseum (Chrysanthemum coccineum** in some books or catalogues). The basic details are height 2–3 ft, spacing 1½ ft, flowering period May–June. Good singles include **'Brenda'** (deep pink), **'E. M. Robinson'** (pale pink), **'Bressingham Red'** (crimson) and **'Kelway's Glorious'** (scarlet). The best double red is **'Lord Rosebery'** — **'Vanessa'** is a yellow-centred pink double.

SITE & SOIL: Well-drained soil is essential — thrives best in full sun.

PROPAGATION: Divide clumps in spring.

Ranunculus aconitifolius 'Flore Pleno'

RANUNCULUS   Buttercup, Bachelor's Buttons

Buttercups are grown in gardens everywhere, but unfortunately they are nearly always present as undesirable weeds in lawn, bed or border rather than as decorative plants. There are, however, several Garden Buttercups — the well-known Turban Buttercup planted as small clawed tubers (page 121), the yellow-flowering Great Spearwort grown around pools and lakes, and the Bachelor's Buttons cultivated in the herbaceous border. Bachelor's Buttons are bushy plants which produce masses of small double flowers in summer. They require moist soil and some form of support for the flower stems. The blooms are excellent for cutting and arranging indoors.

VARIETIES: R. aconitifolius is commonly called White Bachelor's Buttons — basic details are height 2 ft, spacing 1½ ft, flowering period May–July. Grow the double variety **'Flore Pleno'**. Yellow Bachelor's Buttons **(R. acris 'Flore Pleno')** flowers later, beginning in June and continuing until August. The Lesser Celandine **(R. ficaria 'Aurantiacus')** is a dwarf orange-flowering plant which blooms in March and April — plant it at the front of the border or in the rockery.

SITE & SOIL: Any moisture-retentive soil will do — thrives in sun or partial shade.

PROPAGATION: Divide clumps in autumn or spring.

R. acris 'Flore Pleno'

Rodgersia pinnata superba

RODGERSIA   Rodgersia

Rodgersia is a wise choice if you have a large border to fill and want a plant which bears bold and colourful leaves as well as summer flowers. The blooms are tiny, appearing in plume-like spikes, and the large divided leaves give Rodgersia an exotic look. It is slow growing, requiring both light shade and moist soil to make it feel at home. Add plenty of compost, leaf mould or peat at planting time and mulch around the leaves in spring. Water in dry weather and cut back the stems in autumn.

VARIETIES: If you can grow only one variety then choose **R. pinnata superba** — height 3–4 ft, spacing 4 ft, flowering period July–August. The toothed and divided leaves are bronze-coloured when young and the flowers are deep pink. **R. aesculifolia** is somewhat similar, its large Horse Chestnut-like leaves displaying a metallic bronzy sheen but its flowers are white. Other garden species include **R. podophylla** (3–4 ft, cream flowers) and the largest-leaved Rodgersia of all — **R. tabularis** (3–4 ft, white flowers).

SITE & SOIL: Any moisture-retentive soil will do — thrives best in partial shade.

PROPAGATION: Divide clumps in autumn or spring.

R. aesculifolia

Rudbeckia 'Goldsturm'

RUDBECKIA   Coneflower

A popular perennial, used to provide long-lasting colour in late summer and autumn. Plant breeders have been able to produce some excellent compact varieties to replace the old-fashioned sorts and there are double-flowered types now available. But the colour range has not really been extended — the Rudbeckias remain either yellow or orange. The blooms last well in water — flower-heads which are not cut for indoors should be removed once the petals have faded. Add organic matter at planting time and stake the stems to support the large heads. Cut the plants down to ground level in late autumn.

VARIETIES: R. fulgida (R. deamii) produces dark-centred star-like flowers — plant details are height 2–3 ft, spacing 2 ft, flowering period July–September. The old favourite variety **speciosa** has now been replaced by **'Goldsturm'** (2 ft high, 5 in. blooms). The giants are varieties of the green-centred **R. laciniata** — height 2½–7 ft, spacing 2–3 ft, flowering period July–September. At the back of the border grow **'Autumn Sun'** or **'Golden Glow'**. For the middle of the border there is the more compact **'Goldquelle'** (2½ ft, double-flowered).

SITE & SOIL: Any reasonable garden soil will do — thrives in sun or light shade.

PROPAGATION: Divide clumps in autumn or spring.

R. fulgida

Salvia superba 'East Friesland'

SALVIA   Perennial Sage

The word Salvia to most gardeners means the bright red annual which is seen in flower beds everywhere. The herbaceous perennial members of the group are blue — much less well known but no less valuable in the garden. The slender spikes above the grey-green leaves bear hooded tubular flowers about ½ in. long — the plants are easy to grow provided that the soil is well drained, and there is no need to lift and divide the clumps every few years. The spikes of the taller varieties may need staking on exposed sites and after flowering the faded heads should be removed.

VARIETIES: The species you are most likely to find is **S. superba** **(S. virgata nemorosa)** — plant details are height 3 ft, spacing 1½ ft, flowering period July–September. The blooms are bluish purple — for a darker and brighter colour grow one of the more compact varieties — **'East Friesland'** (1½ ft) or the May-flowering **'May Night'** (1½ ft). **S. haematodes** (3 ft) has attractive lavender flowers but is short-lived — **S. patens** (2 ft) has bright blue flowers but is not completely hardy.

SITE & SOIL: Any well-drained soil will do — thrives in sun or light shade.

PROPAGATION: Sow seeds under glass in April (S. haematodes) or divide clumps in autumn or spring.

S. superba

Saponaria officinalis

SAPONARIA   Soapwort, Bouncing Bet

The common names of Saponaria are a guide to some of its properties. Stir a handful of cut leaves in a bowl of water and the lather produced reveals why it is called Soapwort. Leave a clump to grow undisturbed in the border for a few years and the sight of its stems springing up amongst other plants reveals why it is also called Bouncing Bet. It is really too invasive for the choice border, but it remains a charming cottage garden plant. The erect stems bear lance-shaped leaves and in summer a terminal cluster of flowers. It is completely trouble-free — merely cut down the stems to ground level in the autumn.

VARIETIES: The species grown in gardens is **S. officinalis**—height 2–3 ft, spacing 2 ft, flowering period July–September. The pink single-flowered species is one of our native flowers, found wild in hedges and woodland, as well as being a popular plant in cottage gardens, but it has now been largely superseded by the double-flowering varieties — **'Rosea Plena'** (pink), **'Rubra Plena'** (red) and **'Alba Plena'** (white). For details of the Rock Soapwort see page 103.

SITE & SOIL: Any reasonable garden soil will do — thrives in sun or light shade.

PROPAGATION: Divide clumps in autumn or spring.

S. officinalis

Saxifraga umbrosa

SAXIFRAGA   Saxifrage

Nearly all of the Saxifrages belong in the rock garden (see page 103) rather than the herbaceous border, but there are a few which are too large or too invasive for the average rockery and are used for edging or ground cover. These Border Saxifrages form rosettes or clumps of leaves from which arise branching slender stems bearing masses of starry flowers. They require moisture-retentive soil and some shade — remove the stems when the flowers have faded.

VARIETIES: By far the most popular of the Border Saxifrages is London Pride **(S. umbrosa)**. Rosettes of dark green leaves cover the ground all year round and in early summer dainty sprays of pink flowers arise — height 1 ft, spacing 1½ ft, flowering period May–July. There is a variegated version with its leaves splashed with yellow **('Variegata')** and a dwarf version with deep pink flowers **(primuloides 'Elliott's Variety')**. S. fortunei (1–1½ ft) is quite different to the well-known London Pride — the glossy leaves are lobed and deciduous, and the white flowers are about 1 in. across. The flowering sprays appear in October and November.

SITE & SOIL: Any humus-rich soil will do — thrives best in partial shade.

PROPAGATION: Divide clumps or rosettes in spring.

S. umbrosa

Scabiosa caucasica 'Clive Greaves'

SCABIOSA Scabious

Scabious does not produce an abundance of blooms at any one time, and yet it remains a favourite herbaceous border perennial. There are two basic reasons for its popularity — flowering begins in late June and continues until the first frosts arrive, and the large flowers are excellent for arranging indoors. The frilly-edged 'pincushions', blue or white and up to 4 in. across, last a long time in water and can also be dried for winter decoration. Plant in the spring and add compost, peat or leaf mould to the planting mixture. Dead-head faded blooms and cut down the stems once the floral display is over. Keep watch for slugs in the spring.

S. caucasica

VARIETIES: The basic species is **S. caucasica** — height 2–3 ft, spacing 1½ ft, flowering period June–October. It bears large lavender-coloured flowers but it has now largely been replaced by its named varieties. The one you are most likely to be offered is **'Clive Greaves'** — mid-blue, large-flowered and long-stemmed. There are a few white varieties, such as **'Miss Willmott'** and **'Bressingham White'** and there are several deep violet types to choose from — pick **'Moerheim Blue'** or **'Imperial Purple'**.

SITE & SOIL: Any well-drained, non-acid soil will do — thrives best in full sun.

PROPAGATION: Divide clumps in spring.

Schizostylis coccinea 'Mrs Hegarty'

SCHIZOSTYLIS Kaffir Lily

An out-of-the-ordinary perennial which will add colour to the middle of the border at the end of the season. Rising above the grassy foliage are the flowering spikes which look like miniature Gladioli — each of the blooms on the spikes has the appearance of a Crocus. The underground rhizomes indicate a relationship to the Iris and yet its common name reveals none of these associates — Schizostylis is called the Kaffir Lily! The 1½ in. blooms are pink or red and are recommended as cut flowers. In spring plant the rhizomes about 1 in. below the soil surface — choose a moist site or add plenty of organic matter before planting. Water in dry weather and dead-head faded blooms. Cut down the stems when the floral display is over and protect the crowns with peat.

S. coccinea

VARIETIES: The basic details of **S. coccinea** are height 2 ft, spacing 1 ft, flowering period September–November. **'Major'** is the variety usually grown — its flowers are large and deep red. **'Mrs Hegarty'** is a useful pink variety which blooms earlier than the others. **'Viscountess Byng'** (pink) is frowned upon because it does not bloom until November.

SITE & SOIL: Rather fussy — a well-drained but moisture-retentive soil is necessary. Thrives in sun or light shade.

PROPAGATION: Divide clumps in spring.

Plants for Sunny Dry Sites

Acanthus spinosus	Iris hybrids
Achillea spp.	Kniphofia uvaria
Alstroemeria aurantiaca	Liatris spicata
Anaphalis triplinervis	Limonium latifolium
Bergenia cordifolia	Liriope muscari
Catananche caerulea	Macleaya spp.
Centaurea dealbata	Nepeta mussinii
Centranthus ruber	Oenothera spp.
Cortaderia selloana	Papaver orientale
Dianthus spp.	Physalis franchetii
Doronicum plantagineum	Potentilla hybrids
Echinops ritro	Salvia superba
Eryngium spp.	Saponaria officinalis
Euphorbia spp.	Sedum spectabile
Gaillardia aristata	Stachys spp.
Geranium spp.	Tradescantia virginiana
Gypsophila paniculata	Verbascum hybridum

SEDUM   Stonecrop

The Sedums are a large group of fleshy-leaved plants which thrive in hot and dry conditions — their ability to cover rocks and walls is responsible for the common name. Many are rock garden plants but some Sedums, known as Ice Plants, are grown in the herbaceous border. The flower-heads of the Ice Plants are large plates of tiny flowers, their appearance in late summer acting as a magnet for the butterflies in the neighbourhood. These Border Sedums are tough plants, shrugging off drought and pests which would cripple more delicate perennials.

VARIETIES: The popular Ice Plant is **S. spectabile** — height 1–2 ft, spacing 1 ft, flowering period August–October. The flower-heads measure 4–6 in. across and the varieties generally differ in flower colour rather than plant form. Choose from **'Brilliant'** (deep pink), **'Carmen'** (rose-red), **'Meteor'** (carmine-red) and **'Ruby Glow'** (red). There is one variety which does stand out from the others — **'Autumn Joy'**. It is tall (2 ft) and the 8 in. heads are salmon-pink at first, turning rusty brown in autumn. The leaves also change, becoming brownish purple at the end of summer. The Purple-leaf Ice Plant is **S. maximum 'Atropurpureum'** (height 1½ ft, pink flowers, purplish red leaves).

SITE & SOIL: Any well-drained soil will do — thrives best in full sun.

PROPAGATION: Divide clumps in autumn or spring.

Sedum spectabile 'Autumn Joy'

S. spectabile 'Meteor'

SIDALCEA   Prairie Mallow

Sidalcea looks like a small and dainty Hollyhock, but its appearance belies its strong constitution. It is not troubled by disease and is long-lived, growing almost anywhere. From a clump of rounded, basal leaves the strong stems with their terminal flowering spikes appear. Each saucer-shaped bloom is about 1½ in. across and the petals have a silky texture. It is a middle-of-the-border perennial which is generally not fussy about soil type, but it is not happy in dry, sandy land and the floral display will be poor if it is grown in deep shade. There is only one important rule to remember — cut down the stems to ground level once flowering is over. Failure to do so may result in a reduction in the number of stems next year.

VARIETIES: The Garden Sidalceas are varieties of **S. malvaeflora** — height 2–4 ft, spacing 1½ ft, flowering period June–August. The flower colours range from shell pink (**'Loveliness'**, 2½ ft) to deep red (**'Croftway Red'**, 3 ft). Between them are the favourites **'Rose Queen'** (4 ft, rose-pink) and **'Elsie Heugh'** (3 ft, pink). There is just one variety outside this pink and red range — **'William Smith'** (3 ft, salmon).

SITE & SOIL: Any reasonable soil will do — thrives in sun or partial shade.

PROPAGATION: Divide clumps in spring.

Sidalcea malvaeflora 'Rose Queen'

S. malvaeflora

SOLIDAGO   Golden Rod

Walk along any suburban street in August and you will find Golden Rod in full flower, a bright yellow foil between the other perennials. In most cases S. canadensis is grown — tall, weedy and frequently badly staked. Don't judge all Golden Rods from such specimens — these days there are many compact hybrids which have a much more attractive appearance. All Solidagos are easy to grow — their feathery plume-like flower-heads standing above the narrow leaves. Cultivation offers no problems — mulch in spring, provide some form of unobtrusive support for the stems, water in dry weather and cut down the shoots in autumn.

VARIETIES: The modern hybrids (**S. hybrida**) have been derived from the original species, such as **S. canadensis**, **S. virgaurea** and **S. brachystachys**. The basic details of the hybrids are height 1–7 ft, spacing 1–2 ft, flowering period July–September. Choose just what you want — a dwarf (**'Golden Thumb'**, 1 ft) or a giant (**'Golden Wings'**, 6 ft), a bush with fluffy, Mimosa-like flowers (**'Goldenmosa'**, 2½ ft) or an upright plant (**'Peter Pan'**, 3 ft). Colours vary, ranging from golden yellow (**'Lena'**, 2½ ft) to lemon yellow (**'Lemore'**, 1½ ft).

SITE & SOIL: Any well-drained garden soil will do — thrives in sun or light shade.

PROPAGATION: Divide clumps in autumn or spring.

Solidago 'Goldenmosa'

S. hybrida

STACHYS   Lamb's Ears, Big Betony

Stachys lanata

Two quite different garden plants bear the name Stachys. The more popular one is a grey-leaved ground cover or edging plant known as Lamb's Ears or Lamb's Tongue. Flowers are borne in whorls on upright spikes but these blooms are insignificant — this perennial is grown for its attractive evergreen silvery foliage. The second Stachys is much less commonly seen — Big Betony is grown for the spikes of showy pink or purple flowers it bears in summer rather than for its plain green leaves. All varieties of Stachys hate heavy soils and the flowering spikes should be cut down once the blooms have faded.

VARIETIES: Lamb's Ears is the common name for **S. lanata (S. olympica)** — height 1½ ft, spacing 1 ft, flowering period July–August. The leaves are covered in woolly hairs and the pale purple flowers are small. The non-flowering **'Silver Carpet'** (4 in.) is grown as a carpeting plant. Big Betony is called **S. macrantha (Betonica macrantha)** in the catalogues — height 2 ft, spacing 1½ ft, flowering period May–July. The lilac flowers are large and tubular — the variety **'Rosea'** produces pink blooms.

SITE & SOIL: Any well-drained garden soil will do — thrives in sun or partial shade.

PROPAGATION: Divide clumps in autumn or spring.

S. macrantha

STOKESIA   Stokes' Aster

Stokesia laevis

Stokes' Aster provides something different for the front of the border, and is a good choice if your soil is light and free-draining. The 3 in. blooms are often described as looking like the flowers of the Cornflower or the China Aster, but in fact they are unique. They first appear in July and the flowering period extends until the first frosts arrive — cut some of the blooms for arranging indoors. Mulch in spring and water during dry spells. Dead-head faded blooms and cut down the stems to ground level in early winter. It is a hardy plant, but it is a good idea to cover the crowns with peat or bracken if your garden is exposed or in a frost pocket.

VARIETIES: There is just one species — **S. laevis (S. cyanea)**. The basic details are height 1–1½ ft, spacing 1½ ft, flowering period July–October. The leaves are long and narrow and the flowers are large and saucer-shaped with deeply-notched petals. The colour of the species is pale mauve, but there are varieties available in different colours — **'Blue Star'** (light blue), **'Blue Moon'** (mid-blue), **'Superba'** (lavender-blue) and **'Alba'** (white).

SITE & SOIL: Any well-drained garden soil will do — thrives best in full sun.

PROPAGATION: Divide clumps in spring.

S. laevis

THALICTRUM   Meadow Rue

Thalictrum aquilegifolium 'Album'

A light and airy plant for the back of the border — a pleasant contrast to the heavy-leaved and large-flowered types which usually dominate the row next to the fence. The stems are slender and the dainty leaflets have the appearance of Columbine or Maidenhair Fern. The foliage is used for flower arranging and so are the large heads of tiny flowers. Most varieties need moisture-retentive soil, so add peat or well-rotted compost at planting time. Provide support for the stems and cut down in autumn.

VARIETIES: **T. dipterocarpum** bears 6 in. heads of lavender flowers with prominent yellow stamens. The basic details are height 5 ft, spacing 2 ft, flowering period June–September. If you have space for only one Thalictrum, then choose the variety **'Hewitt's Double'** (3 ft). The Columbine Meadow Rue **(T. aquilegifolium)** is earlier flowering, producing masses of fluffy flowers in white, mauve, pink or purple in late spring. Some well-known varieties are **'Thundercloud'** (2½ ft, deep purple), **'Dwarf Purple'** (2½ ft, mauve) and **'Album'** (3 ft, white). The all-yellow Thalictrum is **T. speciosissimum** (5 ft).

SITE & SOIL: Any reasonable garden soil will do if humus is added — thrives in sun or partial shade.

PROPAGATION: Divide overgrown clumps in autumn or spring, otherwise sow seeds under glass in spring.

T. dipterocarpum

TIARELLA   Foam Flower

Evergreen perennials with foliage which turns bronzy or red in winter have a useful part to play in the herbaceous border, providing colour when all around them everything is dead or bare. Tiarella fulfils this role and has the added advantage of revelling in partial shade. In early summer the spikes of small frothy flowers appear — hence the common name. There is nothing imposing about Tiarella — it is a dainty ground cover or edging plant for the front of the border.

VARIETIES: The most popular species is **T. cordifolia** — height 8 in., spacing 1½ ft, flowering period May – June. The tiny flowers are white and star-like, and the large lobed leaves turn bronze in winter. It spreads quite rapidly and so is a good choice if you want a carpeting evergreen. **T. wherryi** (height 1 ft, spacing 1 ft, flowering period June – September) grows in tufts and is not invasive like its more widely-grown relative. The flowers are tinged with pink and the leaves turn reddish in winter. **T. polyphylla** is rather similar but taller, with flowering spikes growing 1 – 2 ft high.

SITE & SOIL: Any moisture-retentive garden soil will do — thrives best in partial shade.

PROPAGATION: Divide clumps in autumn or spring — T. wherryi should be raised from seeds sown under glass in March.

Tiarella cordifolia

T. cordifolia

TRADESCANTIA   Spiderwort

Spiderwort is a grow-anywhere plant — in wet or dry soil, in full sun or partial shade, the three-petalled flowers begin to appear in early summer and the floral display continues until autumn. The silky petals surrounding the showy stamens are open for only a day, but the clusters of buds in each flower-head ensure a continuous succession of flowers. Purple is the usual colour but there are named varieties in white, pink, blue, mauve and violet. The leaves are sword-shaped, 1 ft tall and attractive to slugs in the spring. An easy plant — supply the ideal conditions of moist soil and partial shade if you can, support the stems and cut back to ground level in late autumn.

VARIETIES: There is a single species — **T. virginiana (T. andersoniana)**. The basic details are height 1½ – 2 ft, spacing 1½ ft, flowering period June – September. Popular varieties include **'Leonora'** (violet-blue), **'Osprey'** (white), **'Isis'** (deep blue), **'J. G. Weguelin'** (sky blue), **'Purple Dome'** (purple) and **'Purewell Giant'** (carmine).

SITE & SOIL: Any reasonable garden soil will do — thrives in sun or partial shade.

PROPAGATION: Divide clumps in autumn or spring.

Tradescantia virginiana 'Isis'

T. virginiana

TROLLIUS   Globe Flower

In early summer globular flowers which look like giant buttercups appear on the erect stems. These blooms measure 2 in. or more across, and although often recommended as cut flowers they do not last well in water. This plant will flourish only where its basic requirement can be satisfied — adequate moisture. If your soil is not plentifully supplied with humus, add peat or compost at planting time. Trollius is an excellent plant for growing in boggy ground by the side of ponds or lakes. Mulch in spring and water in dry weather. Cut the stems down to ground level in autumn.

VARIETIES: The hybrids of **T. europaeus** may be listed under **T. cultorum** or **T. hybridus** in the catalogues. Basic details are height 1½ – 2½ ft, spacing 1½ ft, flowering period May – June. Colours range from cream to orange — **'Alabaster'** (pale cream), **'Canary Bird'** (pale yellow), **'Goldquelle'** (bright yellow) and **'Orange Princess'** (bright orange). **T. ledebouri** is a taller plant with later and more open flowers — height 2½ – 3 ft, spacing 1½ ft, flowering period June – August. The variety you are most likely to find is **'Golden Queen'** (bright orange with prominent yellow stamens).

SITE & SOIL: Moisture-retentive soil is essential — thrives in sun or partial shade.

PROPAGATION: Divide clumps in autumn or spring.

Trollius ledebouri

T. hybridus

VERBASCUM   Mullein

Hybrid Mulleins look most attractive in the catalogue photographs, and garden centres offer a range of named varieties. Before you buy one for the back of the border, however, you should know the disadvantages. In rich soil Verbascum tends to produce a disappointing floral display, and plants sometimes die at the end of the flowering season — Hybrid Mulleins tend to be short-lived. If your soil is well drained and you accept the need to replace plants occasionally, the Mulleins offer a wide range of colours and heights for the border. From the basal rosette of woolly leaves arise the much-branched flowering stems, bearing 1 to 1½ in. saucer-shaped blooms. Provide some form of support for these stems and cut them down to just above ground level in autumn. Keep watch for caterpillars.

VARIETIES: Nearly all named varieties belong to **V. hybridum** — height 3–6 ft, spacing 2 ft, flowering period June–August. The shorter ones include **'Gainsborough'** (3–4 ft, yellow), **'Pink Domino'** (3–4 ft, rose-pink), **'Mont Blanc'** (3–4 ft, white) and **'Cotswold Queen'** (3–4 ft, apricot). The best of the giants is **'C. L. Adams'** (6 ft, yellow) — other tall ones are **'Miss Willmott'** (6 ft, white) and **'Harkness Hybrid'** (6 ft, yellow).

SITE & SOIL: Most well-drained garden soils will do — thrives best in full sun.

PROPAGATION: Take root cuttings in winter.

Verbascum 'C. L. Adams'

V. hybridum

VERONICA   Speedwell

The Garden Speedwells have a remarkable range of heights — you can buy alpine varieties which grow no more than 1 in. high or border plants which reach 5 ft. The flowers are borne on tall and narrow spikes and most species appreciate moisture-retentive soil. The main enemy is poor drainage — waterlogging in winter is the usual cause of death. Mulch in spring and water when the weather is dry. Provide support for tall-growing species and cut stems back in autumn.

VARIETIES: The earliest to flower is the pale blue **V. gentianoides** (height 2 ft, spacing 1½ ft, flowering period May–June). **V. incana** flowers a little later (height 1–1½ ft, spacing 1 ft, flowering period June–July) — look for its silvery leaves and blue flowers. **'Wendy'** is a popular hybrid. **V. spicata** grows to the same height as V. incana and flowers at the same time, but its leaves are green and its flowers may be pink or white as well as blue. One of the brightest of all Veronicas is **V. teucrium 'Crater Lake Blue'** (1½ ft, ultramarine) and the popular tall one is **V. virginica 'Alba'** (5 ft, white).

SITE & SOIL: Any well-drained garden soil will do — thrives in sun or light shade.

PROPAGATION: Divide clumps in autumn or spring.

Veronica gentianoides

V. spicata

VIOLA   Violet

Do not expect the Perennial Violas to produce the large and colourful blooms associated with the Pansies and Violas grown in parks and gardens as bedding plants. The old-fashioned Violets, once so popular and now uncommon, produce blooms which are ½ in. or 1 in. in diameter. Use them for ground cover or edging at the front of the border — they will flourish in most soils but they do need good drainage and some shade. Mulch in spring and water when the weather is dry in summer. Dead-head regularly and every three years lift and divide the clumps.

VARIETIES: **V. odorata** is the Sweet Violet which was so adored by the Victorians. The basic details are height 4–6 in., spacing 1 ft, flowering period February–April and again in autumn. The leaves are heart-shaped and the flowers blue or violet. Other colours are available — **'Christmas'** (white) and **'Coeur d'Alsace'** (pink). **'Czar'** (purple) has the reputation for being the most fragrant. **V. cornuta** is the Horned Violet — height 6 in.–1 ft, spacing 1 ft, flowering period May–July. Named varieties include **'Alba'** (white), **'Jersey Gem'** (purple) and **'Lilacica'** (lilac).

SITE & SOIL: Any well-drained soil will do — thrives best in light shade.

PROPAGATION: Divide clumps in autumn or plant basal cuttings in a cold frame in summer.

Viola odorata

V. cornuta

CHAPTER 4

INCREASING YOUR STOCK

There are several methods of raising new plants, but there is no 'best' way. Sowing seeds is a relatively inexpensive way of producing large numbers of flowers for the garden – it is the standard way for annuals but beset with drawbacks for most perennials. Border and rockery perennials require a vegetative (non-seed) means of propagation if you want to reproduce a named variety – seed rarely produces plants which are completely true to type. Dividing up a mature clump is, of course, the easiest method of vegetative propagation, but not all perennials can be split up in this way and even when practical you have to disturb an established plant. Cuttings are a much more practical proposition in most cases if you want lots of new plants – the cuttings are usually taken from non-flowering shoot tips but roots, leaves and small basal shoots are also used. Don't try to guess the correct method to use. Look up the plant in the A-Z guide and employ the recommended technique.

SEED SOWING

Looking through the seed catalogues is one of the joys of gardening. Many gardeners begin their horticultural experience with a packet of Virginia Stock or Nasturtiums, and perhaps we move too quickly to buying in bedding plants and container-grown specimens — forgetting the thrill of starting from scratch. Growing plants from seed is perfectly straightforward if you follow a few simple rules. The first decision to make is whether you are going to raise the seedlings indoors for planting out later (the Half Hardy Annual Technique) or sow the seeds outdoors (the Hardy Annual or the Biennial Technique).

Half Hardy Annual Technique

Uses
- Half hardy annuals for bedding out in late spring.
- Hardy annuals for growing in cold and wet sites.
- Hardy annuals for early flowering.
- Perennials where trueness to varietal type is not important.

Timing
- March – April (check A – Z guides for possible variations).

1 **CONTAINERS** Use a seed tray, pan or ordinary flower pot. Drainage holes or cracks are necessary. Wash used containers before filling — soak clay pots overnight.

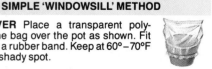

2 **COMPOST** A peat-based seed compost provides an ideal medium for germination — sterile, light and consistent. Fill the container with Baby Bio Seed and Cutting Compost. Firm lightly with a piece of board. Sprinkle the compost with water the day before seed sowing — it should be moist (not wet) when you sow the seeds. Scatter them thinly and cover with a thin layer of compost — small seeds should not be covered. Firm lightly with a board. Now choose the standard 'under glass' method or simple 'windowsill' method.

STANDARD 'UNDER GLASS' METHOD

3 **COVER** Place a sheet of glass over the tray or pot and put brown paper on top. Keep at 60°–70°F and wipe and turn the glass every day.

4 **LIGHT** As soon as the seedlings break through the surface, remove the paper and prop up the sheet of glass. After a few days the glass should be removed and the container moved close to the light. Keep the compost moist but not wet.

SIMPLE 'WINDOWSILL' METHOD

3 **COVER** Place a transparent polythene bag over the pot as shown. Fit with a rubber band. Keep at 60°–70°F in a shady spot.

4 **LIGHT** As soon as the seedlings break through the surface, remove the polythene bag and move the pot to a windowsill which does not receive direct sunlight. Turn the pot regularly to avoid lop-sided growth — keep the compost moist but not wet.

5 **PRICK OUT** As soon as the first set of true leaves have opened the seedlings should be pricked out into trays, pans or small pots filled with Potting Compost. Handle the plants by the seed leaves — not the stems. The seedlings should be set about 1½ in. apart. Keep the container in the shade for a day or two after pricking out.

6 **HARDEN OFF** When the seedlings have recovered from the pricking out move, they must be hardened off to prepare them for the life outdoors. Increase the ventilation and move the container to a cool room or to a cold frame. Then move outdoors during daylight hours; finally leaving them outdoors all the time for about 7 days before planting out.

Correct stage for pricking out

Hardy Annual Technique

Uses ● Hardy annuals for growing in flower beds.
● Half hardy annuals where late flowering is acceptable.

Timing ● March – April for hardy annuals, but let soil conditions be your guide. The soil must be warm enough for germination, and dry enough to allow you to make a seed bed. Hold up operations if the weather is cold and wet, even though it may mean being a couple of weeks late — the plants will catch up by flowering time. A good guide that sowing time has arrived is the appearance of annual weeds.
● September is a suitable time for sowing many annuals (e.g Larkspur, Limnanthes, Virginia Stock, Cornflower and Pot Marigold). These autumn-sown annuals will bloom earlier than spring-sown ones.

1 **PREPARE SOIL** A well-made seed bed is necessary so that the seeds will have enough air and moisture, and the tiny roots will secure a proper foothold. Choose a day when the soil is moist below the surface but dry on top. Lightly tread over and then rake until the surface is even and crumbly.

2 **MARK OUT THE BED**
You can scatter seed over the allotted area but this will make thinning and weeding difficult. It is much better to sow the seeds in drills at the recommended distance apart (see A–Z guide). Note that drills are set at different angles to avoid a regimented appearance

Mark out zone for each variety with a pointed stick

Note overlap to avoid sharp dividing lines

Space left for bedding out a half hardy annual in late May or early June

3 **PREPARE SEED DRILLS** The depth of the drill depends upon the size of the seeds. A general rule is to ensure that the seeds will be covered with soil to about twice their size. Remember that you should never water the seed bed after sowing — if the soil is dry then gently water the drills before sowing.

For small seeds

For large seeds

4 **SOW SEED** Seed must be sown thinly. Mix very small seeds with sand to help ensure an even spread. After sowing, carefully rake the soil back into the drill and then firm it with the back of the rake. Apart from gentle watering if there is a long dry spell, nothing further need be done until after germination apart from protecting the area from birds. Cover the surface with twigs or stretch black thread over the seed bed.

5 **THIN OUT** When seedlings reach the stage illustrated on page 82, it is time to start thinning. At the first stage reduce the stand to one seedling every 2 inches. Lift out unwanted plants very carefully — you must not disturb the ones you propose to retain. Repeat this thinning about 10 days later, so that the young plants are at the distance apart recommended for them in the A–Z guide. Thin out September-sown seedlings in autumn.

Biennial Technique

Uses ● Hardy biennials which will be transplanted into beds in autumn.
● Hardy perennials which will be transplanted into pots in autumn. Nearly all named varieties of perennials fail to breed true from seed, but you might not mind having a mixture of colours — let a seed catalogue be your guide. The real problem is that you might have to wait several years before perennials reach flowering size.

Timing ● May – July (check A – Z guide for possible variations).

1 **PREPARE NURSERY BED** This is a special plot of ground set aside for raising seedlings. Follow the rules for preparing the soil for hardy annuals — Step 1 above.

2 **PREPARE SEED DRILLS** Follow the rules for preparing drills for hardy annuals — Step 3 above. The drills should be 1 ft apart and labelled with the name of the variety sown.

3 **THIN OUT** As soon as the seedlings reach the stage shown on page 82 they should be thinned to about 2 in. apart. Firm the soil around plants.

4 **PLANT OUT** In autumn when the plants are 1½ – 2 in. high, lift up each plant with a trowel and transfer it with its soil ball to the bed or border where it is to flower (hardy biennials) or a small pot filled with Potting Compost (hardy perennials). Gently water the plants into their new home.

SEED TYPES

Standard seed Nearly all seed used for propagation is bought in packets shortly before the time of sowing. This seed will have been carefully selected and cleaned by the packager.

Dressed seed The grower will have dusted the seed with a fungicide or insecticide/fungicide before packaging.

Pelleted seed The packager will have coated the seed with a clay mixture to enable the easy handling of small seeds. The chore of thinning is removed — sow at half the final spacing and merely pull out or transplant alternate seedlings after germination.

Saved seed Some seed is usually left over after sowing — nearly every variety can be saved for next year if you put the seed in an air-tight tin and keep in a cool place.

Home-grown seed Annuals and biennials can be propagated from seed collected from plants growing in the garden. Collect the seed when ripe and allow it to dry thoroughly before storing in an air-tight tin in a cool place.

Self-sown seed Many plants produce self-sown seedlings around them — Nature was propagating her own long before Man arrived! These self-sown plants can be left where they are or transplanted to another spot. The drawback is the same as for home-grown seed — the pollen may have come from inferior or even wild plants and the resulting flowers are generally poorer and more varied than those raised from shop-bought seed.

DIVISION

Border & Rockery Perennials

Division is a form of propagation which is often forced upon you. Spreading border perennials will often deteriorate after a few years if not lifted and divided. In this way you can increase your stock and regenerate the plant at the same time.

Choose a mild day in spring or autumn when the soil is moist but not wet. Dig up the clump with a fork, taking care not to damage the roots more than necessary. Shake off the excess soil and study where the basic divisions should be. You might be able to break the clump with your hands, taking off pieces bearing both shoots and roots. If the clump is too tough for this technique then use two hand forks or garden forks. Push the forks back-to-back into the centre of the clump and prise gently apart. Treat the resulting divisions in a similar fashion or tear apart with the fingers. A sharp knife may be necessary for tough rootstocks.

Select the divisions which came from the outer region of the clump — discard the central dead region of an old plant. Replant the divisions as soon as possible and water in thoroughly.

Always check in the A–Z guide before lifting a perennial. Some dislike disturbance and may take several years to recover. Others which can be moved may have a distinct preference for either autumn or spring.

Rhizomes

Carefully dig around the clump of rhizomes and raise them gently so that the roots are retained. Shake off the excess soil and with a sharp knife divide up each rhizome into sections, so that each piece bears leaves or buds above and roots below. Throw away all old and diseased pieces and then replant each section at the same depth as the original plant. Summer is the usual time for dividing rhizomes.

Bulbs and Corms

Most bulbs and corms spread to form clumps in the garden, and these require lifting and dividing every few years. The best time for this task is when the foliage has died down. Lift the clump with a fork and separate with the fingers. Replant the large specimens at once in areas where flowers are required next year, but move the small offsets (bulblets or cormlets) to an out-of-the-way spot. Plant them 2–4 in. deep and leave them undisturbed until they have reached flowering size in 2 or 3 years time. Once they have flowered they can be lifted and moved to the display part of the garden.

CUTTINGS

A cutting is a small piece removed from a plant which with proper treatment can be induced to form roots and then grow into a specimen which is identical to the parent plant. **Stem-tip cuttings** are popular — short pieces of non-flowering shoot tips which are ideally soft and green at the top and rather firm at the base. Some border perennials produce young shoots around the base of the main stems in spring — Lupins, Delphiniums and Paeonies are good examples. These shoots are pulled away or cut off at ground level with a sharp knife to provide **basal cuttings**. A third form of cutting is obtained by gently pulling off a side shoot from a main stem, making sure that some of the old stem ('heel') remains. These **heel cuttings** usually root very easily.

The A – Z guides reveal that you cannot guess the best type of cutting to take nor the best time to propagate it. There are, however, a few general rules. Use a sterile rooting medium and plant the cuttings as soon as possible after severance from the parent plant. Some form of cover will be required to ensure that the cuttings are kept in a humid atmosphere, and do not be tempted to keep pulling at the cutting to see if it has rooted. The appearance of new growth is the best guide.

Stem Cuttings

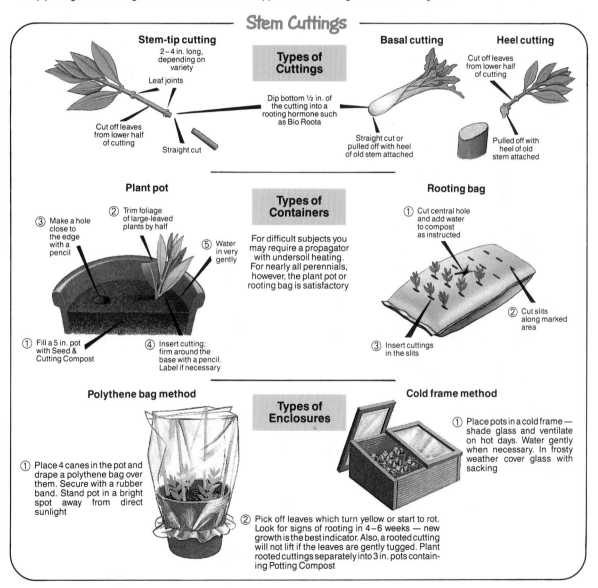

Stem-tip cutting
2–4 in. long, depending on variety
Leaf joints
Cut off leaves from lower half of cutting
Straight cut

Types of Cuttings
Dip bottom ½ in. of the cutting into a rooting hormone such as Bio Roota

Basal cutting
Straight cut or pulled off with heel of old stem attached

Heel cutting
Cut off leaves from lower half of cutting
Pulled off with heel of old stem attached

Plant pot
③ Make a hole close to the edge with a pencil
② Trim foliage of large-leaved plants by half
⑤ Water in very gently
① Fill a 5 in. pot with Seed & Cutting Compost
④ Insert cutting; firm around the base with a pencil. Label if necessary

Types of Containers
For difficult subjects you may require a propagator with undersoil heating. For nearly all perennials, however, the plant pot or rooting bag is satisfactory

Rooting bag
① Cut central hole and add water to compost as instructed
② Cut slits along marked area
③ Insert cuttings in the slits

Polythene bag method
① Place 4 canes in the pot and drape a polythene bag over them. Secure with a rubber band. Stand pot in a bright spot away from direct sunlight

Types of Enclosures
② Pick off leaves which turn yellow or start to rot. Look for signs of rooting in 4–6 weeks — new growth is the best indicator. Also, a rooted cutting will not lift if the leaves are gently tugged. Plant rooted cuttings separately into 3 in. pots containing Potting Compost

Cold frame method
① Place pots in a cold frame — shade glass and ventilate on hot days. Water gently when necessary. In frosty weather cover glass with sacking

Root Cuttings

Some perennials can be propagated by planting sections of their fleshy roots — examples include Phlox, Anchusa and Oriental Poppy. Insert 1 in. pieces vertically into Seed and Cutting Compost for half their length, then cover them completely with a layer of sharp sand. Water in and transplant into individual pots when new top growth appears.

CHAPTER 5
ROCKERY PERENNIALS

'Rockery perennial' is a vague term used to describe a dwarf herbaceous perennial which is suitable for growing in a rock garden – it is impossible to be more precise. Such plants are often referred to as alpines because many of them (the true alpines) were originally collected from the slopes of the Himalayas, Andes, Atlas Mountains, European Alps, Rocky Mountains and so on – the intrepid traveller can still find these true alpines growing in the wild. The Edelweiss of the Swiss Alps has become the classical representative of this group – low-growing and extremely hardy with a passion for sun and gritty, free-draining soil. Many true alpines can be grown outdoors as rockery perennials but some of the choicest examples have to be kept in an alpine house – a cool or cold greenhouse with a low-pitched roof. The reason for housing these difficult plants indoors is that they cannot stand our winter winds, frosts and rain – at home they spend all the winter months tucked up under a thick blanket of snow.

Not all rockery perennials are true alpines. Some come from lowland sites such as deserts and the seashore – others are the product of the plant breeder's art rather than the work of Nature. The Aubrietia in your garden is quite different to its ancestors growing in the wild.

A mixed bag, then, of low-growing but often spreading perennials which are usually grown in a rockery or rock garden. Success with a rock garden depends upon proper siting, construction and planting. . . . and there are pitfalls at each stage. Siting first, and you should pick an unshaded spot as nearly all rockery perennials are sun lovers. A few require shade and these can easily be accommodated against a rock-face which receives little or no sun during the day. Never, never try to build a rockery under trees – the drip from the wet foliage in summer and the blanket of fallen leaves in winter can be fatal.

Having found the right site you must now think about construction. Order your stone – find a local source if you can as the cost of transporting rocks over a large distance can be prohibitive. Slabs weighing between 50 and 250 lb are what you require, and you should not attempt to construct a rockery on your own unless you are used to heavy work. The best of all stone types is tufa, a porous limestone which allows root penetration.

Before you lift a single stone you must make sure that the drainage is adequate. If there is the slightest problem then you must build a soakaway of pebbles or broken bricks on which the rock garden should be constructed. A long time ago Reginald Farrer described badly-made rockeries as dogs' graves, almond puddings and devil's lapfuls, and textbooks provide detailed warnings against such eyesores with the stones sticking upwards. Always try to make the rock garden look like a natural outcrop with the stone slabs sloping gently backwards and with most of the bulk and all of the undersides buried in the earth. Cutting a rockery into a sloping lawn is the easiest situation although with care (and some skill) you can build one on a level site.

Use a planting mixture rather than ordinary soil for building up the structure and for filling the gaps between the stones – mix 2 parts soil, 1 part peat and 1 part grit or coarse sand. Never use fine sand – it would do more harm than good. Planting is the final stage, and it would be a poor rock garden which relied on rockery perennials alone. Dwarf conifers, low-growing shrubs, dwarf bulbs and a few annuals all have an important role to play and there are an infinite number of possible arrangements. The best plan is to go along to your local botanical garden (or the R.H.S. Gardens at Wisley if you are in the London area) and write down the names of the plants you will find in the rock garden.

When you return home, look up the plants in the A-Z guides in this book and in The Tree & Shrub Expert – you will see that some need sizeable planting pockets whereas others prefer crevices. A few must be planted vertically in cracks between the rocks in order to keep winter rain off the leaves.

We have dealt at length with the rock garden but it is not the only or even the best place for rockery perennials in a small garden or a level site. A raised bed or a sink garden shows off tiny, choice alpines to perfection whereas they can be lost amongst the large stones and spreading leafy sheets found in the rock garden. Many alpines flourish in the cracks between the bricks in old walls or the paving stones in pathways, and there is always the front of a small border where they can make middle-of-the-border plants look like giants. Somewhere in every garden there is a place for at least a few rockery perennials.

ACAENA   New Zealand Burr

A low-growing carpeting perennial, useful for growing in the cracks between paving stones or as ground cover in the rockery. It will succeed in dry or poor soil, but Acaena soon dies out if the ground is waterlogged. The dense mat of evergreen leaves spreads quite rapidly and you must take care that it doesn't swamp choice miniature plants growing nearby. The flowers are tiny and insignificant, but they are followed by bristly seeds borne in a burr-like head which is showy and colourful in some species.

VARIETIES: The most popular species is **A. microphylla** — height 2 in., spread 2 ft, flowering period July–September with burrs appearing from August onwards. The leaves are bronzy green and the burrs are deep red. **A. buchananii** has a similar growth habit, but the leaves are silvery green and the burrs are orange. The most vigorous Acaena is **A. novae-zealandiae** — attractive and colourful but very invasive.

SITE & SOIL: Any well-drained soil — thrives in sun or light shade.

PROPAGATION: Divide clumps in autumn or spring.

Acaena microphylla

ACHILLEA   Alpine Yarrow

Most of the varieties of Achillea grow several feet tall and are found in the middle or at the back of the herbaceous border. There is, however, a popular dwarf variety which belongs in the rockery — A. tomentosa. There are several other Alpine Yarrows and all are useful for covering areas of dry sandy soil or crevices between rocks. Flowers are borne on short stems in summer and the plants are easily propagated by division. Sprinkle Slug Pellets around the leaves in spring.

VARIETIES: The basic details of **A. tomentosa** are height 6 in., spread 1 ft, flowering period July–September. The finely-divided greyish leaves form a prostrate mat and the tiny yellow flowers are borne in flat heads which are about 3 in. across. **A. 'King Edward'** (**A. lewisii**) also bears yellow flowers, but it blooms earlier and is a bushier and smaller plant. **A. clavennae** bears white flowers in loose clusters.

SITE & SOIL: Requires well-drained infertile soil in full sun.

PROPAGATION: Divide clumps in spring.

Achillea tomentosa

AETHIONEMA   Aethionema

This shrubby evergreen is an excellent choice for the rock garden or for growing on an old wall. The greyish, fleshy leaves form a dense carpet and for many weeks in spring or summer there is a tightly packed covering of flower-heads. Each head is a spike of tiny flowers, varying in colour from palest pink to deepest rose, depending on the variety chosen.

VARIETIES: At the garden centre you are most likely to find **A. 'Warley Rose'**. The basic details are height 6 in., spread 1 ft, flowering period April–May — the flower colour is rosy red. **A. 'Warley Ruber'** is a similar plant but the blooms are even more striking. **A. pulchellum** is a taller plant (9 in.) which produces dull pink flowers between May and July. The tallest Aethionema is **A. grandiflorum** (1 ft), bearing pale pink blooms throughout the summer.

SITE & SOIL: Any well-drained, non-acid soil — full sun is required.

PROPAGATION: Plant non-flowering cuttings in a cold frame in early summer.

Aethionema 'Warley Rose'

Flowers for Every Season

FEBRUARY – APRIL

(for MAY – JUNE see page 99)
(for JULY – AUGUST see page 105)
(for SEPTEMBER – DECEMBER see page 106)

By careful selection you can ensure that your rockery will have flowers nearly all year round. For each month there is a list of perennials which can be expected to be in full bloom — remember that some of these plants may come into flower earlier and can continue to bloom for many weeks afterwards.

FEBRUARY

Hepatica nobilis	Primula edgeworthii

MARCH

Arabis albida	Primula auricula
Arenaria balearica	Primula juliae
Aubrieta deltoidea	Ranunculus calandrinioides
Hepatica nobilis	Saxifraga (Cushion)
Polygonum tenuicaule	Soldanella alpina

APRIL

Aethionema 'Warley Rose'	Phlox subulata
Alyssum saxatile	Pleione bulbocodioides
Androsace sarmentosa chumbyi	Polygonum tenuicaule
Arabis albida	Primula auricula
Arenaria balearica	Primula juliae
Armeria caespitosa	Pulsatilla vulgaris
Aubrieta deltoidea	Ramonda myconii
Draba aizoides	Sanguinaria canadensis
Erinus alpinus	Saxifraga (Mossy)
Erysimum alpinum	Shortia galacifolia
Hepatica nobilis	Soldanella villosa
Morisia monanthos	Viola biflora
Onosma tauricum	Waldsteinia ternata

ALYSSUM Alyssum

Almost every rockery bears a bright yellow patch of Alyssum saxatile in spring. Grow it by all means, but do not let it dominate the site — so many rockeries are spoilt by allowing Alyssum and Aubrietia to run riot. There are so many choicer if less vigorous alpines to grow which can be relied upon to provide colour when the yellows of Alyssum and the blues of Aubrietia have gone. When not in flower Alyssum is a greyish shrubby perennial which flourishes in poor soil. Trim the stems back once the flowers have faded — in this way you will prolong the life of the plant, keep it within bounds and improve next year's display.

VARIETIES: A. saxatile is the basic species — height 9–12 in., spread 1½ ft, flowering period April–June. When in bloom the heads of bright yellow flowers may completely cover the plant. There are a number of named varieties which make a welcome change from the common-or-garden parent plant which is grown nearly everywhere. **'Citrinum'** bears pale yellow flowers and at the other end of the scale are the buff-coloured blooms of **'Dudley Neville'**. For double flowers choose the variety **'Flore Pleno'** and if space is limited you can plant the dwarf **'Compactum'** which grows only about 6 in. high. All these varieties of A. saxatile make fine rockery or wall plants but if you want a miniature then grow **A. montanum.** This May-flowering alpine grows about 4 in. tall and rarely spreads more than 1 ft.

SITE & SOIL: Any well-drained garden soil will do — add lime if the land is acid. Thrives best in full sun.

PROPAGATION: Sow seeds of species (not named varieties) under glass in spring. With named varieties plant non-flowering cuttings in a cold frame in early summer.

Alyssum saxatile 'Citrinum'

Alyssum saxatile 'Compactum

ANACYCLUS Mt. Atlas Daisy

Some of the rockery perennials in this section are so well known that they require little description, but only a knowledgeable gardener will be able to put a name to this distinctive alpine. In bud only the red undersides of the petals can be seen, but when open the flower is a pure white Daisy. Search for it if you like colourful plants — red buds, large white flowers and grey ferny foliage.

VARIETIES: There is just one species — **A. depressus.** The basic details are height 2 in., spread 1 ft, flowering period June–August. The leaves form a prostrate carpet and the flower stems bear blooms which are 2 in. across. Choose a sheltered spot for this choice plant and dead-head after flowering.

SITE & SOIL: Requires well-drained sandy soil — full sun is essential.

PROPAGATION: Sow fresh seeds under glass in autumn. Alternatively plant non-flowering cuttings under glass in spring.

Anacyclus depressus

ANDROSACE Rock Jasmine

In specialist catalogues you will find numerous species of Androsace listed, but you must choose with care. Most of them are too delicate to grow outdoors — only A. sarmentosa chumbyi is fully reliable without protection from the ruins of a British winter. Some produce neat rosettes of leaves and the remainder have a more trailing growth habit, and all bear tiny, Primrose-like blooms.

VARIETIES: Several varieties of **A. sarmentosa** are available — the one you are most likely to find is **chumbyi.** It grows only 4 in. high but the spread of the neat rosettes of leaves is up to 2 ft. Between April and June the heads of pink flowers appear. **A. lanuginosa** will thrive outdoors if given protection from winter rain — it bears white or pink flowers between June and October.

SITE & SOIL: A well-drained site is essential — add sharp sand before planting. Thrives in sun or light shade.

PROPAGATION: Use rosettes or basal shoots as cuttings — plant in a cold frame in early summer.

Androsace sarmentosa chumbyi

ANTENNARIA   Cat's Ear

An unspectacular rockery plant which has never become popular with British gardeners, but it can be a valuable addition. Its narrow leaves form an ideal carpet to cover the ground over dwarf bulbs and its evergreen growth habit makes it a useful crack-filler between paving stones. It will flourish in poor soil, and in early summer the small flower-heads open with blooms in white, pink or red.

VARIETIES: There is a single species — **A. dioica**. It spreads to form a dense mat of grey-green leaves, reaching about 1½ ft in diameter. The flower stalks appear in May and June — the height of the stalks and the colour of the ¼ in. blooms clustered at the tips depends on the variety chosen. The smallest is **'Minima'** (2 in., pink) — one of the taller ones is **'Rosea'** (6 in., deep pink). Others include **'Nyewood'** (4 in., red) and **'Aprica'** (4 in., white).

SITE & SOIL: Requires well-drained soil and a sunny site.

PROPAGATION: Divide clumps in early autumn or spring.

Antennaria dioica 'Rosea'

ARENARIA   Sandwort

Arenaria is not a showy plant — the leafy prostrate stems form a dense mat and the white blooms borne on the flower stalks are not particularly eye-catching. It has, however, a useful part to play because it will cover rocks which are in either sun or shade. The leaves are evergreen and though the plant eventually spreads over a large area it can easily be kept in check.

VARIETIES: For covering rocks which receive little or no sun choose **A. balearica** (height 1 in., spread 1½ ft, flowering period March–July). The tiny green leaves give the plant a mossy appearance and the small white flowers are borne abundantly on short stalks. For rocks which face the sun choose instead **A. montana** (height 6 in., spread 1½ ft, flowering period May–June). **A. caespitosa 'Aurea'** (proper name **Sagina glabra 'Aurea'**) bears golden grassy leaves.

SITE & SOIL: Requires well-drained moist soil. Needs sun or shade depending on the species.

PROPAGATION: Divide clumps in autumn or spring.

Arenaria balearica

ARABIS   White Rock Cress

Few carpeting plants provide such a splash of colour in spring as the common white form of Arabis as it tumbles over a wall or covers a bank. Unfortunately it is all too often allowed to run wild in a small rockery, where it is invasive and looks untidy when out of flower. To keep the plants in check, the stems should be cut back after flowering. It is an extremely easy plant to grow, which partly accounts for its popularity.

VARIETIES: The Common White Rock Cress is **A. albida (A. caucasica)** — height 9 in., spread 2 ft, flowering period March–April with sporadic blooms until June. The more compact double form (**'Flore Pleno'**) is popular — the blooms are larger but the plant is less free-flowering. White is not the only colour — you can grow the variety **'Rosabella'** (pink) or **'Coccinea'** (red). There is also a slow-growing variety with variegated leaves — **A. albida 'Variegata'**. Avoid A. albida if you want a low-growing compact plant — choose instead a prettier and less rambling species such as **A. blepharophylla** (height 3 in., spread 9 in., flower colour deep rose) or **A. ferdinandi-coburgii 'Variegata'** (height 4 in., spread 1 ft, flower colour white, leaves remain brightly variegated all year round).

SITE & SOIL: Any well-drained garden soil will do — thrives in sun or light shade.

PROPAGATION: Divide clumps in autumn or plant cuttings in a cold frame in late summer. Species (not named varieties) can be raised from seeds sown under glass in spring or summer.

Arabis albida 'Flore Pleno'

Arabis blepharophylla

Building an ideal home for rockery plants

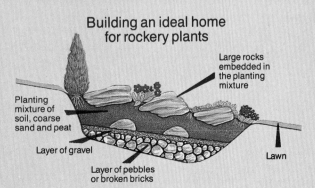

Large rocks embedded in the planting mixture

Planting mixture of soil, coarse sand and peat

Layer of gravel

Layer of pebbles or broken bricks

Lawn

ARMERIA Thrift, Sea Pink

The grass-like leaves of Thrift, densely packed into hummocks, are a common sight in rockeries and around the sea-shore. It is an excellent plant for a dry and sunny spot — in spring or early summer the thin flower stalks appear, each one bearing a globular head of tiny blooms. These flowers may be numerous enough to cover the foliage.

VARIETIES: Our native Thrift is **A. maritima** (height 8 in., spread 1 ft, flowering period May – July). The flower-heads are about 1 in. in diameter — the colour of the species is pink but you can have different colours by choosing a named variety. Pick from **'Alba'** (white), **'Laucheana'** (rich pink), **'Vindictive'** (red) or **'Bloodstone'** (deep red). In some situations a more compact Thrift is required — **A. caespitosa (A. juniperifolia)** is the answer. Basic details are height 3 in., spread 9 in., flowering period April – May. The pink flower-heads are almost stemless.

SITE & SOIL: Requires well-drained soil and a sunny site.

PROPAGATION: Plant basal cuttings in a cold frame in summer.

Armeria maritima

ASTER Mountain Aster

The Asters are well represented in the garden by the Michaelmas Daisies which grace most herbaceous borders, but there is one dwarf species which belongs in the rockery. It is a spreading plant with greyish leaves, and in summer the flowers are large and colourful. If you don't mind having a mixture of flower colours, you can raise this plant from seed — for a single colour you should buy a named variety from your garden centre or nurseryman.

VARIETIES: Specialist nurseries supply such miniature Asters as **A. natalensis** and **A. tibeticus**, but the only one you are likely to find at the garden centre is **A. alpinus**. Its basic details are height 9 in., spread 1½ ft, flowering period July. The flowers measure about 1½ in. across, with pale purple ray petals surrounding the golden eye. Varieties in other colours are available — **'Glory'** (blue), **'Albus'** (white) and **'Wargrave'** (pink).

SITE & SOIL: Requires well-drained soil and a sunny site.

PROPAGATION: Divide clumps in early summer.

Aster alpinus

ASTILBE Astilbe

Astilbes are usually associated with the herbaceous border — 3 ft high plants bearing feathery plumes of flowers in summer. There are also a number of dainty miniatures which grow less than 1 ft tall — choose one if you have a small neat bed or a cool and damp spot in the rockery to fill. They bloom in midsummer when so many other alpines have passed their flowering season and their miniature ostrich plumes make a pleasant change from the usual flower form of rockery perennials. Remember, however, their need for moisture — they will fail in dry conditions.

VARIETIES: One of the most popular rockery Astilbes is **A. chinensis pumila** — height 9 in., spread 1 ft, flowering period July – October. The flowers are pink — for other colours choose a named variety of **A. crispa**. The baby of the family is **A. glaberrima** (height 5 in., spread 5 in., pink and cream flowers in June and July).

SITE & SOIL: Requires moist soil — thrives in light shade.

PROPAGATION: Divide clumps in spring.

Astilbe chinensis pumila

AUBRIETA Rock Cress, Aubrietia

Aubrietia in full flower cascading over a wall or covering a sloping bank is one of the heralds of spring. In the average-sized rockery it certainly has a place, but it should not be allowed to take over. Cut it back once flowering is over so that choicer but more delicate specimens can expand and show their full beauty.

VARIETIES: The basic species is **A. deltoidea** (height 3 in., spread 2 ft, flowering period March – June) but the wild form is not grown. The garden varieties are hybrids of this species — pale purple and pink are the usual colours, but both blue and red are available. A few of the more popular Aubrietias are **'Dr Mules'** (violet), **'Riverslea'** (mauve), **'Dawn'** (pink), **'Crimson Bedder'** (red), **'Triumphant'** (blue) and **'Barker's Double'** (pink).

SITE & SOIL: Any well-drained, non-acid soil — full sun is required.

PROPAGATION: Sow seeds under glass in spring. With named varieties either divide clumps in autumn or plant basal cuttings in a cold frame in summer.

Aubrieta deltoidea

CAMPANULA   Bellflower

No rockery is really complete without at least one species of Campanula, and there are many types from which to make your choice. All need well-drained soil and the addition of lime if the ground is acid. Most species will flourish in light shade and the popular varieties are easy to grow. Slugs are the worst enemy — scatter Slug Pellets around the plants in spring. June and July are the peak flowering months, and Campanulas have a well-earned reputation for bearing masses of blooms. These flowers are of two distinct types, depending on the species. The usual form is a bell, sometimes held erect but more commonly pendent. The other form is a star-like bloom, with C. garganica and C. poscharskyana as examples.

VARIETIES: One of the most popular species is **C. carpatica** — height 10 in., spread 1 ft, flowering period June–September. It bears large cup-shaped flowers in shades ranging from pure white to deep blue. **C. cochlearifolia** (Fairy Thimbles) is a much daintier plant — it spreads as wide as C. carpatica and flowers during the same period, but the height of the flowering stems is only 3 in. and the flowers are small pendent bells in blue or white. If the site is shady, grow **C. muralis** — height 4 in., spread 1 ft, flowering period June–September. It bears masses of purple bell-shaped flowers which cover the leafy trailing stems. **C. poscharskyana** is the one to choose if you want to cover a large area quickly. Its basic details are height 10 in., spread 2 ft and the lavender or white starry flowers appear between June and September. If you want a star-like Campanula which will not spread everywhere, pick instead **C. garganica**, which produces compact tufts and long trails of blue or white blooms between June and August.

SITE & SOIL: Any well-drained, non-acid soil — thrives in sun or light shade.

PROPAGATION: Sow seeds under glass or divide clumps in spring. Alternatively plant non-flowering cuttings in a cold frame in late spring.

Campanula carpatica

Campanula poscharskyana

CERASTIUM   Snow-in-summer

Many books on rockery plants do not mention Cerastium because of its bad habits. But that will not make it go away — this rampant grower can still be seen in rockeries all over the country, spreading like a weed and choking out other plants. The silvery-leaved sheets bearing white flowers in early summer are out of place in the average-sized rock garden, but the ordinary varieties are useful for covering large dry banks.

VARIETIES: You will find Snow-in-summer listed in catalogues or offered for sale at the garden centre under the latin name **C. tomentosum**. Its basic details are height 6 in., spread 2 ft or more, flowering period May–July. The white flowers are about ½ in. across. **C. biebersteinii** is a very similar species but the leaves are larger and woollier. Some books recommend **C. lanatum** because it is much less invasive than the others, but it needs protection from winter rain and is not worth the trouble.

SITE & SOIL: Any well-drained soil — thrives best in full sun.

PROPAGATION: Sow seeds or divide clumps in spring.

Cerastium tomentosum

CYANANTHUS   Cyananthus

Sandwiched between such well-known rockery plants as Campanula and Dianthus in this A-Z guide is the little-known Cyananthus. It is a low-growing, blue-flowering alpine closely related to Campanula, although it usually bears funnel-shaped blooms rather than bells or stars. Cyananthus is well worth growing if you have a moist but free-draining spot to fill with a compact plant.

VARIETIES: The best species to pick is **C. microphyllus**, as it is the one most likely to survive the British climate in winter. Basic details are height 3 in., spread 1 ft, flowering period August–September — the pale purple flowers are about 1 in. across. **C. lobatus** is another prostrate species with erect funnel-shaped flowers but the colour is bright blue and the petals are wider.

SITE & SOIL: Requires well-drained, humus-rich soil — thrives in sun or light shade.

PROPAGATION: Sow seeds under glass in spring or plant basal cuttings in a cold frame in late spring.

Cyananthus microphyllus

DIANTHUS Rockery Pink

The dwarf cousins of the Border Pink, Carnation and Sweet William (page 53) are planted in rockeries to form either neat cushions or spreading carpets of grey or green grassy leaves. The foliage is studded in early summer with sweet-smelling flowers — pink is the usual colour but other shades are available. There is even a yellow Rockery Pink — D. knappii. As a general rule the Rockery Pinks are lime lovers and clay haters, flourishing in a sunny, open situation. They have many uses — covering walls, filling troughs, decorating crazy paving as well as adorning the rock garden. The species can be raised from seed but the named varieties must be propagated from cuttings.

VARIETIES: Our native Maiden Pink **(D. deltoides)** is an old favourite. It is a carpeting plant — height 6 in., spread 9 in., flowering period June–September. The flowers are white, pink or red — for maximum colour choose the brilliant crimson variety **'Flashing Light'**. Another popular species is the Cheddar Pink **(D. caesius)**, which has now been given the tongue-twisting name of **D. gratianopolitanus**. This is the wide-spreading carpeter of the group — height 8 in., spread 2 ft, flowering period May–July. The foliage is narrow and grey. For large flowers, choose the Alpine Pink **(D. alpinus)**. Although the blooms are more than 1 in. across, the compact cushion of foliage is small — height 4 in., spread 6 in., flowering period May–August. A beautiful plant, but it rapidly dies out if the drainage is not perfect. **D. neglectus** forms a neat cushion 6 in. high and 6 in. across, bearing flowers in July and August. It is an oddity — this Dianthus hates lime and the petals are pink or crimson above with a biscuit-coloured reverse.

SITE & SOIL: Thrives in light, chalky soil in full sun.

PROPAGATION: Sow seeds under glass in spring or plant non-flowering cuttings in a cold frame in summer.

Dianthus deltoides 'Flashing Light'

Dianthus alpinus

DODECATHEON Shooting Star

The Shooting Star gets its name from the shape of its showy flowers — the petals of the flowers are swept backwards, revealing the golden anthers. The flowers are borne in a cluster on top of a tall stalk — a group of shooting stars. It is an easy plant to grow if the conditions are suitable — a damp situation (by the poolside is ideal) and some shade. It is an eye-catching specimen in summer when the flowers are present, but in winter the leaves die down and nothing can be seen above ground.

VARIETIES: The most popular species of Shooting Star (American Cowslip) is **D. meadia** — height 1½ ft, spread 1 ft, flowering period June–July. The usual flower colour is rose-purple, but both white and red varieties are available. If your rockery is small **D. pauciflorum** (9 in.) would be more suitable.

SITE & SOIL: Requires a moist but well-drained site — thrives best in light shade.

PROPAGATION: Sow seeds under glass or divide clumps in spring.

Dodecatheon meadia

DRABA Whitlow Grass

Some rockery perennials, such as Cerastium, Arabis and Aubrietia, can become too dominant in the rockery. Draba suffers from the opposite problem — its small cushion of foliage can be overlooked in a large rock garden. It is a plant to grow in the crevices between stones and in trough gardens. Choose with care when buying — many species are not suitable for growing outdoors.

VARIETIES: The easiest one to grow is the largest — **D. aizoides**. The basic details are height 4 in., spread 6 in., flowering period April. The greyish leaves are borne in tight rosettes and the ¼ in. yellow flowers are carried in clusters. The choicest variety is the tiny **D. bryoides imbricata**, with a height and spread of only 2 in. The bright yellow flowers appear on short wiry stems in April — a plant for the sink garden or small rockery.

SITE & SOIL: Any well-drained soil — thrives best in full sun.

PROPAGATION: Sow seeds under glass in spring or plant rosettes as cuttings in a cold frame in summer.

Draba aizoides

DRYAS   Mountain Avens

An excellent ground cover plant — the creeping woody stems bear evergreen leaves which are shiny green above and silvery below. Above these oak-like leaves the large flowers appear on short stalks in late spring, followed by attractive silky seed-heads in summer.

VARIETIES: The popular species is **D. octopetala**, which grows wild in the mountainous regions of Britain and other European countries. The basic details are height 4 in., spread 2 ft, flowering period May – June. The blooms are about 1½ in. in diameter and look like small single roses. There are 8 white petals and a golden centre — a lovely sight when they are numerous enough to cover the foliage of a large specimen. The American **D. drummondii** is similar but the flowers are yellow. The hybrid of these two species is **D. suendermannii** — its flower colour, as one would expect from such a marriage, is cream.

SITE & SOIL: Any well-drained, non-acid soil will do — add some compost or peat at planting time. Full sun is essential.

PROPAGATION: Plant cuttings in a cold frame in summer.

Dryas octopetala

ERIGERON   Fleabane

Erigeron is usually associated with the herbaceous border, but there are a few dwarf species which belong in the rockery. These sun-loving plants are not difficult to grow, and their Daisy-like flowers add colour during the summer months.

VARIETIES: The most popular species is **E. mucronatus** (**E. karvinskianus**) — height 8 in., spread 2 ft, flowering period June – September. The delicate appearance of this plant belies the robustness of its true nature. It can spread quite quickly by means of underground runners and may be too invasive for the small rockery. It flourishes in crevices between rocks, cracks between stones and crannies in walls. A colourful plant — the flowers darken from white to deep pink with age. In a severe winter the top growth may be killed, but new leaves will appear in spring. **E. aureus** is smaller — height 4 in., spread 9 in. with golden flowers in June and July.

SITE & SOIL: Thrives best in light, well-drained soil in full sun.

PROPAGATION: Sow seeds or divide clumps in spring.

Erigeron mucronatus

ERINUS   Summer Starwort

This little alpine is for cracks and crannies in paving and walls and for planting in the rock garden. It is easy to grow but the plants are rather short-lived. This is not really a problem as self-sown seedlings take over, providing small mounds of tiny green leaves. In spring, clusters of small star-shaped flowers appear on short wiry stalks — a splash of white, pink or red which may last until midsummer or even longer.

VARIETIES: A single species is grown — **E. alpinus**. The basic details are height 3 in., spread 6 in., flowering period April – August. The flower colour of the species is pink, but you can buy named varieties in different colours, and a blessing is that these named sorts breed true from seed. The two favourites are **'Albus'** (white) and **'Dr Hanele'** (crimson). **'Mrs Charles Boyle'** is a good pink variety.

SITE & SOIL: Requires well-drained infertile soil — thrives in sun or light shade.

PROPAGATION: Sow seeds in spring where the plants are to flower.

Erinus alpinus

ERYSIMUM   Alpine Wallflower

The Wallflower is one of the most popular of all spring-flowering plants for the bed or border, but its dwarf alpine relative is an uncommon rockery plant. You will certainly be able to recognise it when in bloom — it looks like a miniature version of the ordinary yellow Wallflower in every way — leaf, growth habit and flower shape. An easy plant which will grow in any open sunny situation, but it is not long-lived.

VARIETIES: Some species of Erysimum grow to 1 ft or more, only **E. alpinum** is a rockery dwarf — height 6 in., spread 6 in., flowering period April – May. The fragrant, yellow blooms are about ½ in. across. A number of named varieties are available if the bright yellow colour of E. alpinum does not appeal, but choose with care — some are quite tall. **'K. Elmhurst'** (lilac) may reach 1½ ft and **'Moonlight'** (primrose yellow) grows taller than the species. You are safe with **'Jubilee Gold'** — it only grows 6 in. high.

SITE & SOIL: Any well-drained, non-acid soil will do — thrives best in full sun.

PROPAGATION: Plant cuttings in a cold frame in summer.

Erysimum alpinum 'Moonlight'

GENTIANA Gentian

Quite simply, something is clearly missing if you don't have at least one species of Gentian in your rockery. The blue trumpets of this alpine plant can provide colour from May to September if you grow spring-, summer- and autumn-flowering types. With Gentians you should always look up the likes and dislikes of a particular species before you buy it — one Gentian's meat is another Gentian's poison. Lime is the problem — spring-flowering species either tolerate it or require it, but the autumn-flowering Gentians cannot tolerate it. All of them demand free-draining but not impoverished soil. Add peat and some grit to the soil before planting — most Gentians are rather temperamental and cannot be regarded as 'grow anywhere' plants.

VARIETIES: The easiest one to grow is **G. septemfida** which will give a good display of 1 in. long trumpets in any well-drained soil. Its basic details are height 9 in., spread 1 ft, flowering period July–August. The popular **G. acaulis** (Trumpet Gentian) is a smaller plant (3 in. high) and blooms earlier (May–June), but its flowers are much more eye-catching — 3 in. long trumpets standing upright above the glossy oval leaves. Unfortunately it is unpredictable — in some situations it will not bloom and nobody knows why. If your plants are flower-shy, simply move them to another spot in autumn. **G. verna** is another spring-flowering Gentian — height 3 in., spread 6 in., flowering period May–June. Its star-like flowers are bright blue and borne singly rather than in clusters. An attractive evergreen, but unfortunately the plants are short-lived. The most popular autumn-flowering Gentian is **G. sino-ornata** — height 6 in., spread 1 ft, flowering period September–November. The 2 in. long trumpets are bright blue with pale green stripes — a showy display when little else is in flower in the rock garden. In order to maintain the vigour of this plant, divide the clumps every 3 years.

SITE & SOIL: Well-drained soil is essential — lime should be present for spring-flowering types but the ground must be acid for the autumn-flowering ones. Thrives in sun or light shade.

PROPAGATION: Divide clumps in spring (autumn-flowering Gentians) or midsummer (spring-flowering Gentians). Propagation from seed is difficult.

Gentiana acaulis

Gentiana verna

GERANIUM Rock Geranium

There are several species of Rock Geranium which flourish in the rockery. All are easy to grow if the site is not shady and the soil is free draining. The only enemies are wet ground and slugs in the spring — scatter Slug Pellets around the stems. The lobed leaves are grey or green, depending on the species, and the pink or red flowers are often prominently veined.

VARIETIES: **G. cinereum** is a popular species — height 6 in., spread 1 ft, flowering period May–September. The deep pink 1 in. flowers are dark-centred and veined — the leaves are greyish green. **G. dalmaticum** has the same height and spread, but the flowering period is shorter (June–August) and the pale pink blooms are not veined. The glossy leaves turn red in autumn. A large-flowered variety is **G. subcaulescens 'Splendens'** (deep pink flowers May–September) and **G. 'Ballerina'** (dark-veined lilac flowers May–September) is a popular hybrid.

SITE & SOIL: Any well-drained soil — thrives best in full sun.

PROPAGATION: Divide clumps in autumn or spring.

Geranium cinereum

GEUM Alpine Geum

The ordinary Geums, such as 'Mrs Bradshaw' and 'Lady Stratheden', are a common sight in the herbaceous border, but the dwarf forms are not often grown in the rock garden. There is no particular reason for this — neither of them is difficult and the large yellow flowers are attractive. They are true alpines, growing wild in the Swiss Alps and deserve to be more popular. The blooms are certainly more colourful than those of Edelweiss!

VARIETIES: The species you are likely to find is **G. montanum**. The rough, wrinkled leaves grow in tufts and in summer the short flowering stems appear, bearing 1 in. bowl-shaped yellow flowers. Its basic details are height 9 in., spread 1 ft, flowering period May–July. **G. reptans** has the same basic details but the growth habit is quite different. Long red stolons spread out from the plant, producing rosettes of leaves where rooting takes place.

SITE & SOIL: Any well-drained soil — thrives best in full sun.

PROPAGATION: Divide clumps in spring.

Geum montanum

GYPSOPHILA Baby's Breath

There are several miniature versions for growing in the rockery. Clouds of small white or pink flowers are produced in summer, scaled-down versions of the popular herbaceous border Gypsophila. The most popular rockery species (G. repens) is also the best, and is ideal for trailing over rocks or down a wall. It is a lime-loving plant but alkaline soil is not essential.

VARIETIES: The basic details of **G. repens** (**G. prostrata**) are height 6 in., spread 2 ft, flowering period June – August. The carpet of stems clothed in grey- or blue-tinged foliage spreads over quite a large area. It is usual to grow a named variety — **'Fratensis'** (pink), **'Letchworth Rose'** (pink) or **'Monstrosa'** (white). Other species are less satisfactory, but you can try **G. cerastioides** (height 3 in., spread 1 ft) or the cushion-forming **G. arietioides** (height 2 in., spread 6 in.) if you want something unusual.

SITE & SOIL: Requires well-drained soil and full sun.

PROPAGATION: Plant non-flowering cuttings in a cold frame in early summer.

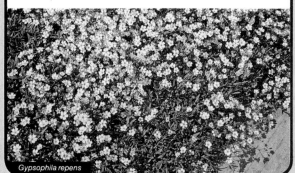
Gypsophila repens

HABERLEA Haberlea

Haberlea is a pretty lilac alpine which offers a challenge. It is very fussy about its environment and will not succeed unless given the right set of conditions. It needs acid soil in a shady spot, and water must not be left to stand in the heart of the rosette of leaves during winter. The best plan is to plant it sideways in a crack between the stones or bricks in a north-facing rockery or wall.

VARIETIES: The usual Haberlea is **H. rhodopensis** — height 4 in., spread 8 in., flowering period May. The stalks bearing clusters of flowers arise from the centre of the rosette composed of dark green leaves. The lilac flowers are tubular and measure about 1 in. across. A white variety (**'Virginalis'**) is available. Pick **H. ferdinandi-coburgii** if you can find it. It is larger than H. rhodopensis and the lilac flowers are flecked with gold.

SITE & SOIL: Requires well-drained but damp soil with little or no direct sun.

PROPAGATION: Plant healthy mature leaves as cuttings in a cold frame in summer. Alternatively divide clumps in autumn.

Haberlea rhodopensis

HELIANTHEMUM Rock Rose

The colourful but lowly Rock Rose (H. nummularium) which is frequently found in rockeries and small beds is really a shrub — see The Tree & Shrub Expert, page 31. It is an extremely useful space-filler, rapidly covering large bare patches and bearing a profusion of flowers between May and July. Dead-head regularly and once flowering is over, cut back all straggly stems.

VARIETIES: The basic details of **H. nummularium** are height 6 in., spread 2 ft, flowering period May – July. Many named varieties are available, ranging in colour from white and yellow to deep red. The popular Rock Rose has two uncommon alpine relatives which are less invasive. **H. alpestre** (height 4 in., spread 1 ft, flowering period June – July) bears yellow, bowl-shaped flowers — similar-shaped flowers are borne by the golden **H. lunulatum** (height 8 in., spread 1 ft, flowering period June – July).

SITE & SOIL: Requires free-draining, non-acid soil — full sun is essential.

PROPAGATION: Plant cuttings in a cold frame in summer.

Helianthemum nummularium 'Ben Afflick'

HELICHRYSUM Everlasting Flower

The usual place to find Helichrysum is in the flower bed — the well-known H. bracteatum is an annual grown for its colourful 'everlasting' flowers which are cut and dried for winter decoration. This half hardy annual has a dwarf perennial relative which can be used to provide ground cover in the rockery.

VARIETIES: The species you are most likely to be offered is **H. bellidioides** — height 3 in., spread 1½ ft, flowering period June – August. It forms a mat of small leaves which are green above and pale grey below. This spreading mat can be invasive and should be kept in check if delicate specimens are growing nearby. In summer the characteristic strawy-petalled flowers appear on short stalks. Unlike its colourful cousin in the flower bed, white is the only colour.

SITE & SOIL: Any well-drained garden soil will do — full sun is essential.

PROPAGATION: Plant cuttings in a cold frame or divide clumps in summer.

Helichrysum bellidioides

HEPATICA Hepatica

There is something especially welcome about a rockery plant which comes into bloom before the flowers of Aubrietia, Alyssum, Arabis and the bulbs have livened up the scene in spring. Hepatica has the added advantage of thriving in partial shade as well as in full sun, and it is therefore surprising that it is not more widely grown. Peat or compost should be added to the soil before planting.

VARIETIES: **H. nobilis (H. triloba)** is the species you are most likely to find. The basic details are height 3 in., spread 1 ft, flowering period February – April. The blue starry flowers, measuring 1 in. across, appear on short stalks above the tri-lobed leaves. White, pink and red varieties are available, but you will have to search to find them. **H. transsilvanica** is a similar plant but the leaves and flowers are larger. Best of all, perhaps, is the lavender-flowered **H. media 'Ballardii'**.

SITE & SOIL: Well-drained but damp soil is required — thrives in sun or partial shade.

PROPAGATION: Divide clumps in autumn.

Hepatica nobilis alba

HYPERICUM St John's Wort

Hypericum is one of the most popular of all shrubs, but the common-or-garden H. calycinum has no place in the rockery. It is far too invasive — there are much choicer types for this situation. All the Hypericums, shrubs and evergreen perennials alike, are easy to grow. They will thrive in any soil which does not become waterlogged in winter, but the dwarf rockery types require rather more sun than their robust brothers in the shrub garden.

VARIETIES: The best rockery shrub is **H. polyphyllum** — height 6 in., spread 1 ft, flowering period July – August. Above the mound of blue-grey leaves the typical Hypericum flowers appear — golden saucers with prominent stamens. **H. coris** is an evergreen perennial rather than a shrub — height 6 in., spread 1 ft, flowering period July – September. The yellow flowers are star-shaped. There is also a ground-cover species — **H. reptans** (height 3 in., spread 1½ ft, flowering period July – September).

SITE & SOIL: Any well-drained soil will do — thrives best in full sun.

PROPAGATION: Plant cuttings in a cold frame in early summer.

Hypericum polyphyllum

IBERIS Perennial Candytuft

Annual Candytuft is usually seen as a colourful mixture of white, pink and red flowers, but Perennial Candytuft comes only in white. This shrubby evergreen is a useful and popular rockery plant — very easy to grow as long as it gets some sun. Dead-head regularly in order to extend the flowering period and spray with an insecticide if holes begin to appear in the leaves.

VARIETIES: Unless you go to a specialist supplier the only species you are likely to be offered is **I. sempervirens**. The flowers are borne in closely-packed heads, each flower exhibiting the 4-petalled arrangement of the Cabbage family. The flowering period is May – June; the height and spread are variable, depending on the variety chosen. The best of all is **'Snowflake'** — height 9 in., spread 1½ ft. Where space is limited, choose instead **'Little Gem'** — height 4 in., spread 8 in.

SITE & SOIL: Any well-drained soil will do — thrives best in full sun.

PROPAGATION: Plant non-flowering cuttings in a cold frame in summer.

Iberis sempervirens 'Snowflake'

IRIS Rockery Iris

Irises come in a bewildering variety of shapes and sizes, and they can be found in several parts of the garden and in two other sections of this book. From the border perennial section you can choose one of the many Dwarf Bearded hybrids of I. pumila — amongst the bulbs there are such rock garden favourites as I. reticulata and I. danfordiae. Described below are the most popular rockery perennials.

VARIETIES: The flowering time for Rockery Irises is May and June. Flower colours and heights are variable — individual plants may differ widely from the following details: **I. cristata** (purple and gold flowers, height 4 in., spread 6 in.), **I. lacustris** (lilac, yellow and white flowers, height 3 in., spread 6 in.), **I. innominata** (gold and brown flowers, height 6 in., spread 9 in.) and **I. douglasiana** (lilac and yellow flowers, height 1 ft, spread 2 ft).

SITE & SOIL: Requires well-drained, lime-free soil — thrives in sun or light shade.

PROPAGATION: Divide rhizomes in late summer every few years.

Iris innominata

LEONTOPODIUM   Edelweiss

Edelweiss is the symbol of alpine flowers. It grows wild in the Alps and rather surprisingly will flourish quite happily in your lowland garden if the site is sunny and the drainage is good. There are many alpines which are more difficult to grow, but there are also many which are more attractive. Edelweiss is interesting rather than beautiful — the greyish white, flat flower-heads are borne on short stalks above the greyish green leaves.

VARIETIES: There is just one species which is widely available — **L. alpinum**, the common Edelweiss of the Swiss Alps. The basic details are height 6 in., spread 9 in., flowering period June – July. The narrow leaves are hoary on top and densely woolly below. They form a rosette from which the furry flower stems appear. The curious flower-heads are about 2 in. across — a central group of small rayless Daisies surrounded by large bracts which appear to be made of grey flannel.

SITE & SOIL: Any well-drained soil will do — requires full sun.

PROPAGATION: Sow seeds under glass in early spring.

Leontopodium alpinum

LEWISIA   Lewisia

Lewisia in bloom is sure to please — yellows and reds predominate and so the flowers may be pink, peach or orange as well as white. The petals are frequently striped — a colourful display for early summer. Unfortunately this American plant is not easy to keep alive in the rockery. The fleshy leaves form a rosette and rotting of the crown takes place if water is allowed to stand in the heart of this rosette during winter. The answer is to plant Lewisia sideways in a crevice between rocks or in a crack between bricks.

VARIETIES: You are most likely to be offered a hybrid of the evergreen **L. cotyledon** — height 1 ft, spread 9 in., flowering period May – June. The other species are more difficult to grow — there is the white-flowering **L. brachycalyx** which blooms in May; the aristocrat of the group is **L. tweedyi** (height 6 in., spread 9 in.) which bears 2 in. silky flowers in April and May.

SITE & SOIL: Requires well-drained soil in full sun.

PROPAGATION: Sow seeds under glass in early spring or plant offsets as cuttings in a cold frame in early summer.

Lewisia cotyledon

LINNAEA   Twin Flower

It is appropriate that this wild flower which grows in the colder regions of Sweden should have been named after Linnaeus, that country's most famous scientist. It is an excellent choice if you have a large damp and shady area to cover. The tangled mat of stems and rounded evergreen leaves spreads quickly, bearing dainty bell-like flowers during the summer months. The soil should not be chalky.

VARIETIES: There is just one species — **L. borealis**. The basic details are height 2 in., spread 2 ft, flowering period May – July. From the prostrate carpet of stems and leaves the short flower stalks appear, each one topped by a pair of pale pink flowers — hence the common name. Make sure you have the right conditions before buying this plant — it would be a waste of money to plant it on a sandy, sunny site.

SITE & SOIL: Requires moist, humus-rich soil in partial shade.

PROPAGATION: Peg down runners with small wire hoops. When rooted, sever from the mother plant and transfer the rooted cutting to its new site.

Linnaea borealis

LITHOSPERMUM   Gromwell

Lithospermum (now re-named Lithodora by the botanists) is a ground cover plant — its blue, funnel-shaped flowers are as bright as anything you will find in the summer rock garden. It requires a sunny spot and humus-rich soil — add peat or compost at planting time. If your soil is chalky, do not plant L. diffusum or its varieties — choose instead the lime-tolerant L. oleifolium.

VARIETIES: The best known species is **L. diffusum**; height 6 in., spread 2 ft, flowering period June – September. The prostrate mat spreads quickly — the leaves are dark green and the blooms deep blue. The species is rarely grown — the choice is between the varieties **'Heavenly Blue'** and **'Grace Ward'**. Most experts vote for 'Grace Ward'. **L. oleifolium** is quite different in colour — the leaves are silvery grey and the flowers change from pink when in bud to pale blue when fully open. Its basic details are height 6 in., spread 1 ft, flowering period May – August.

SITE & SOIL: Any well-drained, moist soil — thrives best in full sun.

PROPAGATION: Plant cuttings in a cold frame in midsummer.

Lithospermum diffusum 'Grace Ward'

LYCHNIS   Alpine Campion

Several Campions are grown in the herbaceous border, ranging in size from the 3 ft tall Jerusalem Cross to the 18 in. Rose Campion. For the rockery there is just a single species — L. alpina. This tiny alpine produces tufts of dark green leaves and in summer clusters of starry flowers appear. Grow it between paving stones or in the rock garden — its compactness makes it an excellent choice for a sink garden. No problems as long as the soil is not chalky and there is no danger of waterlogging. The only difficulty is that the Alpine Campion is short-lived.

VARIETIES: You will find the Alpine Campion listed as **L. alpina** or **Viscaria alpina** — height 4 in., spread 4 in., flowering period May–July. The flower stalks are just a couple of inches high, each one crowned with a group of pink flowers. For other colours choose the variety **'Alba'** (white) or **'Rosea'** (deep pink).

SITE & SOIL: Any well-drained acid or neutral soil will do — thrives best in full sun.

PROPAGATION: Sow seeds under glass in early spring.

Lychnis alpina 'Splendens Plena'

LYSIMACHIA   Creeping Jenny

Creeping Jenny (Moneywort) is the dwarf Lysimachia which grows wild in Britain and has been used in gardens for hundreds of years. Its vigorous trailing stems serve as an effective ground cover for damp places, stifling weeds and providing a display of yellow flowers in summer. It thrives in the moist soil adjacent to ponds, but it will grow quite happily in the rockery if compost is added to the soil before planting.

VARIETIES: The common-or-garden Creeping Jenny is **L. nummularia** — height 2 in., spread 1½ ft, flowering period June–July. The ½ in. flowers are bright yellow saucers and the leaves are bright green. It is a vigorous carpeting plant — far too invasive for a small rockery. Choose instead the yellow-leaved variety **'Aurea'** — it is much less vigorous and its foliage remains attractive all year round.

SITE & SOIL: Requires well-drained, humus-rich soil in a partially shaded spot.

PROPAGATION: Plant cuttings in a cold frame in spring or divide clumps in autumn.

Lysimachia nummularia

MAZUS   Mazus

Mazus is a ground cover plant which does not appear in many gardening books, but it is available from large garden centres. The creeping stems grow rapidly and it is an excellent carpeter but it does need moisture in the soil. Choose it then for a moist, shady spot — use Thymus or Antennaria instead if the site is dry and sunny. The flowers which appear in summer are both attractive and unusual. They look rather like lilac Snapdragons with the lower petals spotted with white and gold.

VARIETIES: The only one you are likely to find is **M. reptans** — height 2 in., spread 1½ ft, flowering period June–August. The slender stems hug the ground, the toothed leaves forming a bronze-tinted green mat. There is another species — **M. radicans**, which used to be called **Mimulus radicans**. The flowers are white with purple spots.

SITE & SOIL: Well-drained, humus-rich soil is required — thrives best in partial shade.

PROPAGATION: Divide clumps in autumn or spring.

Mazus reptans

MIMULUS   Monkey Flower

The trumpet-shaped flowers of Mimulus have a Snapdragon appearance — the colour scheme is basically either red blotched with yellow or a shade of yellow blotched with red, purple or brown. You can grow a variety of the popular M. cupreus (see page 30) as a short-lived perennial instead of treating it as a half hardy annual. There are also rockery perennials, but whichever one you choose must be provided with the basic needs of the Monkey Flower — a moisture-retentive soil and regular watering in dry weather.

VARIETIES: M. primuloides is perhaps the best species to grow — height 4 in., spread 9 in., flowering period May–August. Bright yellow flowers are borne on short stalks arising from the prostrate mat of leaves. **M. luteus guttatus (M. langsdorfii)** produces yellow flowers blotched with dark brown, **M. burnettii** bears bronze-coloured flowers with yellow throats on 9 in. high plants.

SITE & SOIL: A moist soil which is not allowed to dry out is essential — some shade is desirable.

PROPAGATION: Sow seeds under glass or divide clumps in spring.

Mimulus burnettii

MORISIA   Morisia

A neat and compact cushion plant for the cracks in crazy paving or a pocket between stones in the rock garden. It is an uncommon specimen with special needs — sandy soil is essential for its survival and full sun is necessary to ensure that the floral display in spring will be satisfactory. The blooms are stemless, the large yellow flowers arising directly from amongst the tiny toothed leaves. Its early-flowering habit is welcome, but planting Morisia is a waste of time if the soil is heavy.

VARIETIES: There is a single species — **M. monanthos (M. hypogaea)**. The basic details are height 1 in., spread 6 in., flowering period March – May. It is not a true alpine — it grows wild on the Sardinian coast. The clusters of golden blooms show that Morisia is a member of the Cabbage family — there are 4 petals making up each cross-shaped flower.

SITE & SOIL: Requires well-drained, light soil in full sun.

PROPAGATION: Plant root cuttings in a cold frame in late winter.

Morisia monanthos

ONOSMA   Donkey Plant

Each plant needs one particular virtue to earn its place in the rock garden — Onosma's virtue is its long flowering season. The first flowers open in spring and continue to appear until late summer. The narrow, bristly leaves are evergreen and form compact clumps. The upright stalks bearing the flowers bend over at the apex, so that the clusters of long tubular flowers are pendent. Sunny and dry conditions are essential — the place for Onosma is in the crevice between rocks or on a dry wall. This plant does not like being disturbed.

VARIETIES: The most popular species is **O. tauricum** — height 8 in., spread 9 in., flowering period April – August. The yellow flowers are fragrant and about ¾ in. long. **O. albo-roseum** is quite similar but comes into bloom later and the flowers are white with a pink flush at the mouth.

SITE & SOIL: A well-drained, sandy soil and full sun are essential.

PROPAGATION: Plant cuttings in a cold frame in summer.

Onosma tauricum

ORIGANUM   Origanum

The rockery species of Origanum will only flourish in a warm and sunny site — they are not completely hardy and should therefore be covered with a cloche during the frosty days of winter. The flowers are long and tubular, appearing in abundance during summer but there is nothing special about these plants.

VARIETIES: The baby of the family is **O. amanum** — height 2 in., spread 6 in., flowering period July – September. During summer the ground-hugging mat of leafy stems is covered by the elongated pink flowers. **O. dictamnus (Amaracus dictamnus)** is quite different — the plant is larger and the woolly leaves form a rounded clump. The flowers are borne in hop-like heads – small pink blooms emerging from large purplish bracts. **O. vulgare 'Aureum'** is the yellow-leaved form of the common herb Marjoram. The purple flowers are insignificant — it is grown for its colourful foliage.

SITE & SOIL: Any well-drained soil — thrives best in full sun.

PROPAGATION: Plant non-flowering cuttings in a cold frame in late summer.

Origanum amanum

Flowers for Every Season

MAY – JUNE

(for FEBRUARY – APRIL see page 87)
(for JULY – AUGUST see page 105)
(for SEPTEMBER – DECEMBER see page 106)

By careful selection you can ensure that your rockery will have flowers nearly all year round. For each month there is a list of perennials which can be expected to be in full bloom — remember that some of these plants may come into flower earlier and can continue to bloom for many weeks afterwards.

MAY

Alyssum saxatile	Haberlea rhodopensis
Androsace sarmentosa chumbyi	Iberis sempervirens
Antennaria dioica	Iris spp.
Arenaria balearica	Lewisia cotyledon
Armeria caespitosa	Onosma tauricum
Armeria maritima	Penstemon rupicola
Aubrieta deltoidea	Raoulia australis
Cerastium tomentosum	Saxifraga (Encrusted)
Dianthus caesius	Silene acaulis
Dryas octopetala	Uvularia grandiflora
Erinus alpinus	Vancouveria hexandra
Gentiana acaulis	Viola aetolica
Gentiana verna	Viola biflora

JUNE

Arenaria balearica	Helianthemum nummularium
Armeria maritima	Iberis sempervirens
Campanula spp.	Iris spp.
Cerastium tomentosum	Leontopodium alpinum
Dianthus spp.	Linnaea borealis
Dodecatheon meadia	Lychnis alpina
Dryas octopetala	Onosma tauricum
Erigeron mucronatus	Oxalis adenophylla
Erinus alpinus	Primula vialii
Gentiana acaulis	Ranunculus gramineus
Gentiana verna	Sedum spp.
Geranium cinereum	Sisyrinchium angustifolium
Geum montanum	Veronica prostrata

OXALIS   Oxalis

Don't plant a clump of Oxalis unless you know its identity. The species described below are suitable, providing attractive foliage and summer flowers, but there are other types which spread everywhere and can ruin a large part of the rockery. Oxalis is an undemanding plant, but peat or compost should be added before planting.

VARIETIES: **O. adenophylla** is the most popular species grown in the rock garden — the basic details are height 3 in., spread 6 in., flowering period June–July. The greyish foliage dies down in winter — label the site to avoid damaging the roots when weeding in the spring. The flowers are bowl-shaped and shiny, white with attractive pink edging and veining. **O. enneaphylla** has the same growth habit, and the variety **'Rosea'** is popular as a rockery perennial. The rose-pink flowers measure about 1 in. across and the silvery leaves are partially folded. The only spreading species you should grow is **O. chrysantha** — height 2 in., spread 1 ft. This dainty carpeter bears yellow flowers.

SITE & SOIL: Any well-drained soil — thrives best in full sun.

PROPAGATION: Divide clumps in autumn.

Oxalis adenophylla

PENSTEMON   Penstemon

Penstemons are shrubby perennials which bear Snapdragon-like flowers. Their blooms are usually pink or purple, but blue and white varieties are available. Grow one or more of the many rockery species by all means, but they do tend to be delicate. Winter is the trying time, when many specimens are killed by a combination of cold winds, severe frosts and wet ground.

VARIETIES: One of the most highly recommended species is the low-growing **P. rupicola** — height 3 in., spread 1 ft, flowering period May–June. The 1 in. long flowers are pale crimson. **P. pinifolius** is the hardiest of the group — height 6 in., spread 1 ft, flowering period June–September. This late-flowering species bears dark orange ½ in. blooms. There are several others (**P. menziesii, P. newberryi** and **P. scouleri**) which grow about 9–12 in. high and 1-1½ ft across, bearing pink or pale purple flowers in June.

SITE & SOIL: Any well-drained soil — thrives best in a sheltered site in full sun.

PROPAGATION: Plant cuttings in a cold frame in summer.

Penstemon newberryi

PHLOX   Dwarf Phlox

The ever-popular Phlox of the herbaceous border has several dwarf relatives from America which will grace any rock garden. They are easy to grow and will cover rocks or tumble over walls, bearing masses of ½ in. flowers in spring or early summer. These flat floral sheets of white, pink or lavender make a change from the over-used Aubrietia.

VARIETIES: **P. subulata** (Moss Phlox) is the one you are most likely to be offered. It is a carpeting plant — height 3 in., spread 1½ ft, flowering period April–May. There are many named varieties, such as **'Apple Blossom'** (pink), **'Temiscaming'** (red) and **'G. F. Wilson'** (pale purple). **P. douglasii** (Alpine Phlox) has a similar height and spread, but blooms a little later. Again there are many named varieties, and you can choose from white, pink or lavender. If you want an unusual variety, plant **P. nana ensifolia** which spreads to only 6 in.

SITE & SOIL: Any well-drained, moisture-retentive soil will do — thrives best in full sun.

PROPAGATION: Plant cuttings in a cold frame in summer.

Phlox subulata 'Temiscaming'

PLEIONE   Rockery Orchid

A plant for people who want to keep up with the Jones's — a true Orchid which will grow outdoors! All you need is a sheltered site in partial shade — the soil must be enriched with plenty of peat and leaf mould plus some sharp sand. In winter, cover the plant with a pane of glass to keep the soil dry. Your reward will be true Orchid flowers, about 3 in. long, borne on short stems — living proof that not all Orchids come from the jungle.

VARIETIES: **P. bulbocodioides (P. formosana)** and its varieties are the Pleiones which are usually grown outdoors — height 6 in., spread 6 in., flowering period April–May. The showy blooms bear narrow white or pink petals and a large yellow, white or orange central tube. After blooming the wide grassy leaves appear — a showpiece in any garden.

SITE & SOIL: A free-draining soil enriched with humus is required — do not plant in full sun.

PROPAGATION: Plant a detached pseudobulb in a cold frame in spring.

Pleione bulbocodioides

POLYGONUM Rock Polygonum

Polygonum is generally grown as a herbaceous border plant, although the popular P. affine is sometimes planted in the rock garden. This is usually a mistake as the highly invasive species, such as P. affine, can easily overrun the less robust alpines growing nearby. There are just two species which are recommended for the rockery.

VARIETIES: **P. vaccinifolium** is the common rockery type — height 6 in., spread 3 ft, flowering period September – December. In late autumn the upright spikes of small pink flowers and the red-tinged leaves of this evergreen are a welcome sight. It is wide spreading but can be easily kept under control if required — use it to cover large rocks or to cascade over retaining walls. If you want something smaller, choose **P. tenuicaule** — height 4 in., spread 1 ft, flowering period March – April. The white flowers are borne on small upright spikes.

SITE & SOIL: Any well-drained soil — thrives best in full sun.

PROPAGATION: Divide clumps in autumn or spring. Alternatively plant non-flowering cuttings in autumn.

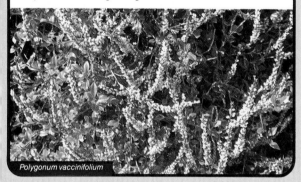
Polygonum vaccinifolium

POTENTILLA Rock Cinquefoil

The shrub forms of Potentilla (The Tree & Shrub Expert, page 45) are much too large for a modest rockery, but there are several species which are small enough to feel at home in such surroundings. These Rock Cinquefoils are generally mat-forming plants which produce a succession of blooms over a long period. These blooms are cup-shaped and often look like tiny single Rose flowers.

VARIETIES: **P. nitida** is the popular one — height 3 in., spread 1 ft, flowering period July – September. The silvery leaves and pale pink flowers are attractive, but it is not a free-flowering plant. Choose the deep pink variety **'Rubra'**. Another mat-forming species is **P. alba** — a glossy-leaved plant with large white flowers. For yellow blooms grow **P. verna nana**. For a non-carpeting type pick **P. alpestris (P. crantzii)** — height 6 in., spread 9 in., flowers orange-centred yellow, July – September.

SITE & SOIL: Any garden soil — thrives best in full sun.

PROPAGATION: Sow seeds under glass in spring or divide clumps in autumn.

Potentilla alpestris

PRIMULA Rockery Primrose

Primula is a large and complex genus. The flowers nearly always have a Primrose shape and they either droop gracefully or are held erect. There are hardly any general rules about cultivation — humus-rich soil and some shade are nearly always needed but the Primulas vary from easy-to-grow favourites which succeed anywhere to some of the so-called Asian varieties which offer a real challenge. The dividing line between the Rockery Primroses and the ones grown in the herbaceous border is not clear-cut. The Common Primrose, Polyanthus and the Drumstick Primrose are often planted in rock gardens, whereas the Auriculas described below are frequently used as front-of-the-border subjects.

VARIETIES: The fleshy-leaved Auricula **(P. auricula)** is an old favourite — height 6 in., spread 6 in., flowering period March – April. Clusters of large flowers in a range of colour combinations are borne on the flower stalks. **P. juliae** has a different growth habit. It is a carpeting plant — height 3 in., spread 1 ft, flowering period March – May. It is best known for its hybrids with their short-stemmed flowers nestling in the leaves — examples are **P. 'Wanda'** (wine-coloured) and **P. 'Victory'** (purple). **P. rosea** (height 6 in., spread 6 in.) is often recommended for its bright pink flowers which appear in the spring, but it will not thrive unless you can provide very moist soil. **P. vialii** is an unusual Primula — quite tall (height 1 ft, spread 1 ft), it flowers in June and July and the flower-heads have the appearance of a Red Hot Poker. **P. marginata** is a small plant (height 4 in., spread 6 in.) which blooms in early April — clusters of sweet-smelling blue or purple flowers above the mealy leaves. **'Linda Pope'** is the best variety. **P. edgeworthii** is a very early Primula, blooming in February. Attractive, with yellow-eyed mauve flowers, but difficult to grow in most areas of Britain. The baby of the family is **P. minima** — height 2 in., spread 5 in., flowering period April – May. The flower stalks bearing large pink blooms arise from the centre of the leaf rosettes.

SITE & SOIL: Well-drained, moisture-retentive soil in light shade is the usual requirement.

PROPAGATION: Plant cuttings under glass in summer or divide clumps after flowering.

Primula 'Wanda'

Primula auricula

PULSATILLA Pasque Flower

The Pasque Flower is one of the gems of the rockery. In spring the flower stems push up through the earth, each one crowned by a silky bud. The buds open into cup-shaped and later star-shaped flowers — each measuring about 3 in. across. The flowers are followed by the emergence of the ferny foliage and the attractive silky seed-heads. It is an easy plant to grow if the site is sunny — the secret of success is to plant Pulsatilla very firmly.

VARIETIES: P. vulgaris (Anemone pulsatilla) is the Pasque Flower which grows wild in Europe. The basic details are height 9 in., spread 1 ft, flowering period April–May. The flower colour is pale purple but you can buy varieties in other colours. If you want a similar-sized Pasque Flower which produces large white blooms, then buy **P. alpina**. Another white species is the diminutive **P. vernalis** (height and spread 6 in.).

SITE & SOIL: Any well-drained sunny site will do – P. vulgaris and P. vernalis need lime.

PROPAGATION: Sow seeds under glass in summer.

Pulsatilla vulgaris

RAMONDA Ramonda

There is something particularly appealing about an alpine bearing flowers which look too big for its body — colourful blooms above a rosette of dark green leaves. Ramonda fits the bill — its 1½ in. flowers are deep lavender with a central boss of bright orange stamens. Unfortunately it is not an easy plant to grow — it requires the same treatment as Haberlea (page 95) to which it is related. To avoid rotting in winter it should be planted sideways in a crack or crevice in a north-facing rockery or wall.

VARIETIES: R. myconii is the most popular variety — height 4 in., spread 9 in., flowering period April–May. The evergreen leaves are rough and crinkled — the flat-faced flowers are deep lavender. Varieties are available — **'Rosea'** (pink) and **'Alba'** (white). The other species are less common — **R. serbica** and **R. nathaliae** are very similar to and no better than R. myconii.

SITE & SOIL: Well-drained but damp soil with little or no direct sun.

PROPAGATION: Plant healthy mature leaves as cuttings in a cold frame in summer. Alternatively divide clumps in autumn.

Ramonda myconii

RANUNCULUS Dwarf Buttercup

Several dwarf relatives of the Buttercup are grown in the rock garden — the taller types belong in the border. But the dividing line between the two groups is not clear-cut — R. ficaria 'Aurantiacus' (see page 75) and R. gramineus (see below) are used as either tall rockery specimens or front-of-the-border plants. Add some sharp sand or grit to the soil before planting.

VARIETIES: R. calandrinioides produces large white flowers above the greyish green leaves — height 6 in., spread 6 in., flowering period February–April. **R. gramineus** blooms later (May–July) and its bowl-shaped flowers are yellow. The shiny blooms are borne in loose sprays above the grassy, bluish leaves. The plant is quite large — height 1 ft, spread 1 ft. **R. montanus** is a neat dwarf — height 4 in., spread 4 in., yellow flowers in spring.

SITE & SOIL: Well-drained soil and sunny site are essential.

PROPAGATION: Sow seeds under glass in spring or divide clumps in autumn.

Ranunculus montanus

RAOULIA Raoulia

Raoulia is a true carpeting plant with a pile which does not exceed ½ in. when in full flower. The tiny leaves and tiny blooms hug the surface over which the living mat has spread — a very effective cover for ground in which dwarf bulbs have been planted. Unfortunately this New Zealand plant is never fully at home in our climate. Casualties occur in very hard winters and a pane of glass should be placed over the plant from autumn until spring to keep off the rain.

VARIETIES: The best-known variety is **R. australis** — height ½ in., spread 1 ft, flowering period May. It is grown mainly for its silvery foliage — the minute pale yellow flowers are of little decorative value. There is a Raoulia which turns into a bright yellow carpet between April and June. This is **R. lutescens** — height ½ in., spread 1 ft. From spring until early summer the flower-heads open and cover the mossy grey-green leaves.

SITE & SOIL: A well-drained, light soil in full sun is required.

PROPAGATION: Divide the mats in autumn.

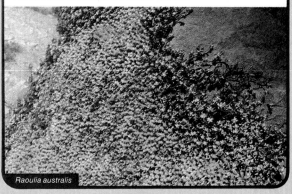
Raoulia australis

SANGUINARIA   Bloodroot

As you would expect from the common name, the root of this N. American plant oozes red sap if it is severed. Sanguinaria is a wide-spreading perennial which belongs to the Poppy family, and has unfortunately inherited the drawback of having flowers with a very brief life span. The flowers may be fleeting but the large white blooms nestling amongst the greyish lobed leaves are extremely attractive. This is not a plant for a sandy pocket in the rockery — grow it in soil enriched with peat or compost.

VARIETIES: There is a single species — **S. canadensis**. The basic details are height 6in., spread 1½ ft, flowering period April – May. The single flowers measure 1½ in. across and last for less than a day — choose instead the longer-lasting and more eye-catching double form **'Flore Pleno'**. Do not disturb after planting — label the plants as the leaves and stems die down in winter.

SITE & SOIL: Acid, humus-rich soil is required — thrives in sun or partial shade.

PROPAGATION: Not easy — carefully divide clumps in spring.

Sanguinaria canadensis 'Flore Pleno'

SAPONARIA   Rock Soapwort

The Soapwort grown in the herbaceous border is S. offici-nalis, an upright and invasive plant which has long been popular in cottage gardens (see page 76). The Rock Soap-wort is also wide-spreading, but it is a low-growing carpeting plant — a splendid choice for covering rocks or tumbling over walls. As you would expect from a perennial which grows wild in the Alps, its two enemies are shade and poor drainage — avoid these and it is trouble-free.

VARIETIES: The basic details of **S. ocymoides** are height 3 in., spread 1½ ft, flowering period July – September. The flowers are pale — for richer pink blooms choose the variety **'Splendens'**. The varieties **'Compacta'** or the red-flowering **'Rubra Compacta'** are useful where a smaller plant is required — or you can choose the bright pink **S. 'Bressingham'** (height 1½ in., spread 9 in., flowering period May – July).

SITE & SOIL: Requires well-drained soil in full sun.

PROPAGATION: Sow seeds under glass in spring or plant non-flowering cuttings in summer.

Saponaria ocymoides

SAXIFRAGA   Saxifrage

The Saxifrages are an extensive and complex range of perennials, a range which is a basic ingredient of both the small and large rock garden. The usual form is low-growing — a group of rosettes or mossy sheets from which starry or saucer-shaped flowers arise. A few exceptions to this general description do occur, but even within the standard pattern there are many variations and so you should choose with care. A few types are often considered as front-of-the-border plants — London Pride and S. fortunei are described on page 74, but the rest are treated as rockery specimens. Some of the best known are dealt with below.

VARIETIES: There are 3 basic groups. The *Encrusted* section contains plants which bear lime-encrusted leaves in the form of a single or many rosettes. The stalked flowers are star-shaped, appearing in May or June. Examples are **S. aizoon (S. panicu-lata)** — height 1 ft, spread 1 ft, sprays of white flowers above silvery rosettes — **'Rosea'** is a pink form; **S. cochlearis** — height 8 in., spread 9 in., sprays of white flowers on red stems above silvery rosettes; and the large **S. cotyledon** (height 2 ft, spread 1 ft) which bears dark green leaves encrusted at the edges. Two named varieties — **'Esther'** (cream) and **'Whitehills'** (white) are popular compact (height 6 in., spread 9 in.) plants. The *Mossy* section contains plants which form hummocks of mossy leaves. The flowers are star- or saucer-shaped and appear in April or May. There is a single species **S. moschata** (height 3 in., spread 1½ ft) with many named varieties — **'Pixie'** (red), **'Peter Pan'** (pink), **'Dubarry'** (red), **'Atropurpurea'** (red), **'Cloth of Gold'** (white flowers, golden foliage) and **'Flowers of Sulphur'** (yellow). Finally, there is the *Cushion* section, containing plants which have lime-coated leaves like the Encrusted section but the flowers appear early, in February – April, and the foliage forms a low cushion. **S. burseriana** (height 2 in., spread 1 ft) blooms in February — the earliest to flower. A little later-blooming and with yellow flowers instead of white is **S. apiculata** (height 4 in., spread 1 ft). **S. 'Elizabethae'** (yellow) is another early flowerer and a popular variety is **S. 'Jenkinsae'** bearing large pink blooms which nestle in the foliage. Equally low-growing (height 1 in.) is the pink-flowered **S. 'Cranbourne'**.

SITE & SOIL: All require well-drained soil. Provide a moist spot with some shade from the mid-day sun — only the Encrusted section thrives in full sun and dry soil.

PROPAGATION: General method is to plant non-flowering rosettes in a cold frame in early summer.

Saxifraga aizoon

Saxifraga 'Elizabethae'

SEDUM Stonecrop

At any large garden centre you will probably be offered a number of different Sedums. The family characteristics are low-growing fleshy leaves with starry flowers in early summer, usually yellow and borne either singly or in flat heads. Look up the properties of the variety you intend to buy or you can well be disappointed — the Ice Plants (S. spectabile and S. maximum) are large plants for the border rather than the rockery — see page 78. For a small and choice rockery you should avoid the Common Stonecrop (S. acre) — a rampant grower which can easily become a weed. Avoiding the pitfalls, you can pick from a wide selection of carpeters which will thrive in cracks and crevices and give that essential alpine touch to the site.

VARIETIES: Too aggressive for most rockeries, **S. acre** is still a useful plant for clothing large areas of walls or dry banks. The basic details are height 2 in., spread over 2 ft, flowering period June–July. Another wide-spreading 'weed' is **S. album** which fortunately has a well-behaved and non-invasive variety — **'Coral Carpet'** (spread 9 in., grey mounds of foliage bearing yellow flowers). **S. dasyphyllum** (height ½ in., spread 1 ft, blue-green leaves, flowering period June, white flowers) is a useful carpeter, but is not as popular as the old favourite **S. spathulifolium** — height 3 in., spread 1 ft, flowering period June–July. The wide mat is made up of silvery rosettes and the yellow flowers are borne in flat heads. The variety **'Purpureum'** has large purple leaves; the foliage of **'Cappa Blanca'** is white. The flowers of **S. spurium** (height 3 in., spread 1 ft) are white, pink or red — a change from the usual yellow. Grow the red-flowered variety **'Schorbusser Blut'**. As a change from the more popular types you can try the semi-trailing **S. ewersii** which bears pink flowers in June.

SITE & SOIL: Requires well-drained soil — thrives best in full sun.

PROPAGATION: Very easy — divide clumps in autumn or spring.

Sedum spathulifolium

Sedum spurium 'Schorbusser Blut'

SEMPERVIVUM Houseleek

The Houseleeks are a common sight amongst the crannies of well-planted rockeries, the thick flower stems rising above the ball-like rosettes of green or coloured leaves. An ideal choice for dry spots — these evergreen succulents withstand summer drought.

VARIETIES: The Common Houseleek **S. tectorum** is the best known — height 3 in., spread 1 ft, flowering period July. Its flowers are rosy purple, quite similar in colour to the blooms of the smaller growing **S. montanum**. In the main the Sempervivums are grown for their showy rosettes rather than for the flowers which appear in June or July. Choose then a Houseleek with decorative foliage — one example is the Cobweb Houseleek **S. arachnoideum** with small rosettes densely covered by white threads. Another group of decorative Houseleeks are the coloured ones — there are **'Othello'** (ruby red rosettes) and **'Commander Hay'** (bronzy red rosettes).

SITE & SOIL: Any well-drained soil will do — full sun is essential.

PROPAGATION: Plant non-flowering rosettes in a cold frame in autumn or spring.

Sempervivum tectorum

SHORTIA Shortia

In complete contrast to the Sedums and Sempervivums on this page, Shortia is a shade-loving plant which detests the presence of lime in the soil. The exposed crevice is not the place for this rockery perennial — it requires cool, peaty earth where it can thrive and display its highly decorative blooms. Dead-head when flowering is over. The shiny rounded leaves are usually tinged with brown or red, and in winter the foliage may turn completely bronze or crimson.

VARIETIES: The basic details of **S. galacifolia** are height 6 in., spread 1 ft, flowering period April–May. The trumpet-shaped flowers measure about 1 in. across — white when first open but changing to pink as the bloom ages. These flowers are borne singly at the top of the flower stems. If you can find it, choose instead the more spectacular **S. uniflora** — height 4 in., spread 1 ft. The flowers are 1½ in. across and the petals are fringed. Their colour is either white or pink.

SITE & SOIL: Well-drained, humus-rich soil is necessary — thrives best in partial shade.

PROPAGATION: Divide clumps in early summer.

Shortia uniflora

Flowers for Every Season

JULY–AUGUST

(for FEBRUARY–APRIL see page 87)
(for MAY–JUNE see page 99)
(for SEPTEMBER–DECEMBER see page 106)

By careful selection you can ensure that your rockery will have flowers nearly all year round. For each month there is a list of perennials which can be expected to be in full bloom — remember that some of these plants may come into flower earlier and can continue to bloom for many weeks afterwards.

JULY

Anacyclus depressus	Leontopodium alpinum
Androsace lanuginosa	Linnaea borealis
Aster alpinus	Lithospermum diffusum
Campanula spp.	Lychnis alpina
Cerastium tomentosum	Lysimachia nummularia
Dianthus spp.	Mazus reptans
Dodecatheon meadia	Mimulus primuloides
Erigeron mucronatus	Onosma tauricum
Erinus alpinus	Penstemon pinifolius
Geranium cinereum	Sedum spp.
Geum reptans	Sempervivum tectorum
Gypsophila repens	Sisyrinchium spp.
Helianthemum spp.	Thymus serpyllum
Helichrysum bellidioides	Verbascum spp.

AUGUST

Acaena microphylla	Helichrysum bellidioides
Achillea tomentosa	Hypericum polyphyllum
Anacyclus depressus	Lithospermum diffusum
Androsace lanuginosa	Mazus reptans
Astilbe chinensis pumila	Mimulus primuloides
Campanula spp.	Origanum amanum
Cyananthus microphyllus	Penstemon pinifolius
Dianthus deltoides	Potentilla nitida
Erigeron mucronatus	Saponaria ocymoides
Gentiana septemfida	Silene maritima
Geranium cinereum	Sisyrinchium spp.
Gypsophila repens	Verbascum 'Letitia'

SILENE Moss Campion

The Campions are easy to grow and most of them have a long flowering season, extending to September or October. They are carpeting plants which are usually planted between rocks, their stems and narrow leaves spreading outwards to form a low carpet from which the star-faced tubular flowers arise. Silene should not be moved.

VARIETIES: Some of the rockery Silenes grow as wild flowers in Britain. One of them is **S. acaulis** (height 2 in., spread 1 ft, flowering period May–June). The tiny green leaves form a mat and above this are the pink flowers, unfortunately less abundant than on the specimens growing wild. Another of our natives is **S. maritima**, the Sea Campion — grow the double-flowering form **'Flore Pleno'**, bearing 1½ in. white blooms and silvery foliage. Its basic statistics are height 6 in., spread 1 ft, flowering period July–October — the same statistics apply to **S. schafta** which produces masses of sprays of deep pink flowers. **'Abbotswood'** is the variety to grow.

SITE & SOIL: Requires well-drained soil in full sun.

PROPAGATION: Plant cuttings in a cold frame in summer.

Silene maritima 'Flore Pleno'

SISYRINCHIUM Pigroot

Pigs, it seems, are fond of digging up and eating the roots — hence the common name. Gardeners are less fond of this rockery perennial, although you should be able to find one or two types at a large garden centre. Its leaves are broadly grassy and its flowers star-shaped, appearing over a long period.

VARIETIES: The smallest species is **S. brachypus** — height 6 in., spread 6 in., flowering period June–October. Yellow blooms appear in succession on the flowering stems. A well-known species is the taller **S. angustifolium** (Blue-eyed Grass) — height 1 ft, spread 9 in., flowering period May–October. **S. bermudianum** is very similar and it is not easy to tell them apart. Both bear blue flowers — look for the yellow eye in the bloom of S. bermudianum. **S. grandiflorum** is a narrow, upright plant, bearing large, bell-shaped purple flowers in March and April.

SITE & SOIL: Requires well-drained, humus-rich soil in a sunny spot.

PROPAGATION: Divide clumps in spring or autumn.

Sisyrinchium brachypus

SOLDANELLA Snowbell

A genus for the connoisseur — dainty bell-like flowers deeply fringed at the margins, drooping gracefully from the top of the upright flower stalks. Lavender-blue is the usual colour but variations are known. They are not plants which can be left to look after themselves — most types require some form of protection against winter rains. Slugs can be a problem by devouring the flower buds — scatter Slug Pellets around the clumps in autumn and winter.

VARIETIES: **S. alpina** (height 3 in., spread 9 in., flowering period March–April) bears all the features of the genus — rounded leathery leaves and pale purple, fringed bells which appear in spring. It is not an easy plant to grow outdoors — you will have more success with the larger **S. montana** (height 4 in., spread 1 ft) which bears ¾ in. bells. The most floriferous and the easiest to grow is **S. villosa** (height 6 in., spread 1 ft). It flowers later than the others (April–May) and is far more robust.

SITE & SOIL: Well-drained, moist soil in light shade is required.

PROPAGATION: Divide clumps in summer.

Soldanella montana

THYMUS Thyme

This well-known culinary herb has many flower garden relatives, some growing as small bushes and others as prostrate mats. It is the carpeting varieties which are widely used in rockeries, producing large sheets of aromatic leaves and a covering of small flowers clustered on short stalks. It can be used to fill gaps in crazy paving or as leafy mats to clamber over rocks. Remove dead blooms with shears when flowering is finished.

VARIETIES: T. serpyllum is the basic species — height 2 in., spread 2 ft, flowering period June–July. Named varieties are usually grown, and you can choose almost any desired shade from white to red — **'Albus'** (white), **'Annie Hall'** (pale pink), **'Pink Chintz'** (deep pink) or **'Coccineus'** (red). For most of the year the plant will not be in flower — if you want coloured foliage choose **T. 'Silver Queen'** (green and white) or the hybrid **T. 'Doone Valley'** (green, blotched gold).

SITE & SOIL: Requires well-drained soil and full sun.

PROPAGATION: Divide clumps in autumn or spring.

Thymus serpyllum

UVULARIA Throatwort

A rarity which appears in few gardens and even fewer books. It is a member of the Lily family, spreading underground by means of rhizomes. The upright stems bear glossy clasping leaves, and in spring these branching stems are topped by long, pendent bells. It is only worth searching for if you have a shady patch of acid soil to fill — it will fail miserably in a small sunny crevice.

VARIETIES: The main species is **U. grandiflora (U. sessiliflora)** — height 9 in., spread 9 in., flowering period May. The stalkless leaves clasp the stem and both the flowers and fruits hang from the tips of the stem like bunches of grapes. The narrow bell-shaped flowers are yellow. **U. perfoliata** is a closely related species with similar flowers; the only major difference is the appearance that the stems pass through the leaves.

SITE & SOIL: Requires well-drained but moist soil — thrives best in partial shade.

PROPAGATION: Divide clumps in summer.

Uvularia grandiflora

VANCOUVERIA Inside-out Flower

Vancouveria is a plant from the damp woodlands of Canada, as one would expect from its name — a useful ground cover for moist and shady places on the rockery, producing carpets of lobed leaves above which rise the wiry flower stems. It is not a particular thing of beauty — just a large-leaved carpeter which your friends will fail to recognise. Vancouveria is closely related to Epimedium (page 55) — both are members of the Barberry family. One is traditionally classed as a border plant and the other as a rockery one — at least it illustrates just how artificial some of the dividing lines really are.

VARIETIES: There is just one species — **V. hexandra**. The basic details are height 9 in., spread 1 ft, flowering period May. The flowers are small and white, and unlike Epimedium the above-ground growth dies down in winter.

SITE & SOIL: Any humus-rich soil — thrives best in partial shade.

PROPAGATION: Divide clumps in spring.

Vancouveria hexandra

Flowers for Every Season

SEPTEMBER–DECEMBER

(for FEBRUARY–APRIL see page 87)
(for MAY–JUNE see page 99)
(for JULY–AUGUST see page 105)

By careful selection you can ensure that your rockery will have flowers nearly all year round. For each month there is a list of perennials which can be expected to be in full bloom — remember that some of these plants may come into flower earlier and can continue to bloom for many weeks afterwards.

SEPTEMBER

Acaena microphylla	Geranium cinereum
Achillea tomentosa	Lithospermum diffusum
Androsace lanuginosa	Origanum amanum
Astilbe chinensis pumila	Penstemon pinifolius
Campanula spp.	Polygonum vaccinifolium
Cyananthus microphyllus	Potentilla nitida
Dianthus deltoides	Saponaria ocymoides
Erigeron mucronatus	Silene maritima
Gentiana sino-ornata	Sisyrinchium spp.

OCTOBER

Androsace lanuginosa	Polygonum vaccinifolium
Astilbe chinensis pumila	Silene maritima
Gentiana sino-ornata	Sisyrinchium spp.

NOVEMBER

Gentiana sino-ornata	Polygonum vaccinifolium

DECEMBER

Polygonum vaccinifolium

VERBASCUM Rock Mullein

The stately 6 ft Mulleins which grace the back of the border have three lowly relatives which are at home in the rock garden. The family traits are there — the need for a sunny home, leaves which are hairy or spiky and a profusion of saucer-shaped blooms.

VARIETIES: The rockery species which is closest in growth habit to the border Mulleins is **V. dumulosum** — height 9 in., spread 1 ft, flowering period June – July. The flowering spikes bearing yellow blooms grow firm and upright from tufts of greyish, woolly leaves. **V. spinosum** is quite different — the leaves are toothed and spiny, and the yellow blooms are borne in loose flower-heads. These two species were accidentally crossed at Wisley Gardens and the resulting hybrid has become the most popular Rock Mullein — **V. 'Letitia'**. The basic details are height 9 in., spread 1 ft, flowering period June – August. It is a shrubby perennial with velvety leaves and is covered by ½ in. yellow blooms in summer.

SITE & SOIL: Requires well-drained soil and full sun.

PROPAGATION: Plant root cuttings in a cold frame in late winter.

Verbascum dumulosum

VERONICA Rockery Speedwell

If drainage is satisfactory then you will have no trouble with Speedwells . . . no trouble to grow them, but you may well have difficulty in keeping them under control. Many are exceedingly invasive, like the small Speedwells in the lawn. The larger Speedwells are grown in the border (page 81), but a few of them, such as V. incana and V. teucrium, are occasionally planted in the larger rockery.

VARIETIES: The basic Rockery Speedwell is **V. prostrata** — height 4 in., spread 1½ ft, flowering period May – July. The basic colour is blue — choose from **'Spode Blue'**, **'Kapitan'** and **'Royal Blue'**. There is also **'Alba'** (white) and **'Mrs Holt'** (pink). **V. filiformis** grows only 1 in. high but it will quickly carpet an area of 3 or more sq. ft — definitely not for the small or choice rockery. For a non-aggressive ground cover, choose **V. pectinata** (height 3 in., spread 1 ft, flowering period May – June). Blue and pink varieties are available.

SITE & SOIL: Any garden soil — thrives in sun or light shade.

PROPAGATION: Divide clumps in spring.

Veronica prostrata

VIOLA Rockery Violet

Violas, Pansies and border Violets have already been described in this book (pages 39 and 81) and they are sometimes planted in the rockery — low-growing plants which produce familiar flat-faced blooms in a multitude of colours. There are also some true Rockery Violets which should be grown.

VARIETIES: Both **V. aetolica** (flowering period May – June) and **V. biflora** (April – May) produce yellow flowers on short stalks. The basic details of these two Rockery Violets are height 2 in., spread 1 ft. In April **V. labradorica 'Purpurea'** (height 3 in., spread 1 ft) bears white-throated violet blooms above purple-tinged leaves. If you see Violet flowers which are white with purple veins, the species is probably **V. cucullata**. Varieties of **V. gracilis** (height 4 in., spread 1 ft, flowering period April – June) are grown in rockeries — good examples are **'Major'** (yellow-eyed purple) and **'Moonlight'** (yellow).

SITE & SOIL: Any well-drained soil — thrives in sun or partial shade.

PROPAGATION: Plant cuttings in a cold frame in summer.

Viola gracilis

WALDSTEINIA Waldsteinia

The first plant mentioned in this chapter on Rockery Perennials was Acaena, the rather uncommon New Zealand Burr which can be used as ground cover — the last plant in the chapter is Waldsteinia, equally effective as a carpeting plant and equally uncommon. The surface-rooting stems produce a mat of lobed leaves which turn golden in autumn.

VARIETIES: The species you are most likely to find is **W. ternata** — height 2½ in., spread 1½ ft, flowering period April – May. The buttercup yellow flowers measure about ½ in. across and are borne in large numbers. It is a grow-anywhere perennial, spreading quite quickly in any soil type and equally happy in sun or light shade. A similar species is **W. fragarioides** — the flowers once again are yellow and saucer-shaped, but the toothed and lobed leaves give the plant a Strawberry look — hence the latin name.

SITE & SOIL: Any well-drained soil — thrives in sun or light shade.

PROPAGATION: Divide the clumps in late summer.

Waldsteinia ternata

CHAPTER 6

BULBS

Even modest beginners feel that they know all about spring-flowering bulbs. Daffodils, Tulips, Crocuses and Snowdrops are planted in a hole which is two or three times deeper than the width of the bulb. This is an autumn task, and after replacing the soil there is nothing more to do until the floral display is over. When the foliage on the Tulips has died down they are lifted and stored for autumn planting – the remainder are left in the ground unless the bed is wanted for other plants.

This child's guide to bulb growing is quite satisfactory as far as it goes, but it leaves out many important points. For instance, some of the Species Tulips should not be lifted every year and there are delicate Daffodils, such as the Tazetta group, which should not be left outdoors in winter. The reason why successful bulb planting is so easy is that very little can go wrong provided the soil is not waterlogged. The purchased Daffodil or Tulip bulb, if healthy and sufficiently large, will have its flowering quality already determined, and the skill of the gardener can have little effect. What happens in future years, however, does depend on you. With proper care and cultivation these bulbs will improve and multiply over the years – with poor handling the stock will quite rapidly deteriorate.

So there are some lessons to be learnt. Make sure that the site is well drained and fairly rich in humus. Bone Meal is the best fertilizer, and fresh manure should never be used. If the ground tends to be damp, Daffodils will do better than Tulips. The choice is up to you, but do buy good-sized bulbs – there is no point in planting tiny daughter bulbs unless you are prepared to grow them on for a couple of years before obtaining satisfactory flowers. Plant to the recommended depth – the figures given in this book refer to the distance between the soil surface and the *bottom* of the bulb. Wherever possible try to naturalise hardy bulbs by planting them in clumps or drifts around trees or on grassy banks where they can be left to grow undisturbed. Scatter the bulbs over the ground and plant them where they fall – in this way the spacings will provide a natural look.

When flowering is over, the leaves must be allowed to remain on the plant. This is the stage when food is produced for next year's bulbs – feeding them with a liquid fertilizer is recommended and never knot the foliage of Daffodils to hasten ripening. If the bed has to be cleared before the foliage has died down, then remove the plants and transfer them to a shallow trench elsewhere in the garden.

So far only the popular spring-flowering bulbs have been mentioned, and apart from summer-flowering Gladioli many gardeners look no further than the denizens of spring. This is a pity, for there are so many other varieties within the vast range of bulbous plants. No other section in this book can match the bulbs for their ability to provide colour in the garden all the year round.

At the heading of this chapter and on the cover of the catalogues the word *bulb* has no botanical significance – it really refers to *bulbous plants*. This section of the world of flowering plants includes all the types which produce fleshy underground organs and which are sold in this dormant state as planting material. Included here are the true bulbs, corms, tubers and some rhizomes. A true bulb consists of fleshy or scale-like leaves or leaf bases arising from a basal plate. Some, such as Lilies, have no outer cover but most others have an outer cover or tunic – examples are Fritillarias, Hyacinths, Grape Hyacinths, Daffodils, Tulips and Bluebells. Within the bulb lies the embryo shoot and flower, and that separates it from the corms – another large group of bulbous plants. A corm is a flattened and thickened stem base, and as the original one becomes exhausted during growth a new one is produced above it. There are a number of attractive corm-producing plants, such as Crocuses and Gladioli.

Tubers are swollen roots or stems. You can tell that it is not a true bulb because there are no overlapping scales or leaves, and you can see it is not a corm because there is no papery coat on the outside. The catalogues contain several examples – Dahlias, Winter Aconites, Tuberous Begonias, Spring-flowering Anemones and Turban Buttercups. The final group of bulbous plants contains the rhizomes – fleshy stems which creep below or on the surface. You will find one popular representative (Lily of the Valley) in this section – most other rhizomes are sold as growing plants.

One final point – don't regard bulbous plants as seeds which can be stored for months on end before planting. A few of the popular ones can be kept in a cool shed for a little while after purchase, but as a general rule this group should be planted as soon as possible after you get them, just like bedding plants.

ACIDANTHERA Acidanthera

Acidanthera has several virtues — its blooms are attractive, highly fragrant and they appear in autumn when most bulbous plants have passed their flowering season. But there is an important drawback — it is a plant of tropical Africa and is half hardy in this country. As a result Acidanthera needs a mild climate and the corms must be lifted before winter frosts arrive. These corms should be stored in a warm and dry place until the spring.

VARIETIES: Just one variety is commonly grown — **A. bicolor murielae**. The sword-like leaves and star-shaped flowers give it a Gladiolus look. The blooms are about 2 in. wide, each white petal bearing a distinct purple blotch at the base.

SITE & SOIL: A corm for warm areas — choose a sunny, south-facing site. Any well-drained soil will do.

PLANT DETAILS: Planting time April. Planting depth 4 in. Spacing 9 in. Height 3 ft. Flowering period September.

PROPAGATION: Remove and plant cormlets in April. Flowering will not take place for several years.

Acidanthera bicolor murielae

ALLIUM Flowering Garlic

There are dwarf Alliums for the rockery and tall ones for the border or shrubbery. All are easy to grow but have never become popular — perhaps the strong onion smell deters many gardeners. The leaves may be wide, like garlic, or narrow like onions. The flowers, too, may be wide- or narrow-petalled.

VARIETIES: The giant is **A. giganteum** (4 ft) — lilac flowers in 4 in. ball-like heads. The largest flower-head is borne by **A. albopilosum** (2 ft) — silvery lilac flowers in 6–9 in. clusters. Good as a cut flower — so is **A. aflatunense** (2½ ft) which produces pink-headed drumsticks. Dwarfs include **A. moly** (9 in., loosely-packed yellow stars) and **A. ostrowskianum** (9 in., loosely-packed pink stars).

SITE & SOIL: Any well-drained soil will do — thrives best in full sun.

PLANT DETAILS: Planting time September–October. Planting depth 3 times the height of the bulb. Spacing 6 in.–1 ft. Height variable — see above. Flowering period June.

PROPAGATION: Divide clumps in autumn every 3 years.

Allium albopilosum

AMARYLLIS Belladonna Lily

The Belladonna Lily is a gamble in our climate. If you have a bed next to a sunny south-facing wall it is well worth the risk — your reward will be a display of large and colourful trumpet-like flowers which will last for about 8 weeks. It has an odd growth habit — the strap-like leaves appear in spring and die down in early summer. A month or two later the thick flower stalk appears, topped by a cluster of 3 or 4 blooms.

VARIETIES: The species grown is **A. belladonna**. The fragrant flowers measure about 3 in. across, pink or salmon with yellow throats. Stake the stems to avoid wind damage and cut them down once flowering is over. Cover the crown with sand, peat or bracken during the winter months.

SITE & SOIL: A bulb for warm areas — full sun is essential. Any well-drained soil will do.

PLANT DETAILS: Planting time July. Planting depth 8 in. Spacing 1 ft. Height 2 ft. Flowering period September–October.

PROPAGATION: Buy new bulbs — Amaryllis hates disturbance.

Amaryllis belladonna

Flowers for Every Season

JANUARY–APRIL
(for MAY–AUGUST see page 114)
(for SEPTEMBER–DECEMBER see page 120)

By careful selection you can have bulbs in bloom all year round. For each month there is a list of bulbous plants which can be expected to be in full bloom — remember that some of these plants may come into flower earlier and can continue to bloom for weeks afterwards.

JANUARY

Cyclamen coum	Galanthus
Eranthis	Iris (Reticulata group)

FEBRUARY

Anemone blanda	Eranthis
Anemone (Poppy-flowered)	Galanthus
Chionodoxa	Iris (Reticulata group)
Crocus	Leucojum (Spring-flowering)
Cyclamen coum	Scilla tubergeniana

MARCH

Anemone apennina	Hyacinthus (Roman)
Anemone blanda	Iris (Reticulata group)
Chionodoxa	Leucojum (Spring-flowering)
Crocus	Narcissus
Cyclamen coum	Puschkinia
Eranthis	Scilla sibirica
Erythronium	Scilla tubergeniana

APRIL

Anemone apennina	Iris (Juno group)
Anemone blanda	Leucojum (Summer-flowering)
Convallaria	Muscari
Crocus	Narcissus
Cyclamen repandum	Ornithogalum
Erythronium	Puschkinia
Fritillaria	Scilla nonscripta
Gladiolus (Species)	Scilla sibirica
Hyacinthus (Dutch)	Trillium
Ipheion	Tulipa

ANEMONE Windflower

There is a place for Anemones in every garden, ranging from the large drifts of blue Daisies naturalised in the shrubberies of country estates to the small clumps of bright saucer-shaped blooms in tiny front gardens. All of them except A. blanda will grow happily in light shade and the popular varieties are excellent for cutting.

VARIETIES: Anemones fall into 2 distinct groups. The *Daisy-flowered* types have many narrow petals surrounding a golden disc, the 1½ in. blooms appearing in spring. The first to flower is **A. blanda** (February – April) which requires full sun as the flowers close in shady conditions. Grow it in the rockery or naturalise it in grassland. The blooms of **A. apennina** (March – April) appear a little later, and this species can be used in rockeries or as ground cover under shrubs. Both these Daisy-flowered Anemones grow about 6 in. tall and the usual colour is blue, although white and pink varieties are available. Plant the twig-like tubers about 2 in. deep in September — space them about 4 in. apart. Much more popular but much less permanent are the *Poppy-flowered* Anemones. The 2 in. bowl-shaped flowers are brightly coloured — white, blue, pink, lavender or red, and they are one of our favourite flowers for cutting and arranging in bowls. Remember to cut the stalks — never pull them. The **de Caen** strain produces single flowers — grow a mixture or choose single colours, such as '**The Bride**' (white), '**Mr Fokker**' (blue) or '**His Excellency**' (red). For semi-double or double flowers choose the **St. Brigid** strain — named varieties include '**Lord Lieutenant**' (blue) and '**The Governor**' (red). Poppy-flowered Anemones grow 6–9 in. tall and can be in bloom from early spring to late autumn if you stagger the planting dates. Planting in November will give you flowers in February — planting in April will give you October flowers. Soak the clawed tubers in water overnight before planting — set them 4 in. apart and 2 in. deep.

SITE & SOIL: Well-drained, humus-rich soil is required — thrives in sun or light shade. The Poppy-flowered Anemones are not long-lived, especially in northern counties — give them a warm, sheltered spot if you can.

PLANT DETAILS: See above.

PROPAGATION: Divide mature clumps in late summer — replant at once.

Anemone blanda

Anemone 'de Caen'

BEGONIA Tuberous Begonia

The Tuberous Begonia is considered by many to be the queen of the summer bedding plants — a dazzling variety of colours to grace beds, borders, hanging baskets or rockeries until the first frosts arrive. They flourish in sun or shade, provided that you enrich the soil with humus before planting and water regularly during dry weather. The flowering period is from late June to September.

VARIETIES: The large-flowered **B. tuberhybrida** is the best-known group, its Rose-like blooms measuring from 3 to 6 in. across. Serrated or smooth-edged petals, self- or bi-coloured — few plants can offer such a range of shapes and colours. Named varieties include '**Sugar Candy**' (pale pink), '**Gold Plate**' (yellow), '**Guardsman**' (vermilion), '**Seville**' (yellow, edged pink), '**Double Picotee**' (cream, edged red) and '**Diana Wynyard**' (white). The plants grow about 1–1½ ft high and should be set 1 ft apart. The tubers are large — 1–2 in. across. Some people prefer bedding Begonias which have a large number of smaller flowers — for them **B. multiflora maxima** is ideal, with masses of double blooms on 6 in. high bushy plants. **B. pendula** bears slender, drooping stems and 2 in. flowers — a good choice for hanging baskets and window boxes. To grow Tuberous Begonias, press the tubers hollow side uppermost into boxes of damp peat in March or April. Keep at 60°–70°F and when leafy shoots appear, transplant the tubers separately into potting compost. Plant out in June when all risk of frost is past. Stake and feed during the growing period, and with B. tuber-hybrida the small female flowers under the large and showy male one should be pinched off whilst still small. Lift the tubers in mid October and keep indoors. Remove the stems after the foliage has died down. Store the tubers in dry peat in a frost-free place over winter.

SITE & SOIL: Requires soil which is rich in organic matter with little or no lime present — thrives best in light shade. Keep the soil moist — water in the morning, not at midday.

PLANT DETAILS: See above.

PROPAGATION: Tubers can be divided when the shoots are small — it is better to buy new tubers.

Begonia tuberhybrida 'Zoe Colledge'

Begonia pendula

BRODIAEA   Brodiaea

A small group of bulbous plants which bear narrow, strap-like leaves and slender flowering stems. The blooms clustered at the top are star-shaped or tubular and they make excellent cut flowers. Brodiaea has a delicate air — grow the bulbs in groups rather than singly.

VARIETIES: **B. laxa (Triteleia laxa)** bears deep lilac tubular flowers in a loose head which looks rather like a miniature Agapanthus (see page 43). **B. tubergenii** is somewhat similar, with pale lilac flowers forming a 3 – 4 in. head. The flowers of **B. grandiflora** are rather different, opening into 1½ in. purplish stars. **B. ida-maia (Dichelostemma ida-maia)** is quite different and most unusual. Each pendent flower consists of a bright red tube with a green and yellow mouth.

SITE & SOIL: A sheltered spot is essential — grow at the base of a south-facing wall. Well-drained soil and full sun are required.

PLANT DETAILS: Planting time September. Planting depth 3 in. Spacing 4 in. Height 1½ – 2 ft. Flowering period May – July.

PROPAGATION: Dislikes disturbance — buy new bulbs.

Brodiaea laxa

CAMASSIA   Quamash

The strange common name is the N. American Indian word for this handsome plant which bears tall spikes covered with starry flowers in summer. It is no bother at all — Camassia will grow in heavy, damp soil and flourishes in either sun or shade. Plant the bulbs where they can be left undisturbed.

VARIETIES: It is generally agreed that the most striking species is **C. leichtlinii** — the upper part of the 3 ft flowering stem is bedecked with 1½ in. white or blue flowers. **C. quamash (C. esculenta)** is usually a little shorter but the flowers are just as numerous, with colours ranging from white to purple. The tallest of the Camassias is **C. cusickii**, producing up to 100 blue flowers on each tall spike.

SITE & SOIL: Any moisture-retentive soil will do — thrives in sun or partial shade.

PLANT DETAILS: Planting time September – October. Planting depth 4 in. Spacing 6 in. Height 2½ – 3½ ft. Flowering period June – July.

PROPAGATION: Divide mature clumps in autumn — replant at once.

Camassia quamash

CANNA   Indian Shot

The flowering spike of Canna looks like a colourful Gladiolus without any of its popularity. The blooms may be large, up to 5 in. across in yellow, pink, red or white, and this plant would certainly be in all the catalogues but for its major drawback. It is not hardy — rhizomes must be started in peat indoors during March and then planted outdoors in early June when all risk of frost is past. Lift the plants in autumn, allow them to dry and then store in sand or peat.

VARIETIES: Many named **C. indica** hybrids are available. They are divided into 2 groups — the *Green-leaved* varieties and the *Coloured-leaved* ones. Canna leaves are extremely large and decorative — choose one of the coloured group. Examples are **'Hercules'** (red flowers, purple foliage), **'Dazzler'** (red flowers, bronze foliage) and **'Tyrol'** (pink flowers, purple foliage).

SITE & SOIL: Use as dot plants in bedding schemes — humus-rich soil and full sun are essential. Not a plant for cold areas.

PLANT DETAILS: Planting time June. Planting depth 2 in. Spacing 1½ ft. Height 3 – 4 ft. Flowering period August – October.

PROPAGATION: Divide rhizomes in early spring.

Canna 'Golden Bird'

CARDIOCRINUM   Giant Himalayan Lily

Imagine a Lily trumpet 6 inches long — now imagine twenty of them borne aloft on a stem above your head! If your garden is a modest one then such a sight will have to remain in your imagination, but if you have the space you can grow the Giant Himalayan Lily.

VARIETIES: The giant is **C. giganteum (Lilium giganteum)**, which grows up to 9 ft tall. The white flowers have purplish markings on the inside and are delicately fragrant — a crown of large bells above the shiny leaves spiralling the towering stem. The 'baby' is **C. cordatum** which only grows 6 ft high. The flowers are fewer in number but no smaller in size.

SITE & SOIL: Well-drained, moisture-retentive soil and light shade are essential.

PLANT DETAILS: Planting time October. Planting depth 6 in. Spacing 3 ft. Height 6 – 9 ft. Flowering period June – August.

PROPAGATION: Buy new bulbs. The bulb dies after flowering — offsets can be planted but will take years to flower.

Cardiocrinum giganteum

CHIONODOXA Glory of the Snow

A popular spring-flowering bulb, but one which is still not seen everywhere like the Crocus and the Snowdrop. It got off to a late start — Chionodoxa was unknown as a garden plant until late Victorian times. Plant the bulbs in large groups and leave them to naturalise in the rockery or the front of the border. The 6-petalled starry flowers are borne in dainty sprays above the strap-like foliage.

VARIETIES: **C. luciliae** is the usual species. About 10 blooms are borne on each flower stalk — pale blue stars with a prominent white centre. Blue is the best buy but there are other varieties — **'Alba'** (white) and **'Pink Giant'** (pink). The largest flowers (1½ in.) appear on **C. gigantea** — **C. sardensis** produces standard-sized blue flowers which have only a small white eye.

SITE & SOIL: Any well-drained soil will do — thrives in sun or light shade.

PLANT DETAILS: Planting time September. Planting depth 3 in. Spacing 4 in. Height 6 in. Flowering period February–March.

PROPAGATION: Divide clumps in May — replant at once.

Chionodoxa luciliae

COLCHICUM Autumn Crocus

Despite its common name and the shape of the flowers, Colchicum is not related to the true Crocus. In autumn the wineglass-shaped flowers appear, the long tubes at the base of the petals extending down into the earth. The size of the open blooms ranges from 2 to 8 in., depending on the species. When winter comes the flowers are gone, and in spring the untidy large leaves appear.

VARIETIES: **C. autumnale** bears 2 in. pink blooms — the prettiest variety is the double-flowering **'Roseum Plenum'** (pink). The giant is **C. speciosum** (Meadow Saffron) with mauve flowers which open out to an 8 in. span. It has many netted and striped varieties, such as **'Violet Queen'** and **'Lilac Wonder'**.

SITE & SOIL: Well-drained, humus-rich soil is required — thrives in sun or light shade.

PLANT DETAILS: Planting time July–August. Planting depth 4 in. Spacing 9 in. Flower height 6–9 in. Flowering period September–November.

PROPAGATION: Divide clumps in July — replant at once.

Colchicum autumnale

CONVALLARIA Lily of the Valley

In spring 2 large lance-shaped leaves appear together with an arching flower stem bearing a number of small, pendent white bells. The sight and the fragrance of these ¼ in. blooms have delighted poets and gardeners for centuries. At weddings it is widely used in bridal bouquets — in the garden it is used to provide ground cover in shady areas.

VARIETIES: There is just one species — **C. majalis**. The plant spreads by means of underground, branching rhizomes. These produce small upright shoots ('pips') which are used for propagation. For large flowers, grow **'Fortin's Giant'** or **'Everest'** — for pink blooms plant **'Rosea'**. Varieties are available with golden-striped leaves.

SITE & SOIL: Moisture-retentive soil is essential — thrives best in partial shade.

PLANT DETAILS: Planting time between October and March. Planting depth 1 in. Spacing 4 in. Flower height 8 in. Flowering period April–May.

PROPAGATION: Divide clumps in September — replant at once.

Convallaria majalis

CRINUM Crinum

It is a pity that Crinum does not have a hardier constitution, as it is undoubtedly one of the finest of all late summer bulbs. These bulbs are expensive and you will be wasting your money unless you can provide a warm and sheltered site close to a south-facing wall.

VARIETIES: The most reliable outdoor species is **C. powellii**. The leaves are long and strap-like, and the short flower stem bears a terminal cluster of flowers. These blooms open in succession, each bud producing a Lily-like trumpet about 4 in. long. White and pink varieties are available, and each plant is a showpiece. Give it plenty of room, water freely in dry weather and cover the crowns with peat or bracken in winter.

SITE & SOIL: Well-drained, moisture-retentive soil in a sheltered sunny spot is essential.

PLANT DETAILS: Planting time April–May. Planting depth 10 in. Spacing 1½ ft. Height 2–3 ft. Flowering period August–September.

PROPAGATION: Buy new bulbs — Crinum hates disturbance.

Crinum powellii

CROCUS Crocus

Everyone can recognise a Crocus, and for many gardeners the choice is a simple one — a purple or yellow variety, or a mixture of both, designed to flower after the Snowdrops and before the Tulips. The full Crocus story is much more extensive — there are varieties to bloom in February with the Snowdrops and others to flower in the autumn with the Dahlias. The wineglass-shaped flowers appear in many colours — bronze, white, pale blue, striped, bi-coloured and blotched as well as the all-too-familiar purple and yellow. The leaves are narrow and continue to grow after the flowers have faded — there is nothing for you to do but to apply a sprinkling of Growmore around the clumps in autumn.

VARIETIES: There are 3 basic groups. The *Winter-flowering* species are small, 3 or 4 in. high, and are well-suited to the rockery. Included in this group are the beautiful **C. imperati** (striped white and purple), **C. susianus** (the Cloth of Gold Crocus with bronze and golden petals) and **C. chrysanthus** plus its host of hybrids. In the catalogues you will find **'E. A. Bowles'** (deep yellow), **'Snow Bunting'** (white), **'Ladykiller'** (purple and white) and many others. The *Spring-flowering Dutch Hybrids* are the most popular, blooming in March and April with large flowers growing 5 in. high. In the catalogues they are sometimes described as Large-flowered Crocuses — pick from **'Enchantress'** (blue), **'Remembrance'** (purple), **'Golden Mammoth'** (yellow), **'Joan of Arc'** (white), **'Little Dorrit'** (lilac), **'Pickwick'** (striped) and the scores of others which are available. The *Autumn-flowering* species, blooming between August and October, offer a much more restricted choice. **C. speciosus** and its hybrids are the most popular, producing attractive flowers in white, lilac or purple.

SITE & SOIL: Any well-drained soil — thrives in sun or light shade.

PLANT DETAILS: Planting time September–October (July for Autumn-flowering Species). Planting depth 3 in. Spacing 4 in. Height 3–5 in. Flowering period February–April (August–October for Autumn-flowering Species).

PROPAGATION: Divide overcrowded clumps in autumn.

Crocus 'Little Dorrit'

Crocus speciosus

CROCOSMIA Montbretia

Montbretia is a must for flower arrangers, but it is also highly decorative in the garden. The plant forms a spreading clump of sword-like leaves and in late summer the wiry flower stems appear. Unfortunately it is not fully hardy — in the south you should leave the dead foliage on the plant over winter and you should cover the crown with bracken, leaves or peat. In colder areas you will have to lift and store the bulbs indoors.

VARIETIES: C. crocosmiiflora is the old favourite, popularly called Montbretia. The upright flower stalks bear trumpet-shaped flowers in zig-zag fashion. The 1½ in. blooms are available in yellow, orange and red shades. **C. masonorum** is a better choice — arching stems bear large flame-coloured trumpets.

SITE & SOIL: Well-drained, humus-rich soil in a sheltered sunny spot is essential.

PLANT DETAILS: Planting time March. Planting depth 3 in. Spacing 6 in. Height 2–3 ft. Flowering period August–September.

PROPAGATION: Divide clumps after flowering every 3 years.

Crocosmia masonorum

CYCLAMEN Cyclamen

For most of us the Cyclamen is a pot plant — large, long-stemmed flowers with swept-back petals rising above heart-shaped decorative leaves. If this flower form appeals to you there are miniature hardy versions with 1 in. flowers to grow outdoors. You can choose your own flowering time — there are winter, spring, summer and autumn varieties.

VARIETIES: Choose from **C. coum** (red, pink or white flowers in December–March; green leaves), **C. repandum** (fragrant red, pink or white flowers in April; marbled leaves), **C. europaeum** (fragrant red flowers in July–September; silver-zoned leaves — the hardiest of all the species) or **C. neapolitanum** (red, pink or white flowers in August–November; marbled leaves).

SITE & SOIL: Well-drained, humus-rich soil in partial shade is required.

PLANT DETAILS: Planting time July–September. Planting depth 2 in. Spacing 6 in. Height 3–6 in. Flowering period see above.

PROPAGATION: Sow seeds under glass in summer — plants cannot be divided.

Cyclamen coum

ERANTHIS Winter Aconite

Plant a group of tubers under shrubs or deciduous trees — in February or even earlier you will be delighted by the glossy yellow carpet of flowers when so much of the garden is bare or dormant. Winter Aconites are often planted with Snowdrops and both bloom at the same time.

VARIETIES: E. hyemalis is the most popular type — 1 in. flowers in lemon yellow with an attractive collar of deeply-divided green leaves. This is the one to choose if you want very early flowers, but it can become a nuisance in confined areas as it produces an abundance of self-sown plants. The hybrid **E. tubergenii** is less invasive, more robust and the flowers are larger. It blooms in March, alongside the fragrant, deep yellow **E. 'Guinea Gold'**.

SITE & SOIL: Any well-drained soil will do — thrives in sun or partial shade.

PLANT DETAILS: Planting time August–September. Planting depth 2 in. Spacing 3 in. Height 3–4 in. Flowering period January–March.

PROPAGATION: Divide tubers in early summer — replant at once.

Eranthis tubergenii

ERYTHRONIUM Dog's-tooth Violet

An excellent plant for the rockery or around the base of trees — it is not a sun-lover but it does relish humus-rich soil. The nodding star-shaped flowers are borne above the attractively-mottled foliage — the common name comes from the shape of the tubers and not the leaves. Let the plants grow undisturbed.

VARIETIES: E. dens-canis is the usual garden type. The rose-coloured flowers measure about 2 in. across and the leaves are mottled with brown markings. There are some attractive varieties, such as **'Pink Perfection'** (pink) and **'Lilac Wonder'** (pale purple). The aristocrat is **E. revolutum 'White Beauty'** — red-eyed, pure white flowers on 1 ft stems.

SITE & SOIL: Well-drained but moist soil is required – thrives best in partial shade.

PLANT DETAILS: Planting time August–October. Planting depth 4 in. Spacing 4 in. Height 6 in. Flowering period March–April.

PROPAGATION: Remove and replant offsets immediately in late summer — never allow Erythronium tubers to dry out.

Erythronium dens-canis

FREESIA Outdoor Freesia

The florist Freesias are well-known as cut flowers for indoor decoration — less well-known are the Outdoor Freesias which can be grown in a sheltered sunny spot in the garden. These Freesia corms have been specially prepared to enable them to flower in our climate — a bright display of richly fragrant blooms in late summer and autumn, but unfortunately the corms have to be discarded once flowering has finished.

VARIETIES: Buy prepared corms of **F. hybrida** — never try to grow ordinary Freesias outdoors unless you live in a specially favoured spot like the Isles of Scilly. The funnel-shaped flowers are borne on one side of wiry stems — the secrets of success are to provide a warm spot and to water regularly in dry weather. A mixture will provide white, red, yellow, blue and lilac flowers.

SITE & SOIL: Light, well-drained soil in full sun is essential.

PLANT DETAILS: Planting time April. Planting depth 2 in. Spacing 4 in. Height 1 ft. Flowering period August–October.

PROPAGATION: Not practical — buy new corms.

Freesia hybrida

Flowers for Every Season

MAY–AUGUST

(for JANUARY–APRIL see page 109)
(for SEPTEMBER–DECEMBER see page 120)

By careful selection you can have bulbs in bloom all year round. For each month there is a list of bulbous plants which can be expected to be in full bloom — remember that some of these plants may come into flower earlier and can continue to bloom for weeks afterwards.

MAY

Brodiaea	Ornithogalum
Convallaria	Scilla nonscripta
Gladiolus (Species)	Scilla peruviana
Hyacinthus (Dutch)	Sparaxis
Ipheion	Trillium
Leucojum (Summer-flowering)	Tritonia
Muscari	Tulipa

JUNE

Allium	Ixia
Brodiaea	Ranunculus
Camassia	Scilla nonscripta
Cardiocrinum	Scilla peruviana
Cyclamen europaeum	Sparaxis
Gladiolus (Species)	Trillium
Iris (Xiphium group)	Tritonia

JULY

Begonia	Gladiolus (Hybrids)
Brodiaea	Iris (Xiphium group)
Camassia	Ixia
Cardiocrinum	Ranunculus
Cyclamen europaeum	Tigridia

AUGUST

Begonia	Cyclamen europaeum
Canna	Cyclamen neapolitanum
Cardiocrinum	Freesia
Crinum	Galtonia
Crocosmia	Gladiolus (Hybrids)
Crocus (Autumn-flowering)	Tigridia

FRITILLARIA   Fritillary

The bell-like blooms of Fritillaria open in spring, hanging downwards from the top of upright stems which bear narrow leaves. There the family likenesses end — it is hard to believe that the stately Crown Imperial and the dainty Snake's Head Fritillary are so closely related. Both of these plants are easy to grow — all they need is a site which is free-draining and receives some sunshine during the day. Every couple of years apply a mulch of well-rotted compost. This does not mean that Fritillarias are trouble-free — you can waste your money if you do not take care at planting time. The bulbs are composed of fleshy scales — do not let them dry out and handle carefully. Put some coarse sand in the planting hole and place the bulb sideways. Cover with sand and then replace the earth.

VARIETIES: **F. meleagris** (Snake's Head Fritillary) is a plant for the rockery, front of the border or naturalising in grass. Each 1 ft stem bears 1 or 2 pendent blooms — 1½ in. bells with a distinctive chequered pattern of purple and white squares. There are several varieties — **'Charon'** is white with dark purple squares and **'Poseidon'** is pale purple with brown squares. It is a pity to grow the all-white varieties such as **'Alba'** and **'Aphrodite'** where the draught-board effect is lost. **F. imperialis** (Crown Imperial) is an imposing plant, quite unlike its close relative. At the top of each stout 3 ft stem is a cluster of pendent blooms — 2 in. cups in yellow, orange or red. The flower-head is unusual — the odour is best described as peculiar and there is a crown of short green leaves. This is certainly not a plant for the rockery — it belongs in the herbaceous or shrub border. There are other species of Fritillaria available but they have neither the hardiness nor the popularity of the pair described above. **F. latifolia** looks like a dwarf Snake's Head Fritillary, and **F. pallidiflora** (1 ft) bears yellow flowers.

SITE & SOIL: Any well-drained soil will do — thrives best in light shade.

PLANT DETAILS: Planting time September–November. Planting depth 5 in. (F. meleagris), 8 in. (F. imperialis). Spacing 6 in. (F. meleagris), 1½ ft (F. imperialis). Height 1–3 ft. Flowering period April.

PROPAGATION: Divide clumps in summer every 4 years.

Fritillaria meleagris

Fritillaria imperialis

GALANTHUS   Snowdrop

The curtain-raiser for the gardening year — small white flowers hanging on 6 in. stems from January onwards. The flowering date depends on the locality and the weather — a time always welcomed as the sign that spring will soon be on its way. Although known to everyone, Snowdrops are sometimes confused with Snowflakes (see page 118). In the Snowdrop flower there are three inner green-tipped petals surrounded by three longer outer ones which are all-white.

VARIETIES: The Common Snowdrop is **G. nivalis**. The 1 in. flowers are single — the best variety is the tall **'S. Arnott'** (10 in.) which bears larger flowers than the species. There is a double form (**'Flore Pleno'**) with globular flowers. The Giant Snowdrop **(G. elwesii)** is no larger than G. nivalis 'S. Arnott'.

SITE & SOIL: Moist soil and light shade are required.

PLANT DETAILS: Planting time September–October. Planting depth 4 in. Spacing 3 in. Height 5 in. (G. nivalis), 10 in. (G. elwesii). Flowering period January–March.

PROPAGATION: Divide mature clumps immediately after flowering — replant at once.

Galanthus nivalis 'S. Arnott'

GALTONIA   Summer Hyacinth

The Summer Hyacinth is a splendid plant for the middle or back of the herbaceous border, or it can be grown between shrubs. In summer the tall flower stalk is clothed with 20 or more pendulous white bells, each about 1½ in. long. The leaves are long and strap-like — the effect is that of a giant and elongated Hyacinth.

VARIETIES: The only species you are likely to find is **G. candicans** (Hyacinthus candicans). The leaves are about 2 ft long and the flowers are white with green markings. Much more imposing than an ordinary Hyacinth, of course, but it is also less fragrant. Despite its size it is an easy plant to grow, provided you remember to plant the bulbs deeply enough (6–8 in.) and leave the clumps to grow undisturbed.

SITE & SOIL: Any reasonable soil — thrives best in full sun.

PLANT DETAILS: Planting time March–April. Planting depth 6–8 in. Spacing 1 ft. Height 3–4 ft. Flowering period August–September.

PROPAGATION: Dislikes disturbance — buy new bulbs.

Galtonia candicans

GLADIOLUS Sword Lily

Gladiolus is one of the few flowers which need no description, but the differences between the varieties are enormous. The height of the thick flower stalk which rises from the corm may reach little more than 1 ft or as much as 5 ft. The open, trumpet-shaped flowers range from the width of an egg-cup to the size of a saucer, and the colours span the rainbow. The common family features are upright, sword-like leaves and six-petalled flowers which all point the same way. There are one or two hardy species but these are not the ones you see in every street in the land. These popular ones are the half-hardy hybrids, planted in spring to flower in summer and then lifted at the end of October. The corms are stored in a cool but frost-free place for planting out in the following spring. These showy plants are easy to grow in good soil and a sunny situation — remember to water thoroughly during dry weather once the flower spikes have appeared. They cannot be faulted as cut flowers but they do have a few drawbacks as bedding plants for garden display — careful staking is sometimes necessary and the blooming period for an individual flower spike lasts for only a fortnight. Still, they do provide a bold splash of colour during those two weeks and the trick is to stagger the planting dates so that a succession of blooms is obtained.

FLOWER SIZES

GIANTS
over 5½ in.

LARGE
4½–5½ in.

MEDIUMS
3½–4½ in.

SMALLS
2½–3½ in.

MINIATURES
less than 2½ in.

VARIETIES: There are 5 main groups. The most popular one contains the largest plants with the showiest flowers — the *Large-flowered Hybrids*. These grow 3–4 ft high; space them 6 in. apart. The triangular flowers are 4½–7 in. wide and the list of varieties is enormous. Three well-known ones are **'Oscar'** (bright red), **'Peter Pears'** (orange, peach and red) and **'Flower Song'** (frilled, golden yellow), but there are scores of others. The *Primulinus Hybrids* grow 1½–3 ft high; space them 4 in. apart. The top petal of each flower is hooded, and the flowers are loosely arranged on the stem. The average bloom width is 3 in. and good examples are **'Joyce'** (deep pink and yellow) and **'Columbine'** (pale pink and white). Staking is not necessary, and it is not often needed for the third group, the *Butterfly Hybrids*. These grow 2–4 ft high; space them 4–6 in. apart. The two basic features of most of these hybrids are the close packing of the flowers on the stem and the striking colours of the throats. These features can be clearly seen in such varieties as **'Melodie'** (pink petals, scarlet throat) and **'Confetti'** (pink petals, yellow throat). The *Miniature Hybrids* are like small Primulinus varieties — height 1–2½ ft, spacing 4 in., flower size 2 in., frequently frilled or ruffled. Examples include **'Bo Peep'** (apricot) and **'Greenbird'** (sulphur yellow). The final group of Gladioli are the *Species* — less highly bred than the hybrids and capable of living outdoors all year round. The hardiest is **G. byzantinus** (2 ft; small red flowers in June) — the most popular are the varieties of **G. colvillii** (2 ft; small flowers in April–June; protect the crowns with bracken or ashes in winter).

SITE & SOIL: Any well-drained fertile soil will do — thrives best in full sun.

PLANT DETAILS: Planting time March–May (Hybrids), October (Species). Planting depth 4–5 in. Spacing 4–6 in. Height see above. Flowering period July–September (Hybrids), April–June (Species).

PROPAGATION: Plant cormlets in April–May. Flowering will take place in about 2 years.

Gladiolus 'Flower Song'

Gladiolus 'Columbine'

Gladiolus 'Melodie'

Gladiolus 'Greenbird'

Gladiolus byzantinus

Gladiolus colvillii

HYACINTHUS   Hyacinth

Many great gardeners of today began their horticultural education when, as small children, they potted Hyacinths in bowls of bulb fibre. An indoor pot plant *par excellence* — leafless flower stalks bearing 30 or more star-faced bells and a fragrance which can fill the room. Outdoors they are spring bedding plants with a lot of merit — neat and compact habit, a long blooming period, a wide range of colours and a sweet smell. They have never been able to match Tulips, Daffodils or Crocuses in popularity despite these merits — the reason probably lies in the high cost of the bulbs compared with other spring favourites. In most soils you can leave the bulbs of Dutch Hyacinths outdoors over winter, but the display will not be as good in the second year. It is generally better to lift the bulbs after flowering and let the foliage die down. The bulbs should then be stored in dry peat until planting time comes round again. There are two secrets of success to follow when planting Hyacinths. Don't pick the large bulbs which are used for indoors — choose instead the medium-sized ones. Secondly, add well-rotted compost or peat to the soil before planting.

VARIETIES: H. orientalis is the Dutch or Common Hyacinth. In April or May the tightly-packed flower-heads appear, ranging in colour from white to purple. Choose from **'L'Innocence'** (white), **'Yellow Hammer'** (creamy yellow), **'Gipsy Queen'** (orange), **'Pink Pearl'** (pink), **'Jan Bos'** (red), **'Ostara'** (blue) and **'Amethyst'** (violet). There is also the Roman Hyacinth **(H. orientalis albulus)** — its flowers are much less tightly packed and appear earlier than the blooms of the Dutch Hyacinth. There are white, pink and purple varieties, all noted for their intense fragrance.

SITE & SOIL: Any reasonable garden soil adequately supplied with humus will do — thrives in sun or light shade.

PLANT DETAILS: Planting time September–October. Planting depth 6 in. Spacing 8 in. Height 6in.–1 ft. Flowering period March–April (Roman Hyacinths), April–May (Dutch Hyacinths).

PROPAGATION: Plant offsets in autumn.

Hyacinthus orientalis 'Anne Marie'

Hyacinthus orientalis albulus

IPHEION   Spring Starflower

There is nothing complex about this delightful plant apart from its name. It will flourish in a sunny rockery or at the front of the border, each bulb sending up several stalks in spring — a 2 in. fragrant star-shaped bloom crowning each stalk. A lowly, easy-to-grow subject which has been saddled with such names as Ipheion uniflorum, Brodiaea uniflora, Milla uniflora and Triteleia uniflora. Any of these names may crop up in the catalogue, plus the common names Spring Starflower and Flower of the Incas!

VARIETIES: I. uniflorum bears pale blue flowers — the best variety is **'Wisley Blue'** (deep blue). The narrow, pale green leaves emit an onion-like smell when crushed.

SITE & SOIL: Any well-drained soil will do — thrives in sun or partial shade. Dislikes an open, windy site.

PLANT DETAILS: Planting time September–October. Planting depth 2 in. Spacing 4 in. Height 6 in. Flowering period April–May.

PROPAGATION: Divide in autumn every 3 years. Replant at once.

Ipheion uniflorum

IXIA   Corn Lily

The Corn Lily produces six-petalled stars on wiry stems in early summer. The colours are usually bright — yellow, orange, pink or red and the centre is generally dark red or brown. Its home is S. Africa and it is not really happy under our conditions. The flowers close when the sun goes in and it will die if overwintered in cold districts. The best plan is to plant in early spring and then lift the corms in summer when the foliage has died down. Store in a dry place.

VARIETIES: I. hybrida is available as a number of named varieties such as **'Hogarth'** (yellow) and **'Vulcan'** (red), but is usually sold as a mixture which produces a host of 1 in. flowers in various colours. **I. viridiflora** bears green blooms.

SITE & SOIL: A light, well-drained soil in full sun is essential.

PLANT DETAILS: Planting time March. Planting depth 3 in. Spacing 4 in. Height 1–1½ ft. Flowering period June–July.

PROPAGATION: Remove cormlets when plants are lifted in summer. Store over winter and plant in spring.

Ixia viridiflora

IRIS Iris

The stately Irises which grow to a height of 3 ft or more in the centre of the herbaceous border belong to the *Rhizome* group — the *Bulb* group are smaller and belong in the rockery or the front of the border. Many useful varieties belong here — dwarfs which peep through the snow in January to large-flowered plants which bloom in July to the delight of the gardener and flower arranger. Survival over the winter can be a problem — a few types are rather tender and nearly all of them require sandy, well-drained soil to prevent rotting.

VARIETIES: There are 3 basic sections. The *Reticulata* group are dwarfs with flower stems 4–6 in. high and bloom in late winter or early spring. There are 2 old favourites — **I. danfordiae** (February–March, yellow scented flowers) and **I. reticulata** (February–March, purplish blue scented flowers with yellow markings). The flowers are about 3 in. across — for larger and earlier flowers grow **I. histrioides 'Major'** (January–February, blue flowers with white and gold markings). Plant the round bulbs 2 in. deep in September–October — set them 4 in. apart. The *Juno* group has distinctive bulbs — at the base there are thick roots which should not be broken when planting. The flowers are quite small (2–3 in.) but the flower stems are taller than the Reticulatas, reaching 1–1½ ft. Set out the bulbs in September or October, planting them 2 in. deep and 6–9 in. apart. A neglected group — few gardeners will know **I. bucharica** (April, cream and yellow flowers) and **I. aucheri** (April, lilac and yellow flowers). The summer-flowering *Xiphium* group are popular, especially as cut flowers. The many named varieties in this large group should be planted 4–6 in. deep in September or October, leaving about 6 in. between them. The flower stalks grow 1–2 ft high. Earliest to flower are the Dutch Hybrids (June) — **'Wedgwood'** (pale blue) is the favourite variety, but white, yellow, purple and blue types are available. The Spanish Hybrids bloom a few weeks later in early July — generally smaller in all their parts than the Dutch sorts. The largest plants and the largest blooms (5 in. across) are borne by the English Hybrids which bloom in July.

SITE & SOIL: Well-drained, light soil is essential — chalk or lime is desirable. Thrives best in full sun.

PLANT DETAILS: See above.

PROPAGATION: Divide bulbs after foliage has died down — store until planting time in autumn.

Iris reticulata

Iris xiphium 'Wedgwood'

LEUCOJUM Snowflake

It is easy to confuse Spring Snowflake with a tall-growing Snowdrop. Both appear in early spring and both bear nodding flowers made up of 6 white petals. You will know it is Leucojum if all the petals are the same size and all bear a green spot at the tip. It is a plant which does not like disturbance — put the bulbs in as soon as they are available.

VARIETIES: The Spring Snowflake is **L. vernum** — a tolerant plant which will thrive in both shade and moist soil. The cup-shaped flowers are about ¾ in. across, borne on upright stalks above the strap-like leaves. The Summer Snowflake **(L. aestivum)** has similar but larger flowers — **'Gravetye Giant'** is the best variety.

SITE & SOIL: Well-drained soil in sun or partial shade.

PLANT DETAILS: Planting time August–September. Planting depth 4 in. Spacing 4 in. (Spring Snowflake), 8 in. (Summer Snowflake). Height 8 in. (Spring Snowflake), 2 ft (Summer Snowflake). Flowering period February–March (Spring Snowflake), April–May (Summer Snowflake).

PROPAGATION: Divide mature clumps when foliage has died down — replant at once.

Leucojum vernum

MUSCARI Grape Hyacinth

A useful and popular clump-forming plant, producing splashes of blue in the rockery or at the edges of beds and borders. Nobody sings its praises and it has none of the glamour of many of the bulbs in this chapter, but our gardens would be poorer without it. The tiny, bell-like blooms are clustered at the top of each flower spike — an excellent choice for use in miniature arrangements indoors.

VARIETIES: The standard choices are **M. armeniacum** (9 in., blue flowers with a white rim) and **M. botryoides** (7 in., sky blue flowers). If you prefer novelties, look through the catalogues for **M. comosum 'Plumosum'** (1 ft, feathery blue flowers) or **M. tubergenianum** (6 in., dark blue flowers above pale blue ones on the spike).

SITE & SOIL: Any well-drained soil will do — thrives best in full sun.

PLANT DETAILS: Planting time September–October. Planting depth 3 in. Spacing 4 in. Height 6 in.–1 ft. Flowering period April–May.

PROPAGATION: Divide clumps in autumn every 3 years.

Muscari armeniacum

NARCISSUS Narcissus, Daffodil

One of the easiest and certainly the most popular of all spring-flowering bulbs — the common name 'Daffodil' is used when the central cup is as long as or longer than the petals. Plant the bulbs as soon as you can in the autumn and then leave them undisturbed to spread over the years — tiny ones in the rockery and larger ones in grassland or border. Do not remove the leaves until they are completely brown.

VARIETIES:

TRUMPET NARCISSI (DAFFODILS) One flower per stem — cup at least as long as the petals. Height 1–1½ ft. Examples are **'King Alfred'** (yellow), **'Beersheba'** (white) and **'Newcastle'** (bi-colour).

LARGE-CUPPED NARCISSI One flower per stem — cup more than ⅓ the length of the petals. Height 1–2 ft. Examples are **'Carlton'** (yellow), **'Silver Lining'** (white) and **'Fortune'** (bi-colour).

SMALL-CUPPED NARCISSI One flower per stem — cup less than ⅓ the length of the petals. Height 1–1½ ft. Examples are **'Frigid'** (white), **'Mahmoud'** (bi-colour) and **'La Riante'** (bi-colour).

DOUBLE NARCISSI More than one ring of petals — cup and petals indistinguishable. Height 1–1½ ft. Examples are **'Golden Ducat'** (yellow), **'Snowball'** (white) and **'Texas'** (bi-colour).

TRIANDRUS NARCISSI Usually several flowers per stem — drooping flowers and slightly reflexed petals. Height 6 in.–1½ ft. Examples are **'Liberty'** (yellow), **'Thalia'** (white) and **'Dawn'** (bi-colour).

CYCLAMINEUS NARCISSI One flower per stem — drooping flowers with long trumpets and strongly reflexed petals. Height 6 in.–1 ft. Examples are **'Peeping Tom'** (yellow) and **'Tête-à-Tête'** (bi-colour).

JONQUILLA NARCISSI (JONQUILS) Several flowers per stem — cup shorter than the petals — fragrant. Height 6 in.–1 ft. Examples are **'Sweetness'** (yellow), **'Golden Sceptre'** (deep yellow) and **'Bobbysoxer'** (bi-colour).

TAZETTA NARCISSI Several flowers per stem — cup shorter than the petals which are often frilled — very fragrant. Generally too tender for growing outdoors. Height 1½ ft. Examples are **'Soleil d'Or'** (yellow), **'Paper White'** (white) and **'Geranium'** (bi-colour).

POETICUS NARCISSI Usually one flower per stem — white petals with a frilled red-edged cup. Height 1½ ft. Examples are **'Actaea'** (yellow cup) and **'Pheasant's Eye'** (red cup).

DWARF NARCISSI Various species and hybrids which do not grow taller than 8 in. Included here are Hoop Petticoat (**N. bulbocodium**), Angel's Tears (**N. triandrus albus**), **N. minimus, N. cyclamineus** and **N. 'February Gold'**. The dwarfs are early flowering.

SITE & SOIL: Any well-drained garden soil will do — thrives in sun or light shade.

PLANT DETAILS: Planting time August–September — the earlier the better. Planting depth 4–7 in. Height 3 in.–2 ft. Flowering period March–April.

PROPAGATION: Lift overcrowded or 'blind' clumps in late summer — divide and plant offsets.

Narcissus 'King Alfred'

Narcissus 'Fortune'

Narcissus 'La Riante'

Narcissus 'Golden Ducat'

Narcissus 'Actaea'

Narcissus 'February Gold'

NERINE Nerine

Nerines are usually considered to be too tender to grow outdoors, but there is one hardy species which can be relied upon to display its eye-catching flowers in the garden. They appear in the autumn — clusters of long-lasting blooms at the top of a leafless stalk. Strap-shaped leaves appear in late summer, grow during winter and spring and then die down in summer. Protect the crowns with peat or bracken in winter.

VARIETIES: N. bowdenii is the species to grow. The flowers measure about 3 in. across — long, spidery petals which are twisted and reflexed. The colour is deep pink — grow **'Pink Triumph'** for silvery pink blooms. Plant the bulbs in a sheltered spot — preferably close to a south-facing wall.

SITE & SOIL: Well-drained soil and full sun are essential.

PLANT DETAILS: Planting time April–May. Planting depth 4 in. Spacing 6 in. Height 2 ft. Flowering period September–October.

PROPAGATION: Divide overcrowded clumps in spring — replant at once.

Nerine bowdenii

ORNITHOGALUM Star of Bethlehem

Several species are too tender to grow outdoors — Chincherinchee (O. thyrsoides) is grown as a pot plant and sold as a cut flower. There are three species which are hardy, however, and two of them are native to Britain. The star-shaped flowers appear in spring, and are always a combination of white and green.

VARIETIES: O. nutans is the best one to buy — about a dozen pendent blooms are borne on each stem — 1 in. bells with pale green backs. **O. umbellatum** grows to the same height (1 ft) but it has a different habit — the flat white stars face upwards and open during the day. Plant it with caution — it can easily become a weed. **O. balansae** (6 in.) is a dwarf for the rockery — the white petals are striped with green.

SITE & SOIL: Any well-drained soil will do — thrives in sun or partial shade.

PLANT DETAILS: Planting time October. Planting depth 2 in. Spacing 4–6 in. Height 6 in.–1 ft. Flowering period April–May.

PROPAGATION: Divide clumps in summer — replant at once.

Ornithogalum umbellatum

PUSCHKINIA Striped Squill

It is strange that this close relative of the Bluebell is so rarely grown. Puschkinia is an excellent subject for the rockery — a trouble-free, low-growing plant which bears its attractive blooms early in the year. It spreads quite rapidly by means of offsets which can be used to increase your stock.

VARIETIES: The species grown as a garden plant is **P. scilloides (P. libanotica)**. Each stem carries about 6 flowers which are open starry bells — each petal is pale blue with a central dark blue stripe — colourful and easy, yet hardly known by gardeners. Plant in groups for maximum effect, and add compost or peat to the soil before putting in the bulbs. There is a variety (**'Alba'**) which bears white petals.

SITE & SOIL: Any well-drained soil will do — thrives in sun or light shade.

PLANT DETAILS: Planting time September–October. Planting depth 2 in. Spacing 3 in. Height 4 in. Flowering period March–April.

PROPAGATION: Divide clumps in summer — replant at once.

Puschkinia scilloides

Flowers for Every Season

SEPTEMBER–DECEMBER

(for JANUARY–APRIL see page 109)
(for MAY–AUGUST see page 114)

By careful selection you can have bulbs in bloom all year round. For each month there is a list of bulbous plants which can be expected to be in full bloom — remember that some of these plants may come into flower earlier and can continue to flower for weeks afterwards.

SEPTEMBER

Acidanthera	Cyclamen europaeum
Amaryllis	Cyclamen neapolitanum
Begonia	Freesia
Canna	Galtonia
Colchicum	Gladiolus (Hybrids)
Crinum	Nerine
Crocosmia	Sternbergia
Crocus (Autumn-flowering)	Tigridia

OCTOBER

Amaryllis	Cyclamen neapolitanum
Anemone (Poppy-flowered)	Freesia
Colchicum	Nerine
Crocus (Autumn-flowering)	Sternbergia

NOVEMBER

Colchicum	Cyclamen neapolitanum

DECEMBER

Cyclamen coum

SCILLA Bluebell, Squill

Bluebells are a common springtime sight in both woodland and gardens. Upright stems above strap-like leaves bear drooping flowers — bells or stars in shades of blue. But not all Scillas are the same — there are winter-flowering dwarfs for the rockery and the traditional Bluebells under trees, around shrubs or naturalised in short grass. These Bluebells flower in mid spring — for early summer flowering choose the Cuban Lily. Thus both height and flowering season cover a wide range, and so does flower colour — there is white, pink and purple as well as the familiar blue. Most Scillas are easy to grow — they can be left in the ground to spread into large clumps over the years and only the Cuban Lily needs a cover of peat, ashes or leaves as winter protection. The only thing you have to remember is that the bulbs are susceptible to decay when out of the soil. Always plant as soon as possible after purchase.

VARIETIES: The earliest and smallest Squill is **S. tubergeniana** — spacing 3 in., height 3 in., flowering period February–March. The flowers are pale blue with dark blue stripes — clearly a close relative of Puschkinia (see page 120). The place for this species is amongst the Snowdrops and Winter Aconites. A lovely display in late winter, but the favourite early-flowering Squill is another one — **S. sibirica** (Siberian or Spring Squill). The basic details are spacing 4 in., height 6 in., flowering period March–April. There are white and pale blue forms but to see the Siberian Squill at its best you should pick the bright blue **'Spring Beauty'**. Another useful early-flowering Squill is **S. bifolia** which bears deep blue stars in March on 6 in. stems. The best known species is, of course, our native English Bluebell. It has other common names, such as Wild Hyacinth, and a host of latin names — **S. nonscripta**, **S. nutans**, **Hyacinthus nonscriptus** and **Endymion nonscriptus**. An unfortunate mouthful, but any one of them may appear in the catalogues. Details are spacing 4 in., height 9 in., flowering period April–June. Flowering at the same time is the larger Giant Bluebell **(S. campanulata** or **Endymion hispanicus)**. Excellent blue, pink and white varieties are available. Last of all in the blooming league comes **S. peruviana** (Cuban Lily) — spacing 6 in., height 1 ft, flowering period May–June, when clusters of pale blue flowers appear.

SITE & SOIL: Any well-drained, moist soil will do — thrives in sun or light shade.

PLANT DETAILS: Planting time August–September. Planting depth 4 in. See above for other details.

PROPAGATION: Divide overcrowded clumps in August or September — replant at once.

Scilla sibirica

Scilla nonscripta

RANUNCULUS Turban Buttercup

The semi-double flowers of the Turban Buttercup are popular for cutting as they last a long time in water. It is also a colourful plant in the garden, each stem bearing several 3 in. flowers in white, pink, orange or red. Except for a few very mild areas it is half hardy in Britain — the routine is to plant the tubers, claw side downwards, in spring and then lift them in October after the foliage has died down. The tubers should be stored over winter in dry peat or sand in a frost-free place.

VARIETIES: R. asiaticus is bought as a mixture of coloured varieties. The leaves are deeply divided. Well-rotted compost or peat should be added to the soil — soak the tubers in water for several hours before planting.

SITE & SOIL: Any well-drained soil will do — thrives best in full sun.

PLANT DETAILS: Planting time March–April. Planting depth 2 in. Spacing 6 in. Height 1 ft. Flowering period June–July.

PROPAGATION: Divide tubers after lifting. Replant in spring.

Ranunculus asiaticus

SPARAXIS Harlequin Flower

If you want to grow bulbs which can be planted in the rockery or front of the border and then left to look after themselves, then Sparaxis is not for you. In the colder areas, this colourful plant must be grown indoors — in milder regions it can be grown outdoors in a sheltered, south-facing site. Even then you will have to follow an unusual routine — the corms are lifted in midsummer when the foliage has died down and kept dry until replanted in November.

VARIETIES: S. hybrida is bought as a mixed selection — white, yellow, orange, red, purple or pink blooms are borne on wiry stems. Some flowers may be plain — others extremely colourful with yellow throats and black collars.

SITE & SOIL: Well-drained soil and full sun are essential.

PLANT DETAILS: Planting time November. Planting depth 3 in. Spacing 4 in. Height 1 ft. Flowering period May–June.

PROPAGATION: Remove cormlets when plants are lifted in summer. Replant in November.

Sparaxis hybrida

STERNBERGIA Yellow Star Flower

At first glance Sternbergia looks like a late-flowering Crocus — the leaves are narrow and the flowers have the familiar wineglass shape. Look closely and you will see that Sternbergia blooms are borne on a stem and not on an extension of the petal tube like a Crocus flower. This is a splendid plant to grow in a rockery which has free-draining soil and is sun-baked in summer. It is notoriously slow to establish — do not lift after planting.

VARIETIES: **S. lutea** is the most popular species — 2 in. flowers of glistening gold are borne in autumn. It is hardy in most parts of Britain. Dead-head once flowering is over, but do not remove the leaves. The best variety to grow is **angustifolia**.

SITE & SOIL: Well-drained, chalky soil and full sun are essential.

PLANT DETAILS: Planting time August. Planting depth 5 in. Spacing 5 in. Height 6 in. Flowering period September–October.

PROPAGATION: Buy new bulbs — Sternbergia hates disturbance.

Sternbergia lutea

TIGRIDIA Tiger Flower

Just when you think that all the bright flowers have gone, Tigridia comes into bloom at the end of summer. The flower is a thing of exotic beauty. Measuring about 4 in. across, the 3 outer petals are large and single-coloured — white, yellow, mauve or red. The 3 inner petals are small and splashed with dark red and purple. The throat is also blotched — hence the common name. Plant it in the spring and lift in October. Keep the corms in dry peat or sand.

VARIETIES: **T. pavonia** is the only species grown. It is hardy in sheltered sites in mild areas — leave it in the ground if you are brave, lucky and knowledgeable. The blooms last only for a day, but they are borne in succession.

SITE & SOIL: A well-drained, sheltered spot in full sun is essential.

PLANT DETAILS: Planting time April. Planting depth 4 in. Spacing 6 in. Height 1½ ft. Flowering period July–September.

PROPAGATION: Remove offsets when plants are lifted in autumn. Replant in spring.

Tigridia pavonia

TRILLIUM Wake Robin

Trillium is not a common plant as it demands a special environment — it will only flourish if you grow it in a woodland where it can have leafy shade above and leaf mould below. Trillium is certainly attractive when well grown, with all its parts arranged in threes — 3 broad leaves on each stalk, 3 small green sepals and 3 large petals surrounding the central group of golden stamens.

VARIETIES: The favourite species is the Wake Robin **(T. grandiflorum)** which bears 3 in. flowers — white at first but slowly turning pink with age. The Painted Wake Robin **(T. undulatum)** is rather similar but smaller, with its 1½ in. white petals streaked with purple. Similar in height to T. undulatum is **T. erectum** (1 ft) which bears small wine-coloured blooms.

SITE & SOIL: A well-drained, humus-rich soil is essential — thrives best in partial shade.

PLANT DETAILS: Planting time August–September. Planting depth 3 in. Spacing 1 ft. Height 1–1½ ft. Flowering period April–June.

PROPAGATION: Divide mature clumps in autumn — replant at once.

Trillium grandiflorum

TRITONIA Blazing Star

In its most usual form the blooms of the Blazing Star are about 2 in. across — vibrant orange cups with yellow centres. It is sometimes confused with Crocosmia (page 113) to which it is closely related, but unfortunately Tritonia is even less hardy. Grow it if you live in a mild area — otherwise don't bother to try.

VARIETIES: There is just one popular species — **T. crocata**. The sword-like leaves are erect and each branching flower stem bears a double row of blooms in early summer. If there is a threat of frost, cover the crowns with bracken, peat or ashes. Several named varieties are available — non-orange examples include **'Roseline'** (pink) and **'White Beauty'** (white).

SITE & SOIL: A well-drained, sheltered spot in full sun is essential.

PLANT DETAILS: Planting time September. Planting depth 2 in. Spacing 6 in. Height 1½ ft. Flowering period May–June.

PROPAGATION: Remove offsets after lifting overcrowded clumps. Replant in September.

Tritonia crocata

TULIPA Tulip

The spring garden and the coloured catalogues of nurserymen abound with Tulips — there is no need here to sing their praises nor to illustrate the scores of varieties which are available. Instead this page is devoted to the rules for success together with a simple description of the various groups. Tulips will succeed in any reasonable garden soil which does not become waterlogged. The Garden Hybrid group is by far the more popular — these are grown as bedding plants, going in after the Narcissi and are then lifted when the foliage turns yellow. The dry bulbs are stored in a frost-free place. The Species group has fewer friends although there are many splendid varieties, including dwarfs for the rockery — some can be left in the ground over winter.

SITE & SOIL: Well-drained soil is necessary — thrives best in full sun.

PLANT DETAILS: Planting time November – December (earlier planting can result in frost damage). Planting depth 6 in. Spacing 5 – 8 in.

PROPAGATION: Remove bulblets at lifting time. Dry, store and replant in late autumn.

GARDEN HYBRIDS

SINGLE EARLY TULIPS
9 – 16 in., flowering early – mid April.
Strong-stemmed and useful for early display, but blooms are smaller than later-flowering varieties. Flowers open flat. Examples are **'Keizerskroon'** (yellow and red), **'Brilliant Star'** (red), **'Couleur Cardinal'** (deep red, scented) and **'Bellona'** (golden yellow).

DOUBLE EARLY TULIPS
9 – 16 in., flowering mid April.
Strong-stemmed and useful for early display — the many-petalled blooms are long-lasting. Petals are sometimes frilled. Examples are **'Peach Blossom'** (rosy pink), **'Orange Nassau'** (orange), **'Marechal Niel'** (orange-yellow) and **'Schoonoord'** (white).

TRIUMPH TULIPS
16 – 24 in., flowering end April – early May.
Strong-stemmed and useful for beds which will have to be cleared for summer-flowering bedding plants. Look like small Darwin Tulips. Examples are **'Garden Party'** (pink-edged white), **'Apricot Beauty'** (salmon-pink), **'Korneforos'** (red) and **'Sulphur Glory'** (yellow).

DARWIN TULIPS
24 – 30 in., flowering early – mid May.
Strong-stemmed — the most popular of all garden Tulips. Large flowers — the Darwin Hybrids are even larger. Examples are **'Apeldoorn'** (orange-red), **'Clara Butt'** (pink), **'La Tulipe Noire'** (blackish purple), **'Zwanenburg'** (white) and **'London'** (pink).

LILY-FLOWERED TULIPS
20 – 24 in., flowering end April – early May.
Strong-stemmed — with Darwins, the favourite Tulips for garden bedding. Long flowers with pointed petals reflexed at the tips. Examples are **'West Point'** (deep yellow), **'China Pink'** (pink), **'Queen of Sheba'** (orange and red) and **'White Triumphator'** (white).

COTTAGE TULIPS
24 – 30 in., flowering early May.
Old-fashioned Tulips with long, egg-shaped blooms. Can be mixed satisfactorily with Darwin Tulips. Examples are **'Rosy Wings'** (pink and white), **'Golden Harvest'** (yellow), **'Marshal Haig'** (red and yellow) and **'Greenland'** (pink, cream and green).

REMBRANDT TULIPS
20 – 24 in., flowering mid May.
'Broken' Tulips — petals are flecked or streaked with another colour. The cause is a harmless virus — sometimes called Bizarre Tulips. Examples are **'Absalon'** (yellow and red), **'Cordell Hull'** (white and red), **'Victory'** (yellow and brown) and **'Gloire de Holland'** (violet and white).

PARROT TULIPS
20 – 26 in., flowering mid May.
Weak-stemmed — some support may be needed. Large flowers with frilled petals — bi-colours are common. Examples are **'Texas Gold'** (red-edged yellow), **'Black Parrot'** (blackish purple), **'Firebird'** (vermilion and white) and **'Fantasy'** (pink and green).

DOUBLE LATE TULIPS
16 – 24 in., flowering late May.
Some support needed to protect from wind and rain. Very large flowers — sometimes called Paeony Tulips. Examples are **'Eros'** (rosy pink, scented), **'Nizza'** (yellow and red), **'Moonglow'** (yellow) and **'Symphonia'** (red).

SPECIES

T. kaufmanniana varieties and hybrids are dwarf (6 – 10 in.) and bloom in March. These Water-lily Tulips are ideal in the rockery, the flowers opening into colourful stars. Do not lift in winter — leave them to spread. Well-known varieties include **'Heart's Delight'** (white-edged red) and **'Stresa'** (red and yellow).

T. fosteriana varieties and hybrids are short (12 – 18 in.) and bloom in April. They are grown for their enormous flowers which can reach a span of 10 in. when fully open. Support for such giant blooms is often necessary. Best known is **'Mme Lefeber'** (**'Red Emperor'**) — others include **'Princeps'** (red, sturdy stems) and **'Easter Parade'** (yellow).

T. greigii varieties and hybrids are dwarf (8 – 12 in.) and bloom in May. The flowers are long-lasting — the leaves are often mottled or streaked with brown. A good plant for the rockery — examples include **'Cape Cod'** (red and yellow), **'Red Riding Hood'** (red) and **'Plaisir'** (cream and red).

T. clusiana is known as the Lady Tulip — 8 in. tall and flowering in April. A marked contrast to the many bold and brilliant Tulips — the leaves are grass-like and the slender blooms are white with pink streaks on the outside of the petals.

T. praestans is grown for its pillar-box red flowers borne 3 or 4 to a stem. It grows 1 ft high and flowers in April.

Tulipa 'Peach Blossom'

Tulipa 'London'

Tulipa 'West Point'

Tulipa 'Greenland'

CHAPTER 7
FLOWER CARE

Some flowering plants are virtually trouble-free and can be left to look after themselves, blooming quite merrily year after year. Such types are in the minority and even they require care at buying and planting time.

For the rest there is a collection of straight-forward tasks to carry out – hoeing, watering, feeding, spraying, staking and the rest. None is particularly onerous or back-breaking, but if you ignore an essential task then there can be a great deal of extra work to do at a later stage.

BUYING

As a general rule, you get what you pay for. It is not an absolute rule – there are times when you can be sold rubbish by a reputable garden centre and many gardeners have obtained an excellent group of plants as a bargain offer from a newspaper advertisement. But the general rule still applies – you get what you pay for.

SOURCES OF SUPPLY

GARDEN CENTRE	The great advantage is that you can see exactly what you are buying. As plants are usually sold in containers you can buy perennials at almost any time of the year for planting out. The stock is large and varied, and if the garden centre is a reputable one you can be sure that half hardy annuals will have been properly hardened off. Against all the obvious advantages you must recognise that container-grown plants are more expensive than lifted ones and that you generally need a car to get there. You also cannot expect them to stock all the plants listed in this book — for some you will have to write to a specialist nursery. If something goes wrong, take the plant back to the garden centre and explain the situation. Always keep your receipt as proof of purchase. If it is not your fault then the garden centre will usually replace the item.
HIGH STREET SHOP	In hardware stores, garden shops, department stores, greengrocers and supermarkets you will find a selection of favourite varieties when the planting season arrives. The popular bulbs will be available in spring and perennials will be on offer in autumn and spring, sometimes packed in polythene bags for easy transport. Bedding plants will be there, but don't expect to find unusual varieties. There are advantages — you can pick up a few items when doing the shopping and the prices tend to be inexpensive, but the warm conditions can lead to drying out and premature growth. If something goes wrong and it is not your fault then you can try taking the plant back to the shop. The response, however, will depend on the store and there is no guarantee of replacement.
MARKET STALL	Bedding plants and bulbs are bought from market stalls throughout the country. They tend to be the cheapest source of supply, and the plants are not kept in overheated conditions. But do take care. A great deal of inferior planting material is sold in this way — and you will only have yourself to blame. Feel the bulbs to make sure that they are firm and do not buy boxes of bedding plants if they are in full flower. The golden rule is to buy from a market stall at the beginning of the planting season. If something goes wrong, there is usually very little chance of redress. It would be surprising indeed if the stallholder admitted that his bulbs were diseased or that his plants had not been hardened off properly.
MAIL ORDER NURSERY	Despite the advantages of the garden centre, there is still a place for the reputable mail order nursery. You can make your choice at leisure — checking the plant's requirements in the A – Z guide before filling out your order. In the specialist catalogues you will find varieties unobtainable from your garden centre — but for ordinary gardeners there is the distinct drawback of not being able to inspect before purchase. Also, the stock may arrive when the weather is unsuitable for planting. Of course, these drawbacks do not apply if you are buying seeds. If something goes wrong, write to the company and explain what has happened. Many nurseries will return your money or send you a credit note if they feel that your complaint is a genuine one.
BARGAIN OFFER NURSERY	National newspapers and gardening magazines often have advertisements for 'bargain' offers. Good value offers do sometimes occur but such advertisements must be viewed with caution. Above all, avoid taking all the glowing descriptions too literally. If money is short and you have a large space to fill, the 'bargain' collection is a money-saving way of stocking up with popular varieties. If the stock is dead or badly diseased write to the company and also to the newspaper or journal where the advertisement appeared. If on the other hand the plants are small and there are just a few spindly stems compared to the robust plants offered for sale at your local garden centre, then you have no grounds for complaint. It was a 'bargain' offer and you have no right to expect top-grade plants.

TYPES OF PLANTING MATERIAL

Buy good quality plants rather than unnamed, poor grade stock. Plants rarely fully recover from a poor start in life – check over the specimens you propose to buy, using the notes below as your guide. If you have to buy before you are ready to plant, keep the stock in a cool dark place. Do not disturb the soil, compost or peat around the roots but do keep it moist. If the delay is likely to be more than 3 or 4 days, heel in the plants in a shallow trench.

Container-grown Plants

A container-grown perennial is a plant which has been raised as a seedling or cutting and has then been potted on until it is housed in the whalehide, plastic or metal container on display. It should *not* have been lifted from the open ground and its roots plus surrounding soil stuffed into the container. Such lifted plants are sold and can give success-ful results, but they should neither be called nor be priced as container-grown plants. The true container-grown hardy perennial can be planted at any time of the year as long as the ground is neither frosty nor waterlogged. The most convenient of all the planting types, but also the most expensive.

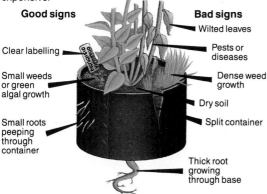

Good signs
- Clear labelling
- Small weeds or green algal growth
- Small roots peeping through container

Bad signs
- Wilted leaves
- Pests or diseases
- Dense weed growth
- Dry soil
- Split container
- Thick root growing through base

Pot-grown Plants

A pot-grown specimen is a miniature version of the container-grown plant. It may be a mature rockery perennial or the juvenile form (seedling or rooted cutting) of a border perennial, annual or biennial. This is the best way to buy a rockery perennial, and it is generally more economical for border perennials than container-grown plants. It is the dearest way to buy annuals, but as there is no check after planting out the flowers are earlier and larger.

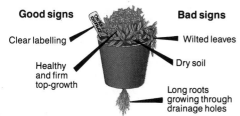

Good signs
- Clear labelling
- Healthy and firm top-growth

Bad signs
- Wilted leaves
- Dry soil
- Long roots growing through drainage holes

Bulbs

Make sure that the bulbs and corms you buy are firm at the base. They should not have started to grow and the surface should be mould-free. Large-sized bulbs are usually the best choice, but buying a mixture of bulbs which you can grow on is the more economical way of covering a large area. Outdoor Hyacinths should be the medium and not the large grade. It is of no importance if Tulips have lost their brown skins. The outer scales of Lily bulbs should be firm and succulent — do not buy bulbs if they are covered with withered scales.

Pre-packaged Plants

The pre-packaged perennial is the standard planting material sold by hardware shops, supermarkets and department stores; they are also available at garden centres. It is a bare-rooted plant with moist peat, sphagnum moss or compost around the roots and the whole plant housed inside a labelled polythene bag. Such plants are cheaper than their container-grown counterparts but there are drawbacks. You can't see what you are buying and premature growth may begin in the warm conditions which occur in the shop. Planting time is the dormant season between autumn and spring.

Good signs
- Plant completely dormant

Bad signs
- Leaf buds beginning to open
- Shrivelled or diseased stems
- Small white roots growing into the damp packing material

Lifted Plants

Small clumps and divisions of large clumps of perennials are sometimes lifted and placed in polythene bags for sale. The problem here is that some roots will have been broken during the transfer and so tap-rooted varieties may take a long time to become established in their new home.

Seeds

The seed packet is one of the corner-stones of gardening and is the standard method for raising annuals and biennials. You can obtain a much wider range of varieties from seed than is possible if you rely on buying bedding plants. Some perennials can be readily raised from seed. Look for types marked F_1 hybrid — this means that the variety has been carefully bred to have more vigour and produce more attractive blooms than the standard types. Expensive, but usually worth the extra cost. Seed Strips and Seed Mats have failed to become popular, but Starter Kits are widely available at seed sowing time. Plastic trays have been filled with Seed Compost and are pre-sown — the transparent lid is used to provide cover during the pre-germination stage. Useful if you are short of time, but the range of plants offered is limited and the cost is under-standably higher than starting from scratch.

Trays

Bedding annuals and biennials are sold in wooden or plastic trays ('flats'). Buy from a supplier with a good reputation or one who has pleased you in previous years — you are bound to be disappointed if the seedlings have not been properly hardened off. Never buy half hardy annuals before the recommended planting time. If you can, buy a whole box and not just a few plants wrapped in newspaper.

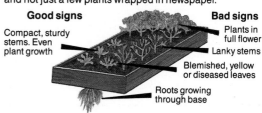

Good signs
- Compact, sturdy stems. Even plant growth

Bad signs
- Plants in full flower
- Lanky stems
- Blemished, yellow or diseased leaves
- Roots growing through base

PLANTING

GETTING THE SOIL READY

DOUBLE DIGGING is recommended to aerate the topsoil and break up the subsoil. The first step is to dig out a trench 18 in. wide and 12 in. deep at one side of the bed or border and transport the soil to the other. Fork over the bottom of the trench to the full length of the prongs, working in garden compost, well-rotted manure, leaf mould or peat. Turn strip A into the trench. Turn over the trench left by the removal of A, again incorporating compost or peat. Turn over strip B and so on, until a final trench is formed which is then filled with the soil from the first one. Do not remove small stones, as they are beneficial in a dry season. Roots of perennial weeds should be removed during digging. To add major plant nutrients, fork 4 oz Growmore per sq. yd into the topsoil, and then let the ground settle for at least 6 weeks before planting.

THE PLANTING OPERATION

The A-Z guide and the soil condition should be your indicators to planting time. The ground must be neither frozen nor waterlogged. Squeeze a handful of soil – it should be wet enough to form a ball but dry enough to shatter when dropped on a hard surface. In well-drained gardens September and October are the best months for planting perennials – with hollow-stemmed plants and in heavy soil areas it is advisable to wait until March or April.

Bedding Plants

In order to induce bushiness, pinch out the growing tips about 10 days before planting. Provided the recommended time has arrived, get on with the job as quickly as possible. These recommended times are April or May for hardy annuals which have been raised indoors, late May or early June for half hardy annuals and September or October for biennials. Water the trays several hours before planting is due to begin, and whilst you are waiting lightly rake over the bed and then firm by gentle treading. Do not add any more fertilizer. Take the tray outdoors and cover with a sheet of paper – dig a hole with a trowel which will be deep enough and wide enough to house the roots without having to bend them. The top of the soil ball should be just below ground level after planting – let that be your guide to the correct depth of the hole. Lift out a plant from the tray by gently prising it up with the trowel and place the young plant into the hole in one operation. Do not lift a clump of plants and leave them by your side to dry out. Return the soil removed from the hole and firm with your fingers. Water in and the job is done. A simple job, but you must learn to do it quickly and you must lift plants by the soil ball or by the leaves – never handle the stem. If your bedding plants are shop-bought and have not been stopped, pinch out the tips about 10 days after planting.

Planting Mixture

Use a planting mixture instead of ordinary soil for filling up the spaces around the new plants. Make up the mixture in a wheelbarrow on a day when the soil is reasonably dry and friable — 1 part topsoil, 1 part moist peat and 3 handfuls of Bone Meal per barrow load. Keep this mixture in a shed until you are ready to start planting.

Bulbs

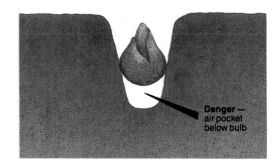

Danger — air pocket below bulb

Autumn is the usual season for planting bulbs but there are exceptions, so check the A-Z guide for the recommended time. Buy your bulbs when you can get on with planting straight away – many bulbs cannot stand being out of the soil for a long period. If you have a large area to plant, dig out the soil to the required depth and cover the base of this planting area with sand. Space out the bulbs to the required distance and press them firmly into the sand. Return the earth and tread down lightly to ensure that no air pockets have been created. It is more usual to plant bulbs individually, and with large bulbs the presence of air pockets is a common cause of failure. Dig a hole with a trowel or bulb planter – make sure that this hole is deeper than the recommended depth. Add sand to the hole and set the bulb firmly on this bed – in this way you can avoid creating an air pocket. Return the soil and press down firmly. Water in after planting.

Pre-packaged Plants • Lifted Plants with large roots beyond the soil ball

If the roots of pre-packaged perennials are dry, stand them in a bucket of water for about 2 hours. Water lifted plants the day before planting. The first step is to mark out the planting stations with canes to make sure that the plants will be spaced out as planned. The next task is to dig a hole for each specimen, and the commonest mistake is to make it too deep or too narrow. For depth use the soil mark on the stem as your guide – for width take the span of the largest roots and then add a few extra inches. With lifted plants do not remove the soil which may be present but do stretch out the roots which stick out from beyond the soil ball. When planting keep all the specimens covered to protect them from drying winds.

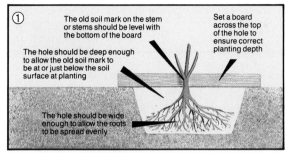

① The old soil mark on the stem or stems should be level with the bottom of the board

Set a board across the top of the hole to ensure correct planting depth

The hole should be deep enough to allow the old soil mark to be at or just below the soil surface at planting

The hole should be wide enough to allow the roots to be spread evenly

② Work a couple of trowelfuls of the planting mixture around the roots. Shake the plant gently up and down — add a little more planting mixture. Firm this around the roots with the fists. Do not press too hard

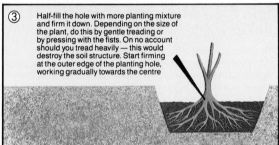

③ Half-fill the hole with more planting mixture and firm it down. Depending on the size of the plant, do this by gentle treading or by pressing with the fists. On no account should you tread heavily — this would destroy the soil structure. Start firming at the outer edge of the planting hole, working gradually towards the centre

④ Add more planting mixture until the hole is full. Firm once again and then loosen the surface. Spread a little soil around the stem so that the surface forms a low dome

When planting is finished, build a shallow ring of soil around the planting hole. This will form a water-retaining basin

Container-grown Plants • Pot-grown Plants • Lifted Plants with compact soil ball

Never regard container-grown and pot-grown plants as an easy way to plant perennials. If the environment around the soil ball is not right then the roots will not grow out into the garden soil. This means that it is not enough to dig a hole, take off the container, drop in the plant and replace the earth. Begin by watering the specimens the day before planting. Mark out the planting sites and then follow the instructions given below.

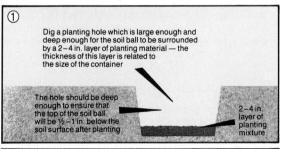

① Dig a planting hole which is large enough and deep enough for the soil ball to be surrounded by a 2–4 in. layer of planting material — the thickness of this layer is related to the size of the container

The hole should be deep enough to ensure that the top of the soil ball will be ½–1 in. below the soil surface after planting

2–4 in. layer of planting mixture

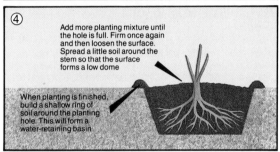

② Lifted Plant or Container-grown Plant Cut down the side of the container or polythene bag when it is stood on the base of the hole. Remove the cover carefully

Pot-grown Plant Gently tap the plant out of the pot and stand the soil ball on the base of the hole

③ Examine the exposed surface of the soil ball. Very gently cut away circling roots but never break up the soil ball

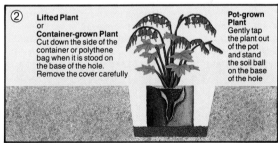

④ Fill the space between the soil ball and the sides of the hole with planting mixture. Do not use ordinary soil — roots may not move from a peat-based compost into mineral soil. Firm down the planting mixture with your fists — do not press too hard

After planting, a shallow water-retaining basin should remain

HOEING & WEEDING

Weeds are a threat to every flower garden and must be kept at bay. They are, of course, unsightly and give a ragged look to the bed or border. With small plants such as rockery perennials, bedding plants and newly-planted border perennials there is an added problem — weeds compete for space, food, water, etc and can harm or even swamp the garden flowers.

There is no single miracle cure for the weed problem — there are a number of interlinked tasks you will have to carry out. At soil preparation time remove all the roots of perennial weeds that you can find. This is especially important if you are going to plant a border which will have to stay undisturbed for several years. If the site is a sea of couch grass then you have a real problem. The best plan is to spray with glyphosate before planting — follow the instructions carefully.

However thoroughly you have removed weeds during soil preparation, additional weeds will appear among the growing plants. Hoeing is the basic technique to keep the problem under control — it must be carried out at regular intervals in order to keep annual weeds in constant check and to starve out the underground parts of perennial weeds. Hoeing can do more harm than good in careless hands — keep away from the stems and do not go deeper than an inch below the surface. Do not bother to hoe as a way of conserving moisture — the old idea of creating a 'dust mulch' is of little value. Wherever possible hand pull or dig out thistles, nettles, docks, bindweed, ground elder and perennial grasses.

Chemicals have a part to play, but must be used with care as they cannot distinguish between friend and foe. Use Weedol to quickly burn off weed growth between plants — paint leaves of perennial weeds with glyphosate. Always read the instructions and precautions before use and label the watering can 'Weedkiller'. Use it for no other purpose. One day there may be a complete chemical answer to the weed problem, but until then the mainstays of weed control must remain hoeing, mulching (see page 129) and hand pulling.

CUTTING

Cutting flowers and decorative leaves to take indoors for arranging is, of course, one of the pleasures of gardening. This form of spring or summer pruning generally does no harm but there are pitfalls. Obviously the garden display is diminished and in the case of newly-planted perennials the loss of stems and green leaves can harm next year's growth. If you have the space and are a keen flower arranger it is worthwhile having a separate bed where plants for cutting can be grown.

WATERING

During the first few weeks of bedding out annuals and the first year of planting perennials it is essential that watering takes place if there is a dry spell in spring or summer. Once plants are established, regular watering will not often be required but drought conditions call for special measures.

A plant should never be left to show visible signs of distress during a prolonged period of drought. Wilting means that you have left it too late — the time to water is when the soil at a few inches depth is dry and the foliage appears dull.

Once you decide to water then water thoroughly — a light sprinkling will do more harm than good. As a rough guide you will need 2 – 4 gallons per square yard — a watering can is often used but a hose pipe is a much better idea unless your garden is very small. Remember to water slowly close to the base of the plant. If you do spray over the foliage then avoid watering in hot sunshine.

How often you will need to water depends upon the soil type — a sandy soil will dry out much more quickly than a loamy one. Low-humus soils also dry out quickly. Never try to keep the land constantly soaked — there must be a period of drying-out between waterings.

Trickle irrigation through a perforated hose laid close to the plants is perhaps the best method of watering. A quick and easy technique popular in America is to build a ridge of soil around the base of a large perennial and then fill the basin with a hose.

DEAD – HEADING

The removal of dead flowers has several advantages — it helps to give the bed or border a well-maintained appearance, it prolongs the floral display and in several cases (Lupin, Delphinium, etc) it induces a second flush of flowers later in the season. Use shears, secateurs,

finger tips or a sharp knife, depending on the variety and care should be taken not to remove too much stem. Obviously dead-heading is not a practical proposition in all cases and with plants grown for their seed pods (Honesty, Chinese Lantern, etc) it must be avoided.

MULCHING

A mulch is a layer of bulky organic material placed on the soil surface around the stems. It is generally not used for annuals, but around herbaceous perennials it provides five positive benefits:

- The soil is kept moist during the dry days of summer.
- Annual weeds are kept in check.
- Soil structure is improved by the addition of humus.
- Plant foods are provided by some mulching materials.
- Frost penetration into the soil in winter is reduced.

Suitable materials for mulching are moist peat, well-rotted manure, leaf mould, properly-made garden compost, Bio Humus, spent hops, mushroom compost and shredded bark. Grass clippings are often recommended and used, but a word of caution is necessary. Add a thin layer at a time and stir occasionally — do not use them if they are weedy or if the lawn has been treated with a weedkiller.

The standard time for mulching is May. Success depends on preparing the soil surface properly before adding the organic blanket. Remove debris, dead leaves and weeds, and then water the surface if it is dry. Apply a spring feed if this has not been done, hoe in lightly and you are now ready to apply the mulch. Spread a 2–3 in. layer around but not touching the stems. Lightly fork this dressing into the top inch of soil during October.

Bearing in mind the value of mulching, it is surprising that it is not more generally practised. It cannot be that the idea is a new one — the Ancient Romans regularly mulched around their plants with stones to keep the surface cool, moist and weed-free. Perhaps, with time, we shall catch up with them.

CUTTING BACK

Very little summer pruning is needed in the bed or border — cutting flowers for indoors and the removal of spent blooms are the only pruning techniques undertaken by most gardeners during the active growing season. Removal of side shoots of Dahlias, Sweet Peas, etc is carried out by exhibitors, but the ordinary gardener only cuts back when growth becomes overcrowded.

It is a different story in the rock garden. Some of the popular spring-flowering types will have formed long and straggly stems during summer, and these should be cut back with shears to make the plant look neater and to ensure that there will be a cushion rather than a ring of flowers next season. Aubrietia is a good example, and cutting back can sometimes induce a second flush of flowers.

RENOVATING

After a few years many border perennials and hardy bulbs need renovation. If the clump is a large one and the central area is bare then the plant requires treatment. Other conditions calling for renovation are overcrowding, whereby the plant has spread into the growing zone of others, and flower deterioration where abundant leaf growth seems to have taken over from bloom development.

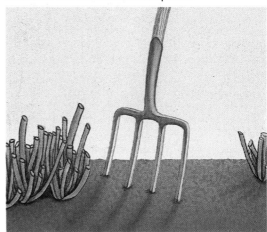

Lift the plant and divide the clump. If active growth has become restricted to the outer ring, remove pieces of shoots with their attached roots and discard the old central section. Do this work in late autumn, but if your soil is heavy and the drainage not particularly good it should be delayed until early spring. Take the opportunity to remove perennial weeds which may have been troubling you for years, and replant the pieces at the same depth as the original clump. Plant firmly, as described in Chapter 4.

A word of caution. Look up the plant in the A – Z guide before attempting renovation work. The correct time may be different from the general rule given above and for some plants lifting is out of the question. It takes several years for such varieties to become established and it would be folly to disturb them just as they were beginning to feel at home.

STAKING

Stakes, wires and other means of support are never things of beauty and can be distinctly ugly when carelessly used, but they are essential for weak-stemmed plants, tall varieties on exposed sites, large-headed flowers and for climbers. Never leave staking until the plant has collapsed. For a few plants, such as Dahlias and Chrysanthemums, the stakes are inserted before planting. With other plants requiring staking, the supports should be put in when the plants are quite small so that the stems can grow through and hide them.

Many forms of support material are available — use the type best suited to the nature of the plant. For many plants requiring staking all you will need is brushwood or pea sticks pushed into the soil around the young plant when the stems are 1–1½ ft high. At all costs avoid the drumstick effect obtained by attaching several stems of a large plant to a single bamboo cane. Try instead to leave the plant open by inserting three or four canes around the stems and enclosing the shoots with twine tied round the canes at 9 in. intervals.

WINTER CARE

For the annuals there is no winter care — their life span is over and their rebirth will be in the spring when the seeds are sown. The half hardy perennials must also leave the garden, but for them there is a stay indoors before being reintroduced into the garden with the return of frost-free weather in the spring. It is unwise to generalise about the proper conditions for half hardy perennials and bulbs which must overwinter indoors. It is a period of rest during which bulbs are kept dry and cool whilst varieties overwintered as green plants are given just enough water to keep them alive. However, you must look up the plant in the A–Z guide to make sure that it is getting the right treatment.

Outdoors the border perennials, rockery perennials and hardy bulbs await the return of spring in the open ground. Most of them have nothing to fear — the snow and frost will do them no harm provided the soil does not become waterlogged — drowned roots kill more plants than frozen ones.

Late autumn is the usual time for cutting back the dead stems of border perennials. Some plants are cut down to ground level and others are left with about 4 inches of stem at the base — the A–Z guide will tell you what to do. This winter clean-up will give the border a neat appearance, but there are a number of exceptions. You should not cut down evergreens and winter-flowering plants, of course, and perennials which are not fully hardy should be cut down in spring.

Forking over is the standard autumn technique to get the soil of the herbaceous or mixed border ready for its winter rest. Choose a day in late autumn when the soil is moist (not wet) and free from frost. Work from the back of the border towards the front or from the centre of the bed to the edges — use a fork to break up the surface crust, turning over the top couple of inches of soil between the plants. Do not disturb the roots, but stop every time you find a perennial weed and dig it out.

Incorporate the mulch you put down in spring into the soil — leave the surface rough. Forking over is an enjoyable job to do on a sunny day in autumn, and it probably does you more good than the plants unless your soil is heavy and prone to severe crusting and mossing over.

Perennials which are not completely hardy present a problem — you can trust to luck but in many areas a severe winter will undoubtedly mean their death. You can cover them with glass cloches but it is more usual to put a blanket of straw, bracken, leaf mould or peat over the crowns. Anchor this cover down with twigs, and don't forget to remove it in spring when new growth begins to appear.

Delicate but hardy alpines need protection from winter rains rather than from frosts. The standard method is to cover the plants with a pane of glass supported by bricks.

FEEDING

Flowers, like all other living things, require food. The production of stems, leaves, roots and flowers is a drain on the soil's reserves of nitrogen, phosphates, potash and several other elements. If one or more of these vital elements run short, then hunger signs appear on the leaves or flowers and both vigour and display are affected. The answer is to apply fertilizer at some stage or stages of the plant's life.

The golden rule is that there is no single technique which can be applied to all plants. The nutrient requirements of a tiny alpine and a large-flowering Chrysanthemum must be different, and yet the alpine is often over-fed and the large perennials starved.

Work a powder or granular fertilizer into the surface during soil preparation prior to planting. The nitrogen content of this fertilizer should never be higher than the phosphate or potash content — for border perennials and bulbs use Growmore, for annuals use Growmore or Bone Meal and for rockery perennials use Bone Meal. Check with the A–Z guides before taking this step — a few plants grow best under starvation or infertile conditions and should not be fed.

Most growing plants will need feeding — with border perennials sprinkle Growmore around the stems in spring and feed large and leafy plants regularly with a liquid fertilizer. Most bulbs also benefit from regular feeding. Annuals require much less feeding as they do not have to build up a storage root system to tide them over the winter. Use a liquid feed such as Instant Bio when the plants are coming into flower — never over-feed or you will get an abundance of leaves and few flowers. Rockery perennials need little or no feeding as a rule — once a year is ample with a potash-rich feed.

A few rules. Work granular or powder fertilizers into the top few inches of soil and never apply when the surface is dry. Keep powders away from stems and leaves.

Foliar feeding is an interesting technique which can be used when root feeding is ineffective. It is useful for all plants when the soil is shallow and where a pest or disease attack has taken place. The response is rapid and root activity is restored — use a watering can or a Bio Hoser and apply Instant Bio as directed.

CHAPTER 8
HOBBY PLANTS

Gardening is a healthy, rewarding and immensely popular hobby. Nearly every garden contains a wide range of plants – each one cared for to ensure that it will at least survive if not flourish. All add to the overall beauty of the garden, but it is quite natural for us to have a few special favourites – those flowers which we would not wish to be without and which receive that extra bit of attention.

For some people this mild favouritism is not enough – the selection, nurture and exhibition of a single plant genus becomes so absorbing that its cultivation is transformed into a hobby in its own right. Of course, not all flowers lend themselves to such devotion – they are simply not challenging enough. Take Nasturtiums as an example. These colourful annuals light up window boxes and flower beds with their bright yellows and reds in summer. Useful and attractive, yes, but their cultivation is so simple and the number of varieties so limited that the gardener is not being tested and there is no feeling that there is more to learn and more skills to acquire. Challenge is needed to transform an activity into a hobby – climbing and sailing are popular hobbies – travelling on escalators and crossing rivers on ferries are not.

At the other extreme from Nasturtiums is the Chrysanthemum – an example of the ideal hobby plant. First of all there is a bewildering multitude of varieties from which to make your choice. Even if you are brilliant enough to know all of the many hundreds of varieties available at present, you would still have a problem keeping up with the stream of new types which flows in every year. Varieties in abundance, and in addition a number of techniques to be learnt if you want to grow these plants to perfection. All of this means that the Chrysanthemum has the essential ingredients of a hobby plant – there are textbooks devoted solely to it plus a specialist national society to keep the enthusiast informed, to update classification when necessary and to hold exhibitions and shows. Competing at the various shows – at national or local level – is an important feature of the Chrysanthemum calendar for the hobbyist. The year is a long one – there are cuttings to strike indoors at the beginning of the season and a variety of jobs, such as soil preparation, planting, staking, stopping, regular feeding, spraying, watering, disbudding, bagging and staging before the stools are lifted and brought indoors in late autumn. During winter there are books, catalogues·and magazines to read and plants to order.

The Chrysanthemum is a half hardy perennial – each year it must be started afresh and then cared for over winter. Activity with the plant is therefore more prolonged than with most garden flowers, and so it is not surprising that nearly all of the hobby plants are half hardy perennials. The Dahlia, like the Chrysanthemum, is overwintered in the dormant state whereas the other two, the Fuchsia and Pelargonium, are kept alive as green plants in a low-activity condition.

There is an exception – the Lily is a bulb. All you have to do here is plant the bulbs in the proper way and at the proper time and up they come, year after year, topped with a crown of beautiful blooms. In fact the Lily isn't quite that simple. Although it does not require lifting in winter it still offers a challenge – many species and varieties are quite temperamental and no one site will suit them all. The spur for the enthusiast is to achieve a representative collection of this extensive group of plants – as with Orchid growing, it is the combination of the intricacies of cultivation and propagation plus the beauty of the flowers which fascinates the Lily devotee.

The grouping of a few well-known plants into a class known as hobby plants is wholly artificial. It is not linked with any natural feature – it merely recognises that the plants concerned have a sizeable and devoted following, and it allows the author to describe the classification, representative varieties and culture in extra detail. In this book the Chrysanthemum, Dahlia, Fuchsia, Lily and Pelargonium have been treated in this way. There are several other popular flowers which could claim to be hobby plants – Sweet Pea, Gladiolus, Iris and Dianthus are obvious examples. For a comprehensive list of up-to-date varieties consult a few specialist catalogues.

One final point – is it a good thing to have a hobby flower rather than a general love of all things in the garden? The answer is that it is not a particularly good thing, but if the charm and challenge of a specific plant gets through to you then nothing will stop you from becoming a keen devotee – a hobbyist in every sense of the word.

CHRYSANTHEMUM Chrysanthemum

The Chrysanthemum fits the definition of a hobby plant exactly — there are innumerable varieties and a long list of technical terms. Both experience and skill are required to ensure success and the plants have been classified into a profusion of groups, classes, sections and subsections. Despite (or because of) this complexity the Chrysanthemum is perhaps Britain's top hobby perennial and is surpassed only by the Rose as our No. 1 garden plant for the enthusiast.

Size and perfection of each bloom rather than the overall appearance of each plant are the aims of the enthusiast, but the Chrysanthemum is also a fine subject for general garden display. It comes in many forms — there is the Annual Chrysanthemum which is a colourful hardy plant raised quite easily from seed, and amongst the herbaceous perennials you will find the Shasta Daisy. But these are merely unimportant relatives of the late summer- and autumn-flowering plants which are raised afresh each year from cuttings.

Technically these are Florists' Chrysanthemums and all bear dark green, lobed leaves. The first choice you will have to make is whether you want an Outdoor or Greenhouse variety — not a difficult decision. The Outdoor Group contains a large number of sections but the basic alternative is between a Small-flowered type for general garden display (and not much work) or a Decorative type with larger blooms which will need staking and stopping. *Staking* will be necessary to support the flower-heads and *stopping* (the removal of the growing tip) is necessary to make the plant flower earlier, improve the shape of the bush and to increase the size of the blooms.

Things are much more difficult if you want flowers for exhibiting — the first stopping and sometimes a second stopping must be timed with great care so that the blooms will be at their best on the day of the show. The varieties grown for exhibition are usually tall and *disbudding* (the removal of every small shoot and flower bud clustered under the central main bud) is necessary to allow the chosen bud to develop fully. This single bloom at the top of each stem may need protection from the elements by *bagging* (the enclosure of the flower in a paper bag) or by covering the plant with polythene sheeting.

So much for the Outdoor types — easy to grow or very demanding, depending on your reason for growing them. The Greenhouse varieties start to come into flower as the Outdoor ones fade in October, and once again the choice is between general display and cut-flower production. For cut flowers choose an Exhibition variety and the ritual of stopping and disbudding is essential; blooms 10 in. or more in diameter can be produced.

Much has been written about the long history of Chrysanthemums in the garden. They were grown in Japan more than 2,500 years ago, but all the spectacular facets of this fascinating flower came with the 20th century.

OUTDOOR VARIETIES

Other names: Early-flowering Chrysanthemums
Border Chrysanthemums

Includes all varieties which bloom in a normal season in open ground before the end of September without any protection.

Small-flowered varieties for garden display

Decorative varieties for garden display

Decorative varieties for cut flowers

Stopping is necessary in the first week of June if no natural breaks have occurred. Disbudding is not required

Stopping is necessary in the first week of June if no natural breaks have occurred. Disbudding is generally not necessary

Stopping and disbudding are required

GREENHOUSE VARIETIES

Other name: Late-flowering Chrysanthemums

Includes all varieties which normally bloom between October and late December under glass.

Flowering pot plants

Decorative varieties for cut flowers

Cascade varieties

Pendulous stems have to be trained

Dwarf varieties of standard types, Charm varieties and Marguerites. Stopping may be necessary but disbudding is not required

Stopping and disbudding are required

CHRYSANTHEMUM PLANTING MATERIAL

ROOT DIVISIONS
In spring the outer portions of last year's stools can be detached, each bearing new shoots and roots. These clumps can be used to propagate all Chrysanthemums, but in practice they are only used for Korean Hybrids. Cuttings are more successful.

ROOTED CUTTINGS
Last season's stools are kept in a cold frame or greenhouse. Cuttings 2–3 in. long are taken in February–April from the new shoots at the base (not the side) of the stems. These are rooted at 50°–60°F and then transferred into 3 in. pots.

SEEDS
Seeds are not used to propagate Chrysanthemums because the plants produced are rarely true to type. The Charm and Cascade varieties are exceptions — these are raised from seed sown in February.

STAKING

Insert a stout bamboo cane to a depth of 12–15 in. *before* planting large-flowered or tall-growing varieties. Tie the stem fairly loosely to the stake, using soft string. Make additional ties as the plant grows. Extra staking in August–September may be necessary.

STOPPING

When the plant is about 8 in. tall, the soft growing tip should be pinched out or *stopped*. This will stimulate the early growth of flower-bearing side shoots (breaks). Do not reduce the number of breaks when growing for garden display — reduce to 8 if growing for cut flowers or 3 if growing for exhibition. In July, pinch out the side shoots which have developed on the remaining breaks.

PLANTING

Plant out rooted cuttings in early May. Water pots thoroughly the day before and use a trowel to dig a hole in the moist ground which is wider but only slightly deeper than the soil ball of the cutting. Never plant Chrysanthemums too deeply. Fill the hole with fine soil and press down firmly. Water in, but do not water again for about a week.

GROWING GREENHOUSE VARIETIES

In April transfer the rooted cuttings from 3 in. to 5 in. pots. In mid May move into 8 in. pots and insert one or more stout canes to support the stems. As with Outdoor varieties, stopping is necessary. In early June move the pots outdoors on to a standing ground of ashes, tiles or concrete. Secure the plants to wires stretched between stout posts. Water regularly, but do not keep the compost constantly soaked. At the end of September bring the pots back indoors. Disbud as necessary. Feed regularly until the buds show colour.

MULCHING

Do not hoe after the middle of June. Keep the soil cool and moist by applying a 2 in. layer of peat or compost around the plants.

WATERING & FEEDING

Water thoroughly during dry spells, but do not keep the ground constantly soaked. Overhead spraying of the foliage is beneficial. Feed every fortnight with a liquid fertilizer, such as Instant Bio, until the buds begin to swell.

PLANTING DISTANCES

Garden display:
12–18 in.
Cut flower production:
18 in. wide rows, plants 15 in. apart.

PESTS & DISEASES

Slugs and birds are serious early pests — young plants can be devoured or stripped. Use Slug Pellets and stretch cotton around the plants. Aphids, capsids, leaf miner and earwigs can all be troublesome. Use a general-purpose insecticide — check that it is suitable for Chrysanthemums. Mildew and grey mould can be prevented by proper management — spray with a systemic fungicide as soon as spots appear. The worst headache is chrysanthemum eelworm, revealed by the blackening of the lower leaves. There is no cure — plants have to be destroyed and the land is unfit for growing Chrysanthemums in future.

SITE & SOIL

Pick a spot which receives at least a few hours sunshine on a bright day. Never plant under trees. Most soils are satisfactory provided they are well-drained. Liming is not necessary — Chrysanthemums prefer slightly acid conditions. In winter dig in plenty of organic matter — there is no need to dig deeper than one spade's depth. Rake in 4 oz of Bone Meal per sq. yd.

STORING STOOLS

In November, cut back the stems to about 6 in. Lift the roots carefully and shake off the soil. Trim off any leaves and tie a label to each stem. These prepared roots (*stools*) should be closely packed into boxes and surrounded by compost. Store the boxes in a cold frame and begin watering when new growth appears.

DISBUDDING

When growing large varieties for cut flowers the aim is to produce one superb bloom per stem. Disbudding is therefore carried out, which means the removal of every unwanted lateral shoot and bud on the stem. This is referred to as *securing the bud*.

BAGGING

Many exhibitors use bags or plastic sheets to protect their outdoor show blooms. Bagging is a popular technique for white or yellow varieties; a greaseproof paper bag is placed over the opening flower bud as soon as the petal colour can be seen.

CHRYSANTHEMUM continued

DECORATIVE TYPES
Medium-flowered: up to 6 in. in diameter
Large-flowered: 6–10 in. in diameter

INCURVED
Florets are turned towards the centre. Bloom forms a tight ball.

Outdoor examples:
Medium-flowered
'Martin Riley' (yellow)
'Nancy Matthews' (white)

Large-flowered
'Derek Bircumshaw' (yellow)
'Evelyn Bush' (white)

INTERMEDIATE
Florets are loosely and irregularly incurved or partly reflexed.

Outdoor examples:
Medium-flowered
'Cricket' (white)
'Claret Glow' (deep pink)

Large-flowered
'Keystone' (purple)
'Escort' (red)

REFLEXED
Florets are turned outwards and downwards from the centre.

Outdoor examples:
Medium-flowered
'Karen Rowe' (pink)
'Regalia' (rosy purple)

Large-flowered
'Tracy Waller' (pink)
'Abundance' (yellow)

SMALL-FLOWERING & SPRAY TYPES

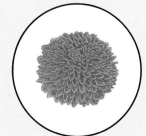

SINGLE-FLOWERED
Not more than 5 rings of ray florets. Central group of disc florets.

Examples:
'Abel Miles' (red)
'Peggy Stevens' (yellow)
'Pat Joice' (pink)
'Ben Dickson' (orange)

ANEMONE-FLOWERED
Not more than 5 rings of ray florets. Central cushion of tubular florets.

Examples:
'Flying Saucer' (white)
'Oliviero' (purple)
'Vivien' (red)
'Beautiful Lady' (pink)

POMPON
Florets are tightly packed (not curled), forming a small globular bloom.

Examples:
'Denise' (yellow)
'Fairie' (pink)
'Cream Bouquet' (cream)
'Bob' (red)

KOREAN HYBRIDS
Late-flowering bushy plants for the open garden — can be left in the soil for 2–3 years. Examples: **'Sunny Day'** (yellow) and **'Caliph'** (red)

SPRAYS
Outdoor and Greenhouse varieties for general display — many small flowers borne on each branched stem. Examples: **'Anne Ladygo'** (pink) and **'Pennine Silver'** (white)

CHARMS
Pot plants producing a domed shape covered with masses of small Daisy-like flowers. Examples: **'Red Charm'** and **'Yellow Charm'**

CASCADES
Pot plants with Charm-like flowers and trailing growth habit. Examples: **'White Cascade'** and **'Pink Cascade'**

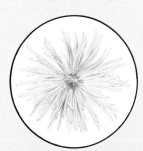

SPIDERY-FLOWERED
Florets are thread-like or spoon-shaped.

Examples:
'Pink Rayonnante' (pink, spidery)
'Pietro' (red, spidery)
'Tokio' (white, spidery)
'Magdalena' (yellow, spooned)

Flower Form

A Chrysanthemum flower is made up of numerous florets. Each floret is really a miniature flower with fused petals, and the shape and type of florets which are present provide the key to identification. They may be small, club-like and on a central disc **(disc florets)** or in a similar position but larger and tube-like **(tubular florets)**. The so-called 'petals' are actually **ray florets**. In a double bloom only ray florets can be seen, and the direction in which these ray florets are curled to make up the bloom is an important recognition point.

Chrysanthemum 'Evelyn Bush'

Chrysanthemum 'Keystone'

Chrysanthemum 'Tracy Waller'

Chrysanthemum 'Peggy Stevens'

Chrysanthemum 'Beautiful Lady'

Chrysanthemum 'Fairie'

Chrysanthemum 'Yellow Rayonnante'

Chrysanthemum 'Anne Ladygo'

Chrysanthemum 'Red Charm'

DAHLIA Dahlia

Dahlias have an interesting history. The first tubers arrived in Europe at the end of the 18th century — sent over to Madrid by the Spanish settlers in Mexico. Andreas Dahl (after whom the plant is named) regarded it as a vegetable rather than a garden flower, but interest switched from the edible tubers to the blooms when the first varieties with large, double flowers were bred in Belgium in 1815. Some of M Donckelaar's novelties were sent to England, and the craze began.

Within a few years nearly every colour we now admire had been introduced, and Victorian catalogues listed hundreds of varieties. The favourites in those days were the Ball and Small Decorative Dahlias — today it is the Large Decorative and Cactus varieties which capture the public fancy. Fashions change, but the popularity of this late summer flower continues to increase.

The reasons for this devotion to the Dahlia are fairly obvious. First of all, the skill of the breeders in England, Holland, Germany, Australia and America has produced a range of sizes and colours unmatched in the world of garden flowers. Plants ranging from dwarf bedders 1 ft high to giants taller than a man — flowers ranging in size from a 2p coin to the largest dinner plate.

Equally important is the time of flowering. From the end of July to the first frosts, Dahlias provide large orbs of colour when so many flowers are past their best. Above all, the Dahlia is an accommodating plant. It likes a good loam but will grow almost anywhere. It relishes sunshine, but can still do well in partial shade. A bed just for Dahlias is really the ideal way of growing them, but they are quite at home in the herbaceous border . . . or even the rockery for dwarf bedding varieties.

An important virtue is the way they put up with the novice or casual gardener. For him, growing Dahlias is a matter of planting the tubers which were dug up last year and stored in the garage. This planting is carried out when the season of frosts is past, and if no tubers are available then a trip to the garden centre offers a wide range of pot tubers or rooted cuttings. With planting out of the way, it's just a matter of staking when the stems threaten to fall over and the foliage is sprayed when blackfly becomes a nuisance. Even with such simple treatment a surprisingly good display can be obtained.

But it need not be an 'easy' plant. For the enthusiast the growing of Dahlias is an exacting and absorbing hobby. There are soil mixtures and composts to prepare in winter, cuttings to raise from tubers, growing points to pinch out, fertilizer to apply, side shoots to remove, plants to disbud, roots to be kept moist and show blooms to stage. There are many challenges for the enthusiast — there is the world record 21 in. bloom to beat, the elusive blue Dahlia to raise and a variety of show awards to win.

But most of the Dahlias will continue to be grown by ordinary gardeners who do not regard growing this plant as their hobby. For them the Dahlia is used to bridge the late summer colour gap in the herbaceous border . . . plus the added benefit of obtaining cut flowers which are large enough to impress the neighbours.

DAHLIA PLANTING MATERIAL

GROUND TUBERS
Usual source: Own garden, dug up in previous autumn and stored over winter.

Every couple of years tubers should be carefully divided. Make sure that each division has a piece of stem with swollen tubers attached.

POT TUBERS
Usual source: Garden shop or mail order nursery.

Pot tubers are convenient and easy-to-handle planting material, but it is more economical to use them to provide cuttings which are then rooted for planting out.

ROOTED CUTTINGS
Usual source: Garden shop or mail order nursery

or

Home-grown — Tubers are planted in moist compost in March under glass to provide 3 in. shoots. These are severed and trimmed, then used as cuttings for potting up and then planting out.

SEEDS
Usual source: Garden shop or mail order nursery.

Bedding varieties (see page 17) can be raised this way. Sow in gentle heat (60°F) in late March, plant out in late May. The flowering period is from late July to November.

FLOWER SIZE

Some catalogues use words to describe the bloom diameters of well-grown Decorative and Cactus varieties. The key below will guide you in making your choice.

Giant	More than 10 in.
Large	8–10 in.
Medium	6–8 in.
Small	4–6 in.
Miniature	Less than 4 in.

PLANT HEIGHT

Some catalogues use words to describe the average height of a variety grown under good conditions. Do remember that the stated height is *only* an average — the actual height achieved by a plant in your garden will depend on the location, weather and cultural conditions.

Tall Border variety	More than 4 ft
Medium Border variety	3–4 ft
Small Border variety	Less than 3 ft
Bedding variety	Less than 2 ft
Lilliput variety	1 ft or less

STAKING

Use a 1 in. square wooden stake for tall varieties — stout bamboo for smaller types. Insert the stake to a depth of 12–15 in. *before* planting. The height should be about 1 ft less than that expected for the plant. When growth reaches 9 in., tie the main stem loosely to the stake, using soft string. Make additional ties as the plant grows. For plants with several main stems a few extra stakes may be required.

PLANTING TUBERS

Plant dormant tubers in mid April — wait until early May in cold northern districts. Dig a hole about 6 in. deep with a spade. Place the tuber in the hole and cover with fine soil. The crown of the tuber should be about 3 in. below the surface. Make sure the soil fills the spaces between the tubers — after filling press the soil firmly with your fingers. Finally, label the stake with the name of the variety. There is no need to water at this stage.

DEAD-HEADING

The regular removal of faded blooms will prolong the flowering life of the plant.

WATERING & FEEDING

Water thoroughly during dry spells. Once the buds have appeared it will be necessary to water every few days if rain does not fall. Feed occasionally from July until early September — use a liquid fertilizer, such as Instant Bio, which has a higher potash than nitrogen content.

PLANTING ROOTED CUTTINGS

Plant in late May in southern districts — wait until early June in the north. Water pots about an hour before planting. Use a trowel to dig a hole which is larger than the soil ball of the cutting. Water in a couple of days after planting. Treat tubers bearing shoots as rooted cuttings.

MULCHING

Do not hoe as plants are shallow rooting. Keep weeds out and moisture in by applying a 2 in. layer of peat or compost around the plants in early July.

PLANTING DISTANCES

Tall Border varieties	3 ft
Medium Border varieties	2 ft
Bedding varieties	1–1½ ft

PESTS & DISEASES

The worst pests — aphids, capsids, red spider mites, caterpillars and earwigs are easily controlled by using a general-purpose systemic spray such as Long-last. In wireworm-infested soil rake in Bromophos before planting. In a wet summer sprinkle Slug Pellets around young shoots. Diseases are rarely serious but two (mosaic and spotted wilt) are due to viruses and there is no cure. Lift the plants and burn. Remember to spray against aphids, which are the virus carriers.

SITE & SOIL

Pick a spot which receives at least a few hours sunshine on a bright day. Do not plant under trees nor in soil which gets waterlogged. Medium loam is ideal, but most soils are satisfactory. In autumn or winter dig in plenty of organic matter such as compost or well-rotted manure — there is no need to dig deeper than one spade's depth. Rake in 4 oz of Bone Meal per sq. yd. after digging.

STORING TUBERS

When the first frosts have blackened the foliage cut off the stems about 6 in. above the ground. Gently fork out the tubers and discard surplus soil and broken roots. Stand tubers upside down for a week to drain off excess moisture. Then place them on a layer of peat in deep boxes and cover the roots (not crowns) with more peat. Store in a cool but frost-free place.

STOPPING

To increase bushiness it is necessary to pinch out the tips of the main stems about 3 weeks after planting.

SIDE-SHOOTING

Long-stemmed plants are needed for indoor decoration and exhibiting — snap away unwanted laterals from the main stem about 2 weeks after stopping.

DISBUDDING

For larger (but fewer) flowers it is necessary to remove the sidebuds, leaving only the terminal flower bud.

DAHLIA continued

I

SINGLE-FLOWERED
One ring of ray florets. Central group of disc florets. Height 1½–2 ft. Blooms up to 4 in. Examples are **'Yellow Hammer'** (yellow), **'Princess Marie José'** (pink) and **'Orangeade'** (reddish orange)

II

ANEMONE-FLOWERED
One or more rings of ray florets. Central group of tubular florets. Height 2–3 ft. Blooms up to 4 in. Examples are **'Vera Higgins'** (bronze), **'Lucy'** (purple and yellow) and **'Comet'** (red)

III

COLLERETTE
One outer ring of flat ray florets plus an inner ring of collar florets and a central group of disc florets. Height 2½–4 ft. Blooms up to 4 in. Examples are **'La Gioconda'** (scarlet and gold), **'Claire de Lune'** (yellow and cream) and **'Chimborazo'** (red and cream)

IV

PAEONY-FLOWERED
Two or more rings of flattened ray florets. Central group of disc florets. Height 2½–4 ft. Blooms up to 5 in. Examples are **'Bishop of Llandaff'** (red), **'Symphonia'** (vermilion) and **'Fascination'** (purple)

V

DECORATIVE
Fully double. Flat ray florets are broad and blunt-ended. Height 3–5 ft. Blooms 3–10 in. or more. Examples are Giant — **'Jocondo'** (purple), Large — **'Thames Valley'** (yellow), Medium — **'Terpo'** (red), Small — **'Gerrie Hoek'** (pink) and Miniature — **'David Howard'** (orange)

Dahlia blooms are made up of miniature flowers known as florets. The types of florets present are a key to identification.

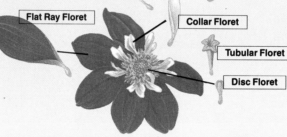
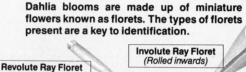

Revolute Ray Floret (Rolled outwards)
Involute Ray Floret (Rolled inwards)
Flat Ray Floret
Collar Floret
Tubular Floret
Disc Floret

VI

BALL
Fully double; ball-shaped — often flattened. Involute ray florets are blunt- or round-ended. Height 3–4 ft. Blooms 3–6 in. Examples are **'Doreen Hayes'** (red), **'Crichton Honey'** (peach and red) and **'Esmonde'** (yellow)

VII

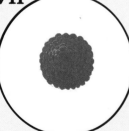

POMPON
Fully double; globe-shaped. Involute ray florets are blunt- or round-ended. Height 3–4 ft. Blooms less than 2 in. Examples are **'Hallmark'** (lavender), **'Willo's Violet'** (pale purple) and **'Noreen'** (pink)

VIII

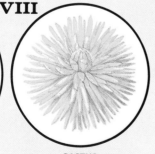

CACTUS
Fully double. Revolute ray florets are narrow and pointed. Height 3–5 ft. Blooms 3–10 in. or more. Examples are Giant — **'Danny'** (pink), Large — **'Irish Visit'** (red), Medium — **'Appleblossom'** (pale pink), Small — **'Doris Day'** (red) and Miniature — **'Pirouette'** (yellow)

IX

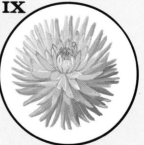

SEMI-CACTUS
Fully double. Pointed ray florets are revolute for half their length or less. Broader than Cactus Dahlia petals. Height 3–5 ft. Blooms 3–10 in. or more. Examples are Giant — **'Hamari Boy'** (yellow), Large — **'Nantenan'** (yellow), Medium — **'Autumn Fire'** (orange-red), Small — **'White Swallow'** (white) and Miniature — **'Yellow Mood'** (yellow)

X

MISCELLANEOUS
Flower form not belonging to Groups I–IX. Examples are Orchid-flowered Dahlias such as **'Giraffe'** (yellow and red), Incurved Chrysanthemum-flowered Dahlias such as **'Andries Wonder'** (salmon), and Star Dahlias which are now rarely seen

Dahlia 'Princess Marie José'

Dahlia 'Comet'

Dahlia 'Chimborazo'

Dahlia 'Fascination'

Dahlia 'Terpo'

Dahlia 'Crichton Honey'

Dahlia 'Willo's Violet'

Dahlia 'Doris Day'

Dahlia 'Nantenan'

FUCHSIA   Fuchsia

No one can decry the beauty of the Fuchsia in flower — beautiful pendent bells with swept-back sepals in a choice of colours. White, mauve, violet, cream, red, pink . . . often with two or even three colours on a single bloom. Of course it deserves a place in a book on flowers, although the tall-growing F. magellanica and its varieties belong in the shrub border and are dealt with in The Tree & Shrub Expert. In this book we are concerned with the large-flowering and colourful varieties of F. hybrida derived from complex crosses involving F. magellanica, F. fulgens and several other species.

These hybrids are not difficult to grow, and have an outstandingly long flowering period — from March to October under glass and from July to October or even later outdoors. There are pests and diseases, of course, as with all living things but the Fuchsia is generally a healthy plant when grown under good conditions. The real problem is hardiness — some varieties are tender and need to be kept indoors for their whole life span in order to flower to their full extent. At the other end of the scale there are many varieties which with proper management will survive outdoors, although frost may cut down the top growth each winter. Between the two are the bedding varieties which will flourish and flower in the garden if planted outdoors in late May or early June and then brought indoors for the winter.

A beautiful flower, then, but it may seem strange that it has been singled out for inclusion with the Hobby Plants. It is not as popular outdoors as the Sweet Pea, the Tulip, the Carnation, etc — all of which have been omitted. Although it does indeed fall down in universal popularity, the Fuchsia does have many of the other attributes of the Hobby Plant. There are innumerable varieties with a complex classification. There is much to learn about flower forms, growth habits and hardiness, and their cultivation can either be easy or exacting — depending on the effect desired. There are varieties and techniques for almost all situations — rockery, flower bed, hanging basket, windowsill, greenhouse or conservatory. You can grow it as a bush or turn it into a standard or pyramid — no wonder its devotees show such enthusiasm. There is a British Fuchsia Society — join if the Fuchsia bug bites you.

FLOWER FORMS

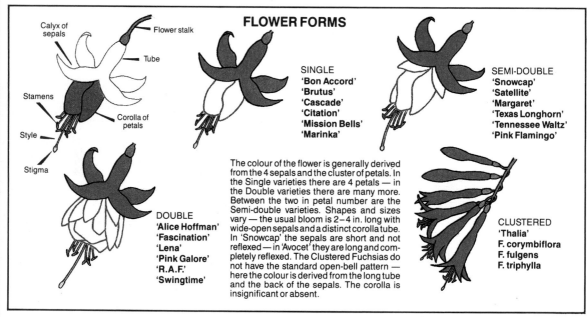

Calyx of sepals
Flower stalk
Tube
Stamens
Corolla of petals
Style
Stigma

SINGLE
'Bon Accord'
'Brutus'
'Cascade'
'Citation'
'Mission Bells'
'Marinka'

SEMI-DOUBLE
'Snowcap'
'Satellite'
'Margaret'
'Texas Longhorn'
'Tennessee Waltz'
'Pink Flamingo'

DOUBLE
'Alice Hoffman'
'Fascination'
'Lena'
'Pink Galore'
'R.A.F.'
'Swingtime'

The colour of the flower is generally derived from the 4 sepals and the cluster of petals. In the Single varieties there are 4 petals — in the Double varieties there are many more. Between the two in petal number are the Semi-double varieties. Shapes and sizes vary — the usual bloom is 2–4 in. long with wide-open sepals and a distinct corolla tube. In 'Snowcap' the sepals are short and not reflexed — in 'Avocet' they are long and completely reflexed. The Clustered Fuchsias do not have the standard open-bell pattern — here the colour is derived from the long tube and the back of the sepals. The corolla is insignificant or absent.

CLUSTERED
'Thalia'
F. corymbiflora
F. fulgens
F. triphylla

LOCATION

OUTDOORS Hardy in most areas of Britain, provided the rules on page 141 are followed	**ROCKERY** Examples: **'Alice Hoffman'** (red sepals, white corolla), **'Tom Thumb'** (red sepals, mauve corolla), **'Lady Thumb'** (red sepals, white corolla) and **'Peter Pan'** (red sepals, purple corolla). **BED or BORDER** Examples: **'Brilliant'** (scarlet sepals, magenta corolla), **'Peggy King'** (red sepals, purple corolla), **'Mrs Popple'** (red sepals, purple corolla), **'Brutus'** (red sepals, purple corolla), **'Tennessee Waltz'** (pink sepals, lilac corolla) and **'Mme Cornelissen'** (red sepals, white corolla).
BEDDING Treat as a summer bedding plant — plant in the garden when all danger of frost is past and take indoors before the first frosts of winter	Examples: **'Avocet'** (red sepals, white corolla), **'Bon Accord'** (white sepals, lilac corolla), **'Royal Velvet'** (red sepals, purple corolla), **'Snowcap'** (red sepals, white corolla), **'Satellite'** (red sepals, white corolla), **'Ting-a-ling'** (white sepals and corolla), **'Mission Bells'** (red sepals, purple corolla), **'Fascination'** (deep pink sepals, pale pink corolla), **'Dollar Princess'** (red sepals, lilac corolla), **'Heidi Ann'** (red sepals, mauve corolla), **'Rufus the Red'** (red sepals and corolla), **'Checkerboard'** (red and white sepals, red corolla), **'Display'** (pink sepals, deep pink corolla) and **'R.A.F.'** (red sepals, pale pink corolla).
GREENHOUSE Not really suitable for outdoors — best treated as an indoor plant	Examples: **'Winston Churchill'** (deep pink sepals, purple corolla), **'Candlelight'** (white sepals, mauve corolla), **'Texas Longhorn'** (red sepals, white corolla), **'Jack French'** (red sepals, purple corolla) and **'Sophisticated Lady'** (pale pink sepals, white corolla).

GROWING FUCHSIAS OUTDOORS

SITE & SOIL

Any reasonable garden soil will do if it is well-drained. Improve its moisture-holding capacity by digging in compost, peat or leaf mould before planting. Add Bone Meal if the soil is infertile. Fuchsias need sun but there can be some shade during part of the day.

PLANTING OUT

Choose with care. Pick an Outdoor variety if you plan to leave the plants in the ground over winter — you have a much wider choice from the Bedding varieties if you propose to bring the plants indoors after the summer display is over. Bedding-out time is between late May and early June when the risk of frost is past. The secret of success for growing Fuchsias as perennials is to plant Outdoor varieties so that about 4 inches of the stem is below ground level. This may seem odd but it does ensure that growth buds will be protected from surface frosts in winter. Water the pots about an hour before planting.

WATERING & FEEDING

Water thoroughly when the weather is dry. Feed occasionally with a liquid fertilizer such as Instant Bio.

PROPAGATION

Use the tips of non-flowering shoots as cuttings. In spring or summer insert 3 in. cuttings in pots of Seed and Cutting Compost — keep in a cold frame or propagator and rooting will take place in about 3 weeks. Pot on the rooted cuttings into 3 in. pots.

WINTER CARE

If you live in a mild region, the Outdoor varieties may over winter as green-leaved shrubby bushes, but in most areas the top growth will be killed. Do not cut down the stems — leave them for protection and delay pruning until spring. As added protection, cover the crowns with bracken, straw or peat. The Bedding varieties will need to be taken indoors during winter. In October lift the plants carefully and transfer them to pots. Store these pots in a greenhouse or well-lit shed for the winter. Keep cool, do not feed and water very sparingly until spring arrives.

PRUNING

With Outdoor varieties which have spent the winter outdoors, cut down the stems to 1 in. above ground level in March.

PESTS & DISEASES

Fuchsias are usually healthy plants but aphids, capsids, red spider mites and caterpillars may attack the leaves. Whitefly can be a menace indoors. Use a general-purpose spray based on a systemic insecticide — Long-last is a suitable example. Rust and grey mould may occasionally attack the leaves — use a fungicide but do check that it is suitable for Fuchsias by reading the label before you buy it.

HEIGHT & SPACING

Bushes: Height 2 ft, spacing 1½ ft.
Standards & Pyramids: Height 3–5 ft, spacing 2½ ft.

FUCHSIA SHAPES

BUSH

To induce bushiness, pinch out the tip after 3 sets of leaves have been formed. This will promote the development of side shoots — when each of these have developed 3 sets of leaves, pinch out the growing tips. The plants should be supported by means of twigs or stakes.

TRAILER

Choose one of the Basket (Trailing) varieties, such as **'Cascade'** (white sepals, red corolla), **'Marinka'** (red sepals, purple corolla), **'Pink Galore'** (pink sepals, pale pink corolla) or **'Swingtime'** (red sepals, white corolla). Pinch out the growing point when the leading shoot has reached the desired level. Pinch out the tips of the side shoots as soon as they have developed 3 sets of leaves.

PYRAMID

Choose a vigorous Upright variety and allow the main stem to grow 2 ft tall. Pinch out the tip — this will promote the development of side shoots. Allow the topmost shoot to grow upwards — pinch out the tips of the others when they have developed 3 sets of leaves. Repeat the process until the pyramid reaches the desired height.

STANDARD

Choose a vigorous Upright variety such as **'Avocet'** or **'Mission Bells'**. Alternatively use a Basket variety such as **'Cascade'** or **'Pink Galore'** — the stem will have to be staked from the start and it will take longer, but a better standard is produced. Place a stout cane next to the plant. Remove side shoots (but not the leaves) from the leading shoot until the desired height is reached. Tie this stem as it grows to the cane. Remove growing point when desired height is reached. Allow 5 or 6 strong shoots to develop to form the head of the standard. Remove leaves from main stem.

Some form of training is required to ensure that the plant will have enough shoots to produce a colourful head of flowers. Training involves pinching out the growing points *(stopping)* to induce side shoot formation. This stopping process must cease before you want the plant to flower — it takes about 7 weeks for a plant to flower after pinching out. Growing the plant as a bush or trailer is the usual outdoor form as top growth may be killed by winter frosts. Standards and pyramids take more than a single season to reach the desired height and shape, so these Fuchsia forms must be kept indoors during winter.

Fuchsia 'Citation'

Fuchsia 'Swingtime'

Fuchsia 'Thalia'

LILIUM Lily

Lilies have fascinated gardeners for over 3,000 years and continue to attract a dedicated band of devotees. It takes time, patience and a great deal of knowledge to build up an extensive collection of these bulbous plants and to grow them to perfection. The older species tend to be rather fussy about their requirements — some need lime whereas others hate it, and they are often prone to disease — L. candidum suffers badly from botrytis and L. auratum is extremely sensitive to virus attack.

So the majority of ordinary gardeners with no special love for the Lily regard it as a difficult plant and leave it at that. It cannot be expected to produce abundant blooms in its first year and it will quickly rot if the soil is not free-draining. The fleshy bulbs packed in peat or wood shavings by the nurseryman must be planted as soon as they have been obtained — no wonder that the average gardener turns to the Tulip, Gladiolus and Iris.

These days, however, the 'hard-to-grow' reputation for all Lilies is quite unfounded. During the past century a number of hardy and tolerant species have been discovered and in the past 30 years the Hybrid Lilies have set new standards in flower size, vigour and disease resistance. Lily flowers vary from 1 in. to 1 ft in diameter with a scent ranging from delightful to disagreeable. The colour range spans the whole floral spectrum with the exception of blue and the large variations in plant height make the modern-day Lily a suitable specimen for many parts of the garden. Dwarfs such as the 1 ft L. pumilum are excellent in the rock garden — the 8 ft giants like L. henryi belong at the back of the border. Between these two extremes are the vast majority of Lilies — 3–6 ft high and at home in the herbaceous border and shrubbery. Lily enthusiasts often grow them in a bed on their own, and by selecting the right varieties there are flowers to be seen and admired from May to October. There are woodland varieties like the Bellingham Hybrids which relish the dappled shade and humusy soil under trees and there are others, such as the 'Empress of China' which must be grown in pots under glass to protect them from the rigours of the weather. There is a Lily for practically every garden, but you will need both space and green fingers to become a serious Lily grower.

FLOWER FORMS

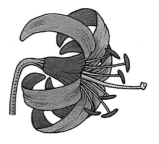

BOWL SHAPED
The petals flare open to produce a wide bowl. The flowers are usually large.
Examples:
L. auratum
L. 'Imperial Gold'
L. 'Imperial Crimson'
L. 'Empress of China'
L. 'Crimson Beauty'
L. speciosum

TRUMPET SHAPED
The petals are grouped together for part of the length of the flower to produce a basal tube.
Examples:
L. longiflorum
L. 'Black Dragon'
L. 'Limelight'
L. regale
L. bulbiferum
L. candidum

TURK'S-CAP SHAPED
The petals are rolled and swept back. The flowers are usually small.
Examples:
L. amabile
L. hansonii
L. martagon
L. tigrinum
L. 'Discovery'
L. monadelphum

Lilium 'Imperial Crimson'

Lilium regale

Lilium tigrinum

GROWING LILIES OUTDOORS

BUYING BULBS

Lily bulbs are made up of fleshy, overlapping scales. There is no outer protective skin and they must therefore not be allowed to dry out. Do not store Lily bulbs — plant them when they arrive. Pick carefully — choose bulbs which are neither bruised nor shrivelled.

PLANTING

The planting season stretches from late summer to early spring — October is the best month. Pick a day when the soil is moist and frost-free. If the bulbs are shrivelled or if the weather is not suitable on the day they arrive, pot up in moist peat before planting out. Most Lilies are stem-rooting, producing roots on the stem just above the bulb as well as at the base. These bulbs will need 6 in. of soil on top of them. A few Lilies, such as L. candidum, are basal-rooting only and they need planting in the autumn and require only 2 in. of soil above them. Sprinkle coarse sand in the bottom of the hole before planting. Spread out the roots and sprinkle sand between them. Finally, refill the hole with soil.

SITE & SOIL

A well-drained site is essential. Most soil types are satisfactory, but light land should be enriched with organic matter and heavy soil will need peat and coarse sand if you wish to take Lily growing seriously. It is impossible to generalise about lime content — many species, such as L. auratum and L. pardalinum, will not thrive if it is present whilst a few others, such as L. candidum, require an alkaline soil. Fortunately most of the modern Lily Hybrids are quite tolerant and are not bothered either way. Most Lilies relish a sunny site but a little shade during the day is not a problem. The lower parts of the plant should be shaded by surrounding shrubs or low-growing perennials. Many varieties are not happy in an exposed situation — choose a sheltered spot.

SUMMER CARE

Lilies must not be allowed to dry out — water thoroughly and regularly during dry weather. Feed occasionally with a liquid fertilizer, such as Instant Bio, and do not hoe — place a mulch around the stems instead. Not all Lilies have to be staked, but if you have a specimen over 3 ft high in an exposed situation then staking will certainly be needed. Stake in March rather than waiting until the stems have been blown over.

DEAD-HEADING

Nip off faded flowers before the seeds form — this will maintain the strength of the plant. At the end of the season allow the stems to die down naturally — cut off at ground level when dead.

PESTS & DISEASES

Slugs are a menace when the shoots are beginning to appear — sprinkle Slug Pellets around the stems. Aphids are easily controlled by spraying and botrytis can be kept in check with a systemic fungicide. It is mosaic virus which threatens the life of the plant — the warning sign is a yellow mottling of the leaves followed by stunting of the plant and a reduction in both flower numbers and quality in subsequent years. There is no cure — lift the bulbs and burn the infected plants.

PROPAGATION

The easiest method is the division of mature clumps in autumn. Replant immediately and accept the fact that the divided parts may not flower next year. Scaling is a popular method — pull off plump scales from a bulb and plant each one in Seed and Cutting Compost so that the bottom half of each scale is buried. Within 6 weeks tiny bulbs will appear at the scale bases — pot up each new plant in 3 in. pots and stand them in a cold frame or cool greenhouse.

Many Lilies can be raised from seed, but named varieties will not come true to type. Sow seeds under glass in autumn.

Lilium 'Enchantment'

SPECIES

L. amabile Height 4 ft. Spacing 1½ ft. Stem-rooting. 3 in. turk's-cap flowers — red with black spots. Disagreeable odour. Flowering period June–July.

L. auratum (Golden-rayed Lily) Height 5–8 ft. Spacing 1 ft. Stem-rooting. 8–10 in. bowl-shaped flowers — white with yellow stripes, brown spots. Fragrant. Flowering period August–September.

L. bulbiferum (Orange Lily) Height 2–4 ft. Spacing 9 in. Stem-rooting. 3 in. trumpet-shaped flowers — orange with purple spots. Flowering period June–July.

L. canadense (Canada Lily) Height 4–6 ft. Spacing 1 ft. Basal-rooting. 2 in. trumpet-shaped flowers — yellow with brown spots. Flowering period September–October. Grow in partial shade.

L. candidum (Madonna Lily) Height 4–5 ft. Spacing 9 in. Basal-rooting. 3 in. trumpet-shaped flowers — pure white. Fragrant. Flowering period June–July.

L. hansonii (Golden Turk's-cap Lily) Height 4–5 ft. Spacing 1 ft. Stem-rooting. 1½ in. turk's-cap flowers — yellow with brown spots. Fragrant. Flowering period June–July.

L. henryi (Henry's Lily) Height 6–8 ft. Spacing 1½ ft. Stem-rooting. 3 in. turk's-cap flowers — yellow with dark red spots. Fragrant. Flowering period August–September.

L. longiflorum (Easter Lily) Height 2½–3 ft. Spacing 9 in. Stem-rooting. 5–6 in. trumpet-shaped flowers — white. Fragrant. Flowering period July–August. Half hardy — grow under glass.

L. martagon (Turk's-cap Lily) Height 3–5 ft. Spacing 1 ft. Basal-rooting. 1½ in. turk's-cap flowers — purplish brown with dark spots. Disagreeable odour. Flowering period June–July.

L. pardalinum (Leopard Lily) Height 3–6 ft. Spacing 1 ft. Basal-rooting. 2½ in. turk's-cap flowers — dark orange with purple spots. Flowering period July.

L. pumilum (Coral Lily) Height 1–1½ ft. Spacing 6 in. Stem-rooting. 1½ in. turk's-cap flowers — scarlet. Flowering period June.

L. regale (Regal Lily) Height 3–6 ft. Spacing 1½ ft. Stem-rooting. 5 in. trumpet-shaped flowers — white with yellow throat. Fragrant. Flowering period July–August.

L. speciosum Height 3–5 ft. Spacing 1½ ft. Stem-rooting. 3–5 in. bowl-shaped flowers — white with red markings. Fragrant. Flowering period August–September. Half hardy — grow under glass.

L. tigrinum (Tiger Lily) Height 3–5 ft. Spacing 1½ ft. Stem-rooting. 3–4 in. turk's-cap flowers — deep orange with purple spots. Flowering period July–September.

HYBRIDS

L. 'Backhouse Hybrids' Height 3–5 ft. Spacing 1½ ft. Basal-rooting. 1½ in. turk's-cap flowers — various colours. Flowering period June–July. Examples: **'Brocade'** and **'Sutton Court'**.

L. 'Bellingham Hybrids' Height 4–7 ft. Spacing 1½ ft. Rhizome-rooting. 3 in. turk's-cap flowers — various colours, all spotted. Flowering period July. Examples: **'Shuksan'** and **'Afterglow'**.

L. 'Fiesta Hybrids' Height 3–5 ft. Spacing 1½ ft. Stem-rooting. 3 in. turk's-cap flowers — various colours. Flowering period July. Examples: **'Adagio'** and **'Many Moons'**.

L. 'Mid-Century Hybrids' Height 2–4 ft. Spacing 1 ft. Stem-rooting. 4–5 in. trumpet-shaped flowers — yellow, orange or red, all spotted. Flowering period June–July. Example: **'Enchantment'**.

L. 'Olympic Hybrids' Height 5–6 ft. Spacing 1½ ft. Stem-rooting. 5 in. trumpet-shaped flowers — various colours. Fragrant. Flowering period July–August. Example: **'Black Dragon'**.

L. 'Parkmannii Hybrids' Height 3–5 ft. Spacing 1 ft. Stem-rooting. 6–7 in. bowl-shaped flowers — various colours. Flowering period July–August. Examples: **'Imperial Crimson'** and **'Pink Glory'**.

PELARGONIUM   Geranium

This plant, with its bright heads of white, pink, red or purple flowers is found in gardens, greenhouses, window boxes, balconies and window sills everywhere. The Geranium is one of our favourite summer bedding plants, but it is not really a Geranium at all — it is the Zonal Pelargonium.

Look at one of the leaves of a typical variety and you will find a horseshoe marking or 'zone' — that is where the name comes from. These Zonal Pelargoniums are classified into three groups with somewhat indistinct dividing lines. The most popular ones belong to the Bedding Geranium group which flourish outdoors as well as under glass — the leaves are usually (but not always) zoned. The second group, the Greenhouse Geraniums, have a similar range of flowers and leaf markings but are disappointing outdoors. The Fancyleaf Geraniums make up the final group — here the leaf marking and colouring is more decorative than the blooms, which are generally (but not always) insignificant.

One of the great attractions of Pelargoniums to the enthusiast is the vast range of varieties which are available, and each year new types appear. No longer need you be content with red or white single flowers — as shown below and on the next page there are many colours and flower shapes to choose from. Indoors the Zonal Pelargonium can be made to bloom at any time of the year provided that the temperature is at least 50°F and the light is bright enough. With care you can have specimens in bloom in the greenhouse for nine months or even longer each year.

The universally popular Zonal types have an aristocratic relation — the Regal or Show Pelargonium. These are the beauties of the Pelargonium world with their shrubby growth, saw-edged leaves and large, bi-coloured ruffled flowers. But they do have problems — they will only succeed in a warm and sheltered spot outdoors and are best grown as indoor plants. The old varieties have a short flowering period of two or three months, but the modern hybrids can be made to flower all the year round as long as there is sufficient light and warmth.

Another relative is the Ivyleaf Pelargonium, bearing fleshy leaves on trailing stems. In Britain it is used for hanging baskets, tubs and clothing trellis work, but in many other countries it is widely used for ground cover. Outside the scope of this book are the Scented-leaf Geraniums — rose-, lemon- and apple-scented foliage much loved by our Victorian ancestors.

You don't need green fingers to succeed with Pelargoniums. They have few pests or diseases and even fewer fussy demands. All they need is plenty of light and a free-draining soil. Propagation is easy — striking late summer. cuttings is the traditional method but the introduction of the F_1 hybrid seed-raised varieties means that you can now produce Zonal Geraniums for your garden as easily as French Marigolds and Snapdragons.

The old favourites like 'Paul Crampel' still dominate the gardens of Britain, but there are now many types from which you can choose. There are Dwarfs which reach only 8 in. There are Stellars, Irenes, Rosebuds, Deacons and so on.... Miniatures growing less than 5 in. and Standards towering to 6 ft or more. Yet the Pelargonium is never truly at home in Britain. It must be lifted from the garden before the first frosts and allowed to sleep indoors until the end of May. Only in particularly favoured spots such as the Isles of Scilly can it grow outdoors as a perennial, and in a wet summer it produces an abundance of leaves and a paucity of flowers.

In the dry and frost-free areas of southern Europe the Pelargonium comes into its full glory. Here the Ivyleaf varieties can be seen cascading from balconies as shrubby perennials and on the hillsides the Zonal Pelargonium has become naturalised in an environment which reminds it of its native South Africa.

PLANT TYPES

BEDDING GERANIUM

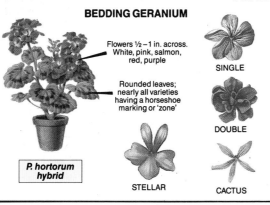

Flowers ½ – 1 in. across. White, pink, salmon, red, purple

Rounded leaves; nearly all varieties having a horseshoe marking or 'zone'

P. hortorum hybrid

SINGLE

DOUBLE

STELLAR

CACTUS

FANCYLEAF GERANIUM

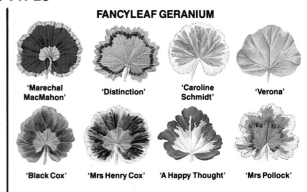

'Marechal MacMahon'

'Distinction'

'Caroline Schmidt'

'Verona'

'Black Cox'

'Mrs Henry Cox'

'A Happy Thought'

'Mrs Pollock'

REGAL PELARGONIUM

Flowers 1½ – 2 in. across. Frilled — white, pink, salmon, red, purple usually marked with darker colour

Serrated leaves

'Elsie Hickman'

P. domesticum hybrid

IVYLEAF PELARGONIUM

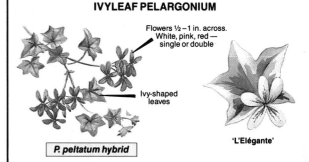

Flowers ½ – 1 in. across. White, pink, red — single or double

Ivy-shaped leaves

'L'Elégante'

P. peltatum hybrid

GROWING GERANIUMS OUTDOORS

SITE & SOIL
Any well-drained garden soil will do – the ideal is a sandy loam. Dig in compost or well-rotted manure before planting. Geraniums do best in full sun, but will tolerate light shade.

PLANTING OUT
Little can go wrong at planting time. All you have to do is choose a day in late May or early June when the danger of frost is past. The soil should be moist and the pots containing the Geraniums should have been watered a few hours before planting is due to begin. Plant firmly – that's all there is to it. Yet failures do occur and the plants seem to stand still instead of growing away. The usual cause is the lack of hardening-off – the plants should have been progressively acclimatised to the new environment and not moved from a warm greenhouse to the cold outdoors in a single day.

PROPAGATION
Geranium cuttings root very easily. Use the ends of green shoots, about 3 – 4 in. long, and insert in Seed and Cutting Compost. Do not use a rooting hormone and do not cover the cuttings – a small Rooting Bag is ideal for Geranium propagation. Take cuttings in July or August – they will root in 2 – 3 weeks after which they should be moved to 3 in. pots containing Potting Compost. During the winter months apply water sparingly and move to a cold frame in early April to harden off the plants for their late May move to the open garden. F_1 Hybrids can be raised from seed – sow under glass in January.

SUMMER CARE
Pinch out the growing tips occasionally to increase the bushiness of the plants. Geraniums can withstand dry conditions better than most plants – constant watering is an easy way to kill them. Leave them alone, but if the dry weather is prolonged then a thorough soaking will be necessary. Feed occasionally with a liquid fertilizer which contains more potash than nitrogen. Remove the dead flowers to prolong the flowering season.

WINTER CARE
Before the first frosts arrive carefully dig up the plants and shake off the soil around the roots. Pot them up singly in Seed and Cutting Compost, using pots which are no larger than necessary to house the roots. Reduce the height of the stems by about a half and cut off all yellowing leaves and dead flower-heads. Put the pots in an unheated spare room or in a cold greenhouse. Do not feed them and water only when it is essential in order to stop the leaves from flagging. In spring move to a well-lit spot and increase the amount of water.

PESTS & DISEASES
The two main pests of Geraniums attack the plants when they are growing under glass. Aphids and whitefly can seriously weaken growth – spray with Bio Flydown. Grey mould is another indoor nuisance – avoid stuffy conditions and spray with a systemic fungicide. Black root rot and foot rot are caused by using non-sterile compost, overwatering or damp air around the plants – there is no cure.

Pelargonium 'Paul Crampel'

BEDDING GERANIUMS
1. Standard Varieties: Height 1-1½ ft, spacing 1 ft. Propagate from cuttings taken in late summer.
   P. **'Paul Crampel'** Bright red, single
   P. **'King of Denmark'** Rose-pink, semi-double
   P. **'Gustave Emich'** Bright red, double
   P. **'Elaine'** Cerise-pink, single
   P. **'Jane Campbell'** Orange, single
   P. **'Queen of the Whites'** White, single
   P. **'Pandora'** Red, single
   P. **'Vera Dillon'** Purple, single
   P. **'Mrs Lawrence'** Pink, double
   P. **'Hermione'** White, double
   P. **'Festiva Maxima'** Purple, double
   P. **'Josephine'** Red, double

2. Irenes: Vigorous; free-flowering. Height 1 – 2 ft, spacing 1½ ft. Flowers semi-double; flower-heads larger than Standard Varieties.
   P. **'Springtime'** Salmon-pink
   P. **'Modesty'** White
   P. **'Surprise'** Pink
   P. **'Electra'** Red with blue overtones
   P. **'Fire Brand'** Red

3. Deacons: Compact. Flower-heads small but very numerous.
   P. **'Deacon Fireball'** Bright red, double
   P. **'Mandarin'** Orange, double
   P. **'Deacon Bonanza'** Bright pink, double
   P. **'Deacon Coral Reef'** Pink, double

4. Rosebuds: Small flowers, centre petals remaining unopened like miniature rosebuds.
   P. **'Red Rambler'** Red
   P. **'Appleblossom Rosebud'** Pink
   P. **'Rosebud Supreme'** Red

5. Cactus: Petals narrow and twisted.
   P. **'Fire Dragon'** Red
   P. **'Noel'** White
   P. **'Tangerine'** Vermilion

6. F_1 Hybrids raised from seed: Can be bought as seeds or bedding plants.
   P. **'Cherie Improved'** Salmon-pink
   P. **'Ringo'** Red
   P. **'Mustang'** Red
   P. **'Bright Eyes'** White-eyed red
   P. **'Sprinter'** Red
   P. **'Carefree Mixed'** Various colours

7. Miniatures & Dwarfs: Height 8 in. or less. Spacing 4 – 6 in.
   P. **'Red Black Vesuvius'** Red
   P. **'Fantasia'** White
   P. **'Pixie'** Salmon
   P. **'Caligula'** Red
   P. **'Grace Wells'** Lilac

FANCYLEAF GERANIUMS
Height 1 – 1½ ft, spacing 9 in. Propagate from cuttings taken in late summer.

Pelargonium 'Carisbrooke'

REGAL PELARGONIUMS
Height 1 – 2 ft, spacing 1 ft. Propagate from cuttings taken in late summer.
   P. **'Aztec'** White with pink blotches
   P. **'Lavender Grand Slam'** Lavender with purple blotches
   P. **'Grandma Fischer'** Orange with brown blotches
   P. **'South American Bronze'** White-edged maroon
   P. **'Geronimo'** Red, frilled
   P. **'Applause'** Pink, frilled
   P. **'Gay Nineties'** White with purple blotches
   P. **'Elsie Hickman'** Vermilion, pink and white
   P. **'Georgia Peach'** Peach, frilled
   P. **'Carisbrooke'** Rose-pink
   P. **'Sue Jarrett'** Salmon-pink with maroon blotches

IVYLEAF PELARGONIUMS
Spread 3 ft. Propagate from cuttings taken in late summer.
   P. **'La France'** Mauve
   P. **'Ville de Paris'** Salmon-pink
   P. **'Abel Carrière'** Magenta
   P. **'Galilee'** Pink
   P. **'Mexicanerin'** Red-edged white
   P. **'Enchantress'** Pink
   P. **'Crocodile'** Foliage white-veined; flowers pale pink
   P. **'L'Elégante'** Foliage white-edged; flowers pale pink

Pelargonium 'Crocodile'

CHAPTER 9

FLOWER GROWER'S DICTIONARY

A

ACID SOIL A soil which contains no free lime and has a *pH* of less than 6.5.

ADVENTITIOUS Term applied to organs produced at a point where such growth would not appear naturally. Roots on an above-ground stem are an example.

AERATION The loosening of soil by digging or other mechanical means to allow air to pass freely.

ALKALINE SOIL A soil which has a *pH* of more than 7.3. Other terms are chalky and limy soil.

ALPINE A rather vague term used to describe low-growing rockery perennials — see page 86.

ALTERNATE Leaves or buds which arise first on one side of the stem and then on the other. Compare *opposite*.

ANNUAL See page 4.

ANTHER The part of the flower which produces *pollen*. It is the upper section of the *stamen*.

ASEXUAL *Vegetative reproduction* — e.g cuttings and division.

AWL-SHAPED A narrow leaf which tapers to a stiff point.

AXIL The angle between the upper surface of the leaf stalk and the stem that carries it. An axillary bud arises in this angle.

B

BASAL SHOOT A shoot arising from the neck or crown of the plant.

BASTARD TRENCHING Another term for double digging — see page 126.

BEARDED A petal bearing a tuft or row of long hairs.

BEDDING PLANT A plant which is 'bedded out' in quantity to provide a temporary display.

BIENNIAL See page 4.

BIGENERIC A hybrid produced by crossing two different *genera* — e.g Heucherella, a hybrid of Heuchera (page 61) and Tiarella (page 80).

BISEXUAL A flower bearing both male and female reproductive organs — compare *dioecious* and *monoecious*.

BLEEDING The abundant loss of sap from severed plant tissues.

BLIND Term applied to a mature bulb which produces normal foliage but fails to flower.

BLOOM Two meanings — either a fine powdery coating or a flower.

BOSS A ring of prominent and decorative *stamens*.

BOTTOM HEAT Undersurface heat provided in the soil by organic fermentation, electric cables or hot water pipes.

BRACT A modified leaf at the base of a flower. A cluster of small bracts is a bracteole.

BREAKING BUD A bud which has started to open.

BUD A flower bud is the unopened bloom. A growth bud or eye is a condensed shoot.

BULB See page 108.

C

CALCAREOUS Chalky or limy soil.

CALCIFUGE A plant which will not thrive in *alkaline soil*.

CALLUS The scar tissue which forms at the base of a cutting.

CALYX The ring of *sepals* which protect the unopened flower bud.

CAMPANULATE Bell-shaped.

CHELATE An organic chemical which can supply nutrients to plants in a soil which would normally lock up the plant-feeding element or elements in question.

CHIMAERA A *mutation* which produces two kinds of tissue — e.g one or more 'wild' coloured petals in a Chrysanthemum.

CHLOROPHYLL The green pigment found in leaves which is capable of using light-energy to transform carbon dioxide and water into carbohydrates by the process known as photosynthesis.

CHLOROSIS An abnormal yellowing or blanching of the leaves due to lack of *chlorophyll*.

CLOCHE A temporary structure of glass or plastic sheets used to protect and hasten the growth of plants in the open.

CLONE A group of identical plants produced by *vegetative reproduction* from a single parent plant.

COMPOSITAE The Daisy Family, in which each flower bears 'petals' which are really *florets*.

COMPOST Two meanings — either decomposed vegetable or animal matter for incorporation in the soil or a potting/cutting/seed sowing mixture made from peat ('soilless compost') or sterilized soil ('loam compost') plus other materials such as sand, chalk and fertilizers.

COMPOUND FLOWER A flower composed of *florets*.

COMPOUND LEAF A leaf composed of two or more *leaflets*.

CORDATE Heart-shaped.

CORM See page 108.

COROLLA The ring of *petals* inside the *calyx* of the flower.

CORONA The trumpet produced in certain flowers, e.g Narcissus.

CORYMB A flat-topped *inflorescence* in which all the flowers open at approximately the same time.

COTYLEDON A seed leaf which usually differs in shape from the true leaves which appear later.

CROCK A piece of broken flower pot used at the bottom of a container to improve drainage.

CROSS The offspring arising from cross-pollination.

CROWN The bottom part of a *herbaceous* plant from which the roots grow downwards and the shoots arise.

CRUCIFERAE The Cabbage or Wallflower Family, in which the flower bears four petals in the shape of a cross.

CULTIVAR Short for 'cultivated variety' — it is a *variety* which originated in cultivation and not in the wild. Strictly speaking, virtually all modern varieties are cultivars, but the more familiar term 'variety' is used for them in this book.

CYME A flat-topped or domed *inflorescence* in which the flowers at the centre open first.

D

DEAD-HEADING The removal of faded flowers.

DECIDUOUS A plant which loses its leaves at the end of the growing season.

DECUMBENT A prostrate stem with an ascending tip.

DENTATE Toothed margin.

DIBBER A blunt-ended wooden stick used to make holes in the soil for transplants.

DIGITATE LEAF A leaf composed of finger-like radiating leaflets.

DIOECIOUS A plant which bears either male or female flowers. Compare *monoecious.*

DISC (DISK) The flat central part of a *compound flower*. It is made up of short, tubular *florets.*

DORMANT PERIOD The time when a plant has naturally stopped growing due to low temperatures and short day length.

DOUBLE A flower with many more than the normal number of petals. When the whole of the bloom appears to be composed of petals it is called 'fully double' — a 'semi-double' flower is the half-way point between a *single* bloom and a fully double one.

DRAWN Term applied to pale and *lanky* seedlings which have been sown too thickly or grown in shady conditions.

DRILL A straight and shallow furrow in which seeds are sown.

E

ENTIRE LEAF An undivided and unserrated leaf.

EVERGREEN A plant which retains its leaves in a living state during the winter.

EVERLASTING Flowers with papery petals which retain some or all of their colour when dried for winter decoration.

EYE Two meanings — a dormant growth bud or the centre of a single or semi-double bloom where the colour of this area is distinctly different from the rest of the flower.

F

FAMILY A group of related *genera.*

FEATHERED A petal on which there are feather-like markings on a ground colour which is distinctly different.

FERTILIZATION The application of *pollen* to the *stigma* to induce the production of seed.

FIBROUS-ROOTED A root system which contains many thin roots rather than a single tap root.

FILAMENT The supporting column of the *anther*. It is the lower part of the *stamen.*

FIMBRIATE Frilly-edged.

FLORE PLENO Term applied to *double* flowers.

FLORET The individual flowers of a *compound flower* or dense flower-head.

FLOWER The reproductive organ of the plant.

FOLIAR FEED A fertilizer capable of being sprayed on and absorbed by the leaves.

FORCING The inducement of flowering before its natural time.

FRIABLE Term applied to crumbly soil.

FROST POCKET An area where cold air is trapped during winter and in which *half hardy* plants are in much greater danger.

FRUIT The *seed* together with the structure which bears or contains it.

FUNGUS A primitive form of plant life which is the most common cause of infectious disease — e.g mildews and rusts. Such diseases are controlled or prevented by means of fungicides.

G

GENUS (plural GENERA) A group of closely-related plants containing one or more *species.*

GERMINATION The emergence of the root and shoot from the seed.

GLABROUS Smooth, hairless.

GLAUCOUS Covered with a *bloom.*

GROUND COLOUR The main or background colour of a petal.

GROUND COVER An ornamental plant which requires little attention and is used to provide a low-growing and weed-proof carpet between other plants.

H

HALF HARDY A plant which will only grow outdoors in Britain when the temperature is above freezing point. The term is not precise — some half hardy plants can be left outdoors in winter in mild regions of the country.

HARDENING OFF The process of gradually acclimatising a plant raised under warm conditions to the environment it will have to withstand outdoors.

HARDY A plant which will withstand overwintering without protection.

HEELING-IN The temporary planting of newly-acquired stock pending suitable weather conditions for permanent planting.

HERBACEOUS A plant which does not form permanent woody stems.

HERMAPHRODITE See *bisexual.*

HIRSUTE Covered with stiff or coarse hairs.

HONEYDEW Sticky, sugary secretion deposited on the leaves and stems by such insects as aphids and whitefly.

HOSE-IN-HOSE A flower which gives the appearance of one bloom inside the other — e.g Canterbury Bell.

HUMUS Term popularly (but not correctly) applied to partly decomposed organic matter in the soil. Actually humus is the jelly-like end-product which coats the soil particles.

HYBRID Plants with parents which are genetically distinct. The parent plants may be different species, cultivars, varieties or occasionally genera.

I

IMBRICATE Closely overlapping.

INFLORESCENCE The part of the plant bearing the flowers — the flower-head.

INORGANIC A chemical or fertilizer which is not obtained from a source which is or has been alive.

INSECTICIDE A chemical used to control insects and other small pests.

INTERNODE The part of the stem between one *node* and another.

INVOLUCRE A ring of *bracts* surrounding a flower or cluster of flowers.

J

JOINT See *node*.

K

KEEL Boat-shaped structure formed by the two lower petals of many members of the *Leguminosae*.

L

LANCEOLATE Spear-shaped.

LANKY Spindly growth — a stem with a gaunt and sparse appearance.

LARVA Immature stage of some insects, popularly known as a caterpillar, maggot or grub.

LATERAL SHOOT A shoot which arises from the side of a main stem.

LEACHING The loss of soluble chemicals from the soil due to the downward movement of water.

LEAFLET One of the parts of a *compound leaf*.

LEAF MOULD Peat-like material composed of partially-rotted leaves.

LEGUMINOSAE The Pea Family. Many have papilionaceous (butterfly-like) flowers — e.g Sweet Pea.

LIGHT Movable part of a cold frame.

LINEAR Very narrow with parallel sides.

LOAM Friable soil which is not obviously clayey nor sandy.

LOBE Rounded segment which protrudes from the rest of the leaf, petal or other plant organ.

M

MONOCARPIC A plant which dies after flowering and seeding.

MONOECIOUS A plant which bears both male and female flowers. Compare *dioecious*.

MULCH A layer of bulky organic matter placed around the stems — see page 129.

MUTATION A sudden change in the genetic make-up of a plant, leading to a new feature which can be inherited.

N

NECTAR Sweet substance secreted by some flowers to attract insects.

NEUTRAL SOIL A soil which is neither acid nor alkaline — *pH* 6.5–7.3.

NODE The point on the stem at which a leaf or bud arises.

NODULE Swelling on the root of a member of the *Leguminosae*.

O

OBLONG Longer than broad, with parallel sides.

OBOVATE Egg-shaped, with broadest end at the top. Compare *oval* and *ovate*.

OFFSET Young plant which arises naturally on the parent plant and is easily separated — e.g bulblet and cormlet.

OPPOSITE Leaves or buds which are borne in pairs along the stem. Compare *alternate*.

ORGANIC A chemical or fertilizer which is obtained from a source which is or has been alive.

OVAL Egg-shaped, with broadest part in the middle. Compare *obovate* and *ovate*.

OVARY The part of the female organ of the flower which contains the *ovules*.

OVATE Egg-shaped, with broadest end at the base. Compare *obovate* and *oval*.

OVULE The part of the female organ of the flower which turns into a seed after *fertilization*.

P

PALMATE Five or more lobes arising from one point — hand-like.

PANICLE An *inflorescence* made up of a number of *racemes*.

PEAT Plant matter in an arrested state of decay obtained from bogs or heathland.

PEDICEL The stalk of an individual flower.

PEDUNCLE The stalk of an *inflorescence*.

PELTATE LEAF A leaf in which the stalk is attached to the undersurface and not to an edge — e.g Nasturtium.

PERENNIAL See page 4.

PERIANTH The outer organs of a flower — the *petals* plus the *sepals*.

PETAL One of the divisions of the *corolla* — generally the showy part of the flower.

PETALOID Term applied to organs which assume the form of petals — e.g *stamens* in double flowers.

PETIOLE The leaf stalk.

pH A measure of acidity and alkalinity. Below pH 6.5 is acid, above pH 7.3 is alkaline.

PICOTEE Term applied to a narrow band of colour on a pale ground at the edge of a petal.

PINCHING OUT The removal between the finger and thumb of the growing tip of the stem to induce bushiness or to hasten maturity.

PINNATE LEAF A leaf with a series of *leaflets* borne on either side of a central stalk.

PIPING A cutting obtained by pulling off the tip of a non-flowering shoot — e.g Pinks and Carnations.

PISTIL The female organ of a flower, consisting of the *stigma*, *style* and *ovary*.

PLUNGE Term applied to the insertion of a potted plant up to its rim in a bed of peat, sand or ashes.

POLLEN The yellow dust produced by the *anthers*. It is the male element which fertilizes the *ovule*.

POLLINATION The application of *pollen* to the *stigma* of the flower.

PRICKING-OUT The first planting out of a seedling or rooted cutting into another container or nursery bed.

PROPAGATION The multiplication of plants.

PROSTRATE Growing flat on the soil surface; procumbent.

PUBESCENT Covered with short, downy hairs.

R

RACEME An unbranched *inflorescence* which bears flowers on stalks.

RADICAL Term applied to a leaf which arises at soil level.

RENIFORM Kidney-shaped.

RETICULATE Marked with a branched network of veins or fibres.

REVERSION A *sport* which has gone back to the colour or growth habit of its parent.

RHIZOME A horizontally-creeping underground stem which produces shoots and roots.

ROSETTE Term applied to a *whorl* of leaves arising at the base of a plant.

RUGOSE Rough and wrinkled.

RUNNER A stem which grows along the soil surface, rooting at intervals.

S

SAGITTATE Arrow-shaped.

SCAPE A leafless flowering stem.

SCREE Bed of gravel, peat and soil for growing *alpines.*

SEED The reproductive unit of a flowering plant.

SEED LEAF See *cotyledon.*

SELF-COLOURED Term applied to a flower of a single uniform colour.

SEPAL One of the divisions of the *calyx.*

SERRATE Saw-edged.

SESSILE Stalkless.

SIMPLE LEAF A leaf which is not *compound.*

SINGLE A flower with no more than the normal number of petals.

SPADIX A fleshy *spike* in which small flowers are embedded.

SPATHE A *bract* surrounding an *inflorescence.*

SPATHULATE Spoon-shaped.

SPECIES Plants which are genetically similar and which breed true to type from seed.

SPIKE An unbranched *inflorescence* which bears stalkless flowers.

SPIT The depth of the spade blade — about 10 in.

SPORT A plant which shows a marked and inheritable change from its parent; a *mutation.*

SPUR A tube-like projection from a flower.

STAMEN The male organ of a flower, consisting of the *anther* and *filament.*

STANDARD Two meanings — either the large upper petal of Sweet Pea-like flowers or a plant with a tall bare stem and a terminal head of leaves and flowers.

STELLATE Star-shaped.

STIGMA The part of the female organ of the flower which catches the *pollen.*

STIPULE A small outgrowth at the base of the leaf stalk.

STOLON A *runner*-like stem which forms roots and produces a new shoot at its tip (not at intervals along its length).

STOOL The *crown* of a border perennial used for *propagation.*

STOPPING See *pinching-out.*

STRAIN A selection of a *variety*, *cultivar* or *species* which is raised from seed.

STRIKE The successful outcome of taking cuttings — cuttings 'strike' whereas grafts 'take'.

STYLE The part of the female organ of the flower which connects the *stigma* to the *ovary.*

SUBSOIL Soil below the fertile top layer.

SUCCULENT A plant with fleshy leaves and/or stems adapted to growing under dry conditions.

SYNONYM An alternative plant name.

SYSTEMIC A pesticide which goes inside the plant and travels in the sap stream.

T

TENDRIL A modified stem or leaf which can wind around a support.

TERMINAL Term applied to organs borne at the tip of a stem.

THROAT The tube formed by the *corolla* of some flowers.

TILTH The crumbly structure of soil at the surface.

TOMENTOSE Densely covered with fine hairs.

TRANSPIRATION The loss of water from the surface of the leaves and stems.

TRANSPLANTING The movement of a plant from one site to another.

TRUSS A flower-head or tightly packed *inflorescence.*

TUBER See page 108.

TUNIC A dry and often papery covering of corms and some bulbs.

U

UMBEL An *inflorescence* in which all the flower stalks are of similar length and arise from the same point.

UNISEXUAL A flower of one sex only — see *monoecious* and *dioecious.*

V

VARIEGATED Leaves which are spotted, blotched or edged with a colour which is different to the basic one.

VARIETY Strictly speaking, a naturally-occurring variation of a species — see *cultivar.*

VEGETATIVE REPRODUCTION Division, cuttings, grafting and layering as distinct from sexual reproduction by seeds.

VIRUS An organism which is too small to be seen through a microscope and which is capable of causing malformation or discoloration of a plant.

W

WEED A plant growing in the wrong place.

WHORL Leaves, petals or branches arranged in a ring.

CHAPTER 10
PLANT TROUBLES

Things occasionally go wrong in even the best cared-for gardens – it is utter nonsense to believe that pests and diseases will only attack sickly plants. However good the beds and borders may appear, you must be on your guard against outside invaders – the insects and fungal diseases which can attack your plants and spoil all your efforts.

This chapter contains a frighteningly large rogues' gallery but you are unlikely to see more than a few in your own garden. It is much more likely that your plants will be harmed by an enemy from within rather than by an outside marauder – these inside causes may be the poor nature of your soil, lack of water, starvation, shade, frost, or you for choosing the wrong plants or doing the wrong things. The golden rule for having healthy flowers is to prevent trouble before it starts and to deal with it quickly once it is seen.

Prevent trouble before it starts

● **Choose wisely.** Don't buy soft bulbs, lanky bedding plants nor disease-ridden perennials — read the rules on page 125. Even if you buy good stock it will not succeed in the wrong location. Use the A – Z guides and avoid types which are too tender for your garden. Don't plant sun-loving annuals under trees — the display is bound to disappoint.

● **Prepare the ground thoroughly.** A strong-growing plant is more likely to recover from a pest or disease attack than a weak specimen. Waterlogging due to insufficient soil preparation is one of the worst problems in clayey soils. Get rid of all weed roots if you propose to plant perennials and add Bromophos to the soil if pests have gnawed roots elsewhere in the garden.

● **Plant or sow properly.** You have chosen the right plants or seeds and the soil is in a fit state to receive them, but trouble lies ahead if you don't bother to follow the rules for good planting laid down in this book. Page 127 tells you how to ensure that there will be no air pockets and that the roots will spread out into the garden soil in the minimum possible time. Seed sowing (pages 82–83) calls for doing the right thing at the right time — sow too early outdoors and the seeds may rot, sow too late and the display may be short-lived. When sowing seed indoors, remember that hardening off will be essential before moving the seedlings outdoors.

● **Never leave rubbish lying about.** Boxes, old flower pots etc are a breeding ground for slugs and woodlice. Rotting plants can be a source of infection and may actually attract pests to the garden.

● **Feed the plants properly.** Shortage of nutrients can lead to many problems — poor growth, undersized blooms, lowered disease resistance and discoloured leaves. Read page 130 and the instructions on the box or bottle — overfeeding can cause scorch and using an unbalanced fertilizer with too much nitrogen will give you lots of leaves and very few flowers.

● **Inspect plants regularly.** Keep watch for trouble and look up the cause in the following pages. Once you have put a name to the problem, act quickly — most pests and diseases can be checked quite easily if treated promptly, but may be difficult or impossible to control if left to get out of hand due to ignorance or neglect.

Deal with trouble as soon as you can

● **Remove occasional problems by hand.** Minor attacks by caterpillar or leaf miner can often be controlled by hand picking. If a plant suddenly dies, dig it up and examine it closely to find the cause. Examine the roots and the earth for soil pests — take remedial action if they are found. Do not replace the dead specimen with a similar plant if the description of the trouble in this chapter calls for a period of quarantine.

● **Keep a small plant-aid kit.** It may be several days before you are able to go to the shops, but a sudden attack by greenfly, caterpillars or slugs calls for immediate action. It is therefore a good idea to keep a small selection of pesticides in the garden shed for emergency use. You will need a bottle of Long-last for all leaf pests, a box of Mini Slug Pellets and a carton of General Purpose Fungicide. Don't buy more than you will need — it is better to buy a new small container each year rather than keep packs from one season to another.

● **Spray properly.** Once pests or diseases have started to take hold it will be necessary to act promptly. Read the label carefully and make sure that the product is recommended for the plant you wish to spray. Follow the instructions — do not make the solution stronger than recommended and never use equipment which has contained a weedkiller.

Pick a time when the weather is neither sunny nor windy and in the flowering season apply the spray in the evening when the bees have stopped working. Use a fine forceful spray and continue until the leaves are covered and the liquid has just started to run off. Do not direct the spray on to delicate open blooms.

After spraying, wash out equipment and wash hands and face. Store packs in a safe place and do not keep unlabelled or illegible packs. Never store pesticides or weedkillers in a beer bottle or similar container.

● **Speed recovery with a foliar feed.** Plants, like humans, can be invalids. The cause may have been a pest or disease attack, and the best way to get things moving again is to use a fertilizer which is recommended for spraying on the leaves — Instant Bio and Fillip are examples.

The major problem with soil pests is that they work unseen. Most of the ones shown below and the swift moth caterpillar (page 152) eat away at roots and by the time the damage becomes obvious the plant may be beyond recovery. Rake Bromophos into the soil before planting and sprinkle Slug Gard around the stems after planting if you know you have a soil pest problem or if the site was recently lawn or rough grassland.

Root Troubles

LEATHERJACKET

Grey or greyish-brown grubs which can be a serious nuisance in herbaceous borders on poorly-drained soil. Leatherjacket attacks are always worst after a wet winter; they are rarely a nuisance in sandy areas. If found at the roots of plants which have failed, sprinkle Slug Gard over the ground and lightly rake in.

1 in. grubs

WIREWORM

These hard, shiny insects are a problem in new gardens and in plots adjoining grassland. They are slow-moving — not active like the friendly centipede. They eat the roots of most flowering plants and may burrow up the stems of Chrysanthemums. Sprinkle Bromophos over the soil surface where they are a problem.

½-1 in. grubs

MILLEPEDE

Various types, both black and spotted, occur in the soil. They tend to curl up when disturbed, and should always be destroyed when found as they damage the underground parts of many plants. Damaged or diseased areas are prime targets. Slug Gard can be used to keep this pest under control.

CUTWORM

These green, grey or brown soil-living caterpillars may be 2 in. long. They gnaw both roots and stems, but their tell-tale effect is to sever seedlings and young bedding plants at ground level. When this happens look for and destroy the cutworms near the attacked plants. Rake in Bromophos as a preventative.

VINE WEEVIL

These wrinkled white grubs attack the roots of many plants, the worst affected being ferns, pot plants and alpines. If a rock plant suddenly dies, search in the soil for the rolled-up grub of the vine weevil. If present, pick out and destroy. Water the soil with spray-strength Hexyl.

CHAFER GRUB

Fat curved grubs feed throughout the year on the roots of herbaceous border plants. Both Chrysanthemums and Dahlias are sometimes killed. If these grubs are found in the soil, or if you intend to plant into newly broken-up grassland, sprinkle Bromophos on to the soil and lightly rake in.

CLUB ROOT

This serious disease of the vegetable garden can affect Wallflowers and Stocks. Below ground roots are swollen and distorted, above ground plants are small and die off earlier than normal. The best precaution is to lime the soil before planting and avoid growing Wallflowers on the same site year after year.

BLACK ROOT ROT

A common disease, affecting Antirrhinum, Begonia, Sweet Pea, Geranium etc. Above ground the leaves turn yellow and wilt. Below ground the roots are blackened. There is no cure, so avoid the causes — unsterilized compost indoors, uncomposted leaf mould outdoors and replanting the same type of plant in infected soil.

CATS

Cats are a pest of annual flowers. Seed beds and newly set out bedding plants are disturbed by their scratching. The resulting root damage can lead to the death of the seedlings. Protection is not easy if cats have chosen your flower bed for their toilet; sprinkle Pepper Dust liberally around the disturbed ground.

MOLES

An invasion by moles can cause havoc. The hills thrown up by their tunnelling are unsightly and cause severe root damage. Small plants may be uprooted. Eradication is not easy — Mole Smokes should be tried first. It may be necessary to set traps or to gas them; this work is best done by a professional exterminator.

Tuber, Corm & Bulb Troubles

Many plants are raised from bulbs, corms, rhizomes and tubers. These fleshy organs are at risk throughout their life cycle. They may be attacked in the soil by swift moth caterpillar, bulb aphid, narcissus fly and eelworm (see below) and by animals searching for food. Root pests such as wireworm, chafer grub and vine weevil (see page 151) will also attack bulbs and corms.

TUBER ROT

Dahlia tubers can be destroyed in store by fungal rots. To prevent this from happening, stand the tubers upside down after lifting and allow them to dry. Clean off all soil. Spray thoroughly with benomyl; leave them to dry before storing in boxes in a dry frost-free place. Inspect tubers from time to time; cut away any diseased parts.

RHIZOME ROT

A destructive disease of Flag Iris, especially in badly drained soil. Leaf tips yellow and wither; later the fan of leaves collapses. A yellowish slimy rot affects the rhizomes. Plants can be saved if the soft diseased areas on the rhizome are cut away as soon as they are seen and the rhizome and soil are treated with a Copper dust.

BULB ROTS

Several serious storage rots affect Tulips and Daffodils. **Narcissus smoulder** causes the bulbs to decay, small fungal growths appearing on the outer scales. **Basal rot** begins at the base of the bulbs of Daffodils and Lilies, the brown rot spreading upwards through the inner scales. **Tulip fire** is the most serious disease of this bulb; small fungal growths appear on outer scales and both shoots and flowers are damaged. If rotting has occurred in the past, immerse bulbs in benomyl shortly after lifting. Repeat dip shortly before planting. Remove rotten bulbs from store.

Narcissus smoulder   Basal rot   Tulip fire

NARCISSUS FLY

Affected Daffodil bulbs are soft and rotten, producing a few leaves but no flowers if planted or left in the soil. The maggots are ½-¾ in. long. Control is not easy; always discard bulbs at lifting or planting time if they are found to be soft. Hoe around the plants as the foliage dies down.

STEM & BULB EELWORM

Affected bulbs of Daffodil, Tulip, Hyacinth etc are soft and rotten. Tell-tale dark rings can be seen in a cut bulb. Daffodil leaves are pale, twisted and bear characteristic small yellow swellings on the surface. Throw away all soft bulbs. Do not plant bulbous plants on affected land for at least 3 years.

CORM ROTS

Several serious storage rots occur on Crocus and Gladiolus corms. **Dry rot** causes many black spots to appear on the corm, which later merge and the tissue completely decays. With **hard rot** the spots are brown and the affected corm becomes shrivelled. The spots of **scab** are round, brown and shiny. **Core rot** is quite different from the other corm diseases — it starts at the central core of Gladiolus corms and then spreads outwards as a moist rot. If rotting has occurred in the past, immerse corms in benomyl shortly after lifting. Repeat dip shortly before planting. Remove rotten corms from store.

Scab

Dry rot   Core rot

SWIFT MOTH

These soil-living caterpillars attack Gladiolus corms, Iris rhizomes and all types of bulbs. Unlike cutworms (page 151) they move backwards when disturbed. If swift moth is known to be a serious problem, rake in Bromophos before planting. Otherwise keep the pest under control by hoeing regularly.

BULB APHID

Colonies of greenfly may develop on Tulip and Lily bulbs and on Crocus and Gladiolus corms in store, sheltering and feeding under the outer scales. Young growth is severely affected when infested bulbs are planted. Rub off aphids before planting; if the aphids are numerous sprinkle bulbs with Gamma HCH dust.

PEA & BEAN WEEVIL

A common pest of the vegetable garden which can be damaging to flowers belonging to the Pea family (Sweet Pea, Lupin etc). Seedlings are most at risk, and should be protected by spraying with Long-last, Hexyl or Fenitrothion if the characteristic U-shaped notches appear on the leaves. Leaves of older plants may be damaged, but spraying here is not usually necessary.

¼ in. brown beetles

Holes in Leaves

Holes and tears in tender leaves are sometimes caused by frost or severe weather, but the usual culprit is an insect pest. Seedlings, small plants and the lower leaves of tall perennials can all be seriously damaged by pests such as slugs, snails, woodlice and vine weevils which feed on the foliage at night and hide under stones, debris etc during the day. Above-ground pests can attack leaves growing at all levels — capsid bugs produce small, brown-edged holes and caterpillars form large holes or even completely skeletonise the foliage. Many types of caterpillar may be found — the angle shades moth attacks the widest range of plants and the vapourer moth can be a nuisance in town gardens. Note that these garden caterpillars are the larval stage of moths rather than butterflies — the abundant cabbage white is the only exception.

CATERPILLAR

Many different leaf-eating caterpillars attack annuals and perennials in the flower garden. Some are uncommon; a few such as the angle shades moth and the cabbage white butterfly can be serious pests. Pick off the caterpillars if this is practical — if damage is widespread spray with a persistent insecticide such as Long-last or Fenitrothion.

ANGLE SHADES MOTH

Smooth caterpillar, about 2 in. long, which can be a serious nuisance on Dahlia, Gladiolus and many perennials.

CABBAGE MOTH

Smooth caterpillar, about 1¼ in. long, which attacks several annuals and perennials. Leaves may be skeletonised.

CABBAGE WHITE BUTTERFLY

Slightly hairy caterpillar, about 1½ in. long, which attacks several annuals and perennials. Leaves may be skeletonised.

VAPOURER MOTH

Colourful caterpillar, about 1 in. long, which feeds on the leaves of many perennials from May until August.

WOODLICE

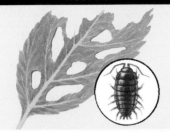

An abundant pest in shady town gardens, hiding under stones or leaves during the day and devouring young leaves of a wide range of flowering plants during the night. Woodlice favour plants which have already been damaged by a previous pest. Control is not easy — do not leave rubbish in the garden and scatter Slug Gard around the plants.

SLUGS & SNAILS

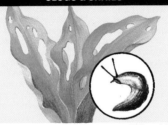

Serious pests, especially on Tulip, Iris, Delphinium, annuals and rock plants. Irregular holes are formed and tell-tale slime trails can be seen. Damage is worst on a shady, poorly drained site. These pests generally hide under garden rubbish during the day, so keeping the area clean and cultivated is the first control measure. Scatter Slug Gard or Slug Pellets around damaged plants.

EARWIG

A familiar pest which attacks Chrysanthemums, Dahlias and several other garden plants during summer and autumn. Males have hooked pincers, females bear straight pincers. They are night feeders, hiding in the petals during the day. To control this pest, shake the stems and then spray plants and ground thoroughly with Long-last or Hexyl.

Leaf not distorted

Leaf distorted

FLEA BEETLE

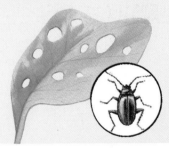

Tiny black or black and yellow beetles attack seedlings of the Crucifer family (Stock, Wall-flower, Aubrietia, Alyssum etc). Numerous, small round holes appear in the leaves. Growth is slowed down and seedlings may be killed. The beetles jump when disturbed. Spray the young plants with Long-last, Hexyl or Liquid Derris as soon as the first signs of damage are noticed.

CAPSID BUG

These little green bugs are a serious pest of Dahlias. Chrysanthemums, Salvias and other flowering plants may be attacked. At first the leaves are spotted; as the foliage enlarges small ragged holes with brown edges are formed. The leaves are distorted and puckered. Spray both the plants and the surface of the soil with Fenitrothion.

Leaf & Stem Troubles

Aphids and powdery mildew are serious problems in a dry summer, and grey mould can be destructive when the weather is wet. Starvation leads to poor leaf and stem development, and traces of lawn weedkiller can lead to severe distortion. The major leaf and stem problems are shown on these two pages — other insects or moulds may occasionally appear but they seldom, if ever, call for treatment.

DAMPING OFF

The damping off fungi attack the roots and stem bases of seedlings. Shrinkage and rot occurs at ground level and the plants topple over. The golden rules are to sow thinly and never overwater. Ensure adequate ventilation under glass. Remove collapsed seedlings immediately; water remainder with Cheshunt Compound.

LEAFHOPPER

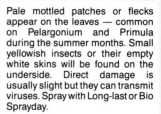

Pale mottled patches or flecks appear on the leaves — common on Pelargonium and Primula during the summer months. Small yellowish insects or their empty white skins will be found on the underside. Direct damage is usually slight but they can transmit viruses. Spray with Long-last or Bio Sprayday.

CHRYSANTHEMUM EELWORM

The leaves develop brown areas between the veins; the plants may be killed if the infestation is severe. Aster and Paeony as well as Chrysanthemum may be attacked. The closely-related leaf blotch eelworm produces similar symptoms on Begonia and ferns. Pick off and burn affected leaves; destroy severely infested plants.

STEM ROT

Several types of stem rot attack garden flowers — all are serious. Part or all of the stem decays and the leaves wilt. Sclerotinia disease is a common cause in herbaceous border plants — Sunflower, Campanula, Chrysanthemum etc. Hard black bodies occur in the pith. There is no cure — lift badly diseased plants and burn.

COLD DAMAGE

A sudden cold snap in spring can affect developing leaves and leaf buds by destroying chlorophyll. The affected leaf, when it expands, may be yellow-edged (Anemone, Sweet Pea etc), almost white (many bedding plants) or white-banded (Daffodils). Pick off badly affected leaves; spray with Fillip to speed recovery.

LEAFY GALL

A mass of shortened shoots with thickened, distorted leaves sometimes develops at the base of the plant. This disease is spread by tools or by taking cuttings from diseased stock, so affected plants should be destroyed and not used for propagation. Susceptible plants are Sweet Pea, Chrysanthemum, Dahlia and Pelargonium.

FROGHOPPER

The frothy white masses ('cuckoo spit') which occur on the stems of Geum, Solidago, Chrysanthemum, and many other flowering plants, are familiar to everyone. Less well known is the cause — pinkish ⅛ in. froghoppers which suck the sap and distort young growth. Hose with water, then spray with Long-last or Hexyl.

PHLOX EELWORM

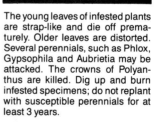

The young leaves of infested plants are strap-like and die off prematurely. Older leaves are distorted. Several perennials, such as Phlox, Gypsophila and Aubrietia may be attacked. The crowns of Polyanthus are killed. Dig up and burn infested specimens; do not replant with susceptible perennials for at least 3 years.

FOOT ROT

The tell-tale sign is the blackening and rotting of the base of the stem. The name depends on the plant affected — geranium blackleg, pansy sickness, campanula crown rot etc. Use sterile compost in seed boxes or pots. Avoid waterlogging. Destroy infected plants and water remainder with Cheshunt Compound or Dithane.

TULIP FIRE

A serious disease of Tulips, causing scorched areas on the leaves and spots on the flowers. Young shoots may become covered with a grey, velvety mould. Rotting of bulbs occurs (see page 152). Cut off diseased emerging shoots below ground level; spray the remaining plants with Dithane. Repeat at 14-day intervals.

APHID

Several species of aphids infest annual and perennial flowers in warm, settled weather. The commonest are the black bean aphid and the peach-potato aphid. Young growth is distorted and weakened; leaves are covered with sticky honeydew which later becomes covered with sooty mould. Keep plants well-watered in dry weather. Spray with Long-last, Bio Sprayday, Malathion or Liquid Derris as soon as colonies start to appear.

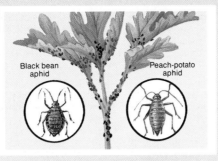

Black bean aphid

Peach-potato aphid

RED SPIDER MITE

If leaves develop an unhealthy bronze colour, look for tiny spider-like mites on the underside of the leaves. The presence of fine silky webbing is a tell-tale sign. In hot settled weather spraying may be necessary — use Long-last or Liquid Derris.

LEAF MINER

Long winding tunnels are eaten in the leaf tissue by small grubs. At first the tunnels appear white, later they turn brown. Chrysanthemum foliage is commonly attacked in this way. The carnation fly behaves rather differently, producing blotches on the leaves and sometimes killing the plant. Pick and destroy mined leaves. Spray with Hexyl.

WILT

Leaves and shoots sometimes wilt badly even though the soil is moist. If the plant is an Antirrhinum, Aster, Sweet Pea, Carnation, Chrysanthemum, Lupin or Poppy then the likely cause is a soil-borne fungus. Tissue inside stem will probably be stained brown. There is no cure. Remove diseased plants — do not grow susceptible plants on the same spot.

VIRUS

Viruses may be carried by insects, tools or fingers. There are many different symptoms of virus infection — leaves may be yellow, covered with yellow spots or patches (**mosaic**), crinkled and distorted or white-veined. Stems may be covered with brown stripes (**streak**) or stunted and distorted. There is no cure; if you are sure of your diagnosis, lift and burn. Buy healthy stock; keep aphids under control.

GREY MOULD (Botrytis)

A destructive disease in wet seasons. Fluffy grey mould appears on the leaves; with many bedding plants (Godetia, Clarkia, Petunia, Zinnia etc) stems are attacked. Remove mouldy leaves and badly infected plants immediately. Spray with a systemic fungicide.

RUST

Look for the tell-tale sign of coloured swellings on the leaves and stems. These raised spots may be yellow, orange or brown. It is a common disease of Antirrhinum, Hollyhock, Pelargonium, Carnation, Chrysanthemum and Sweet William. Pick off and burn diseased leaves; spray with Dithane every 2 weeks.

LEAF SPOT

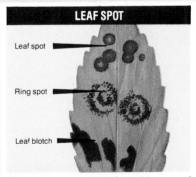

Leaf spot

Ring spot

Leaf blotch

Leaf spot is a family name for a wide group of diseases which appear on many types of flowering plants. Leaf spot (round or oval coloured spots) is an important disease of Pansy, Phlox, Polyanthus, Poppy, Iris and Sweet William. Ring spot (dark concentric rings of spores) is common on Carnation, and leaf blotch (irregular-shaped spots) affects Delphinium. Pick off diseased leaves. Spray with a Copper spray or Dithane, but control may be difficult.

POWDERY MILDEW

The main symptom is a white mealy growth on the leaf surface. It is encouraged by overcrowding and lack of soil moisture. This is the disease commonly seen on Michaelmas Daisy, Delphinium and Chrysanthemum. Spray with a systemic fungicide at the first sign of disease and again 1 week later. Repeat if disease reappears.

DOWNY MILDEW

Less likely to be troublesome in the flower garden than powdery mildew, although Antirrhinum, Sweet Pea, Poppy and Wallflower are often affected in damp weather. Upper leaf surface shows yellow or dull patches; greyish mould growth occurs below. Plants are crippled by a severe attack. Spray with Dithane at the first sign of disease; repeat at 14-day intervals.

Bud & Flower Troubles

Blooms may be poor in size and quantity. They may also be damaged, distorted or spotted. In addition to the pests and diseases shown here, there are other flower enemies illustrated on previous pages — slugs (page 153), eelworm (pages 152 and 154), tulip fire (page 154) and the angle shades moth (page 153).

BIRDS

Birds are extremely selective in their choice of flowers. Nearly all blooms are ignored but Polyanthus, Primula 'Wanda' and Crocus (especially the yellow-flowering varieties) may be stripped of buds and flowers in spring by sparrows and blackbirds. Surprisingly, plants in one garden may be ruined and similar plants next door completely ignored. Control is difficult because netting is unsightly in the flower garden. A bird repellent spray may be tried.

NO FLOWERS

There are several possible reasons why plants may fail to bloom. Some herbaceous border plants dislike being moved and may not bloom during their first year in the garden. Daffodils suffer from a disorder known as grassiness — grass-like leaves and no flowers; there is no cure. Tulips sometimes suffer from blindness. But the most likely cause of failure to flower is the effect of one of the factors in the paragraph below.

FEW FLOWERS

A common problem is the failure of plants to produce the normal number of blooms. The two most frequent reasons are too much shade and too much nitrogen. Some bedding and rockery plants will hardly bloom at all in deep shade — always choose carefully for such locations. Too much nitrogen, due to overmanuring, is the cause of too much foliage and too little bloom; use a fertilizer which has more potash than nitrogen in order to redress the balance. There are many other possibilities — failure to pinch out the growing point of bedding plants to induce bushiness, failure to cut off dead blooms in order to induce repeat flowering and failure to water in dry weather. Bud drop can occur if there is a late frost or even a cold night; Sweet Peas frequently suffer in this way. Finally, an attack by some of the pests and diseases described on this page can reduce the number of blooms.

APHID

Aphids, both greenfly and blackfly, can seriously reduce the quantity and quality of the floral display. When the weather is warm and dry, large colonies of these pests build up on the buds of many types of flowering plants, causing the flowers when they are open to be undersized. In a severe attack the buds may fail to open. Spray with Long-last, Bio Sprayday, Malathion or Liquid Derris when the pests are first seen.

EARWIG

An important pest of Chrysanthemum and Dahlia blooms. At night the petals are eaten, making them ragged and unsightly. During the day the earwigs hide in the heart of the blooms or beneath leaves and other debris on the ground. Clear away rubbish. Shake open blooms, then spray plants and soil thoroughly with Hexyl.

THRIPS

Thrips or thunderflies, swarm over leaves and flowers in a hot summer. The usual symptom is silvery flecking of flowers and leaves. Gladioli are particularly susceptible. Flowers may be ruined by a bad attack. Spray at the first sign of attack with Fenitrothion or Long-last.

CAPSID BUG

¼ in. greenish insects

These active, sap-sucking bugs are a serious pest of Dahlias, Chrysanthemums and many other flowers. Buds may be killed; if they open the flowers are lop-sided. Begin spraying with Fenitrothion as soon as damage appears on the leaves (see page 153). Repeat 2 or 3 times at 14-day intervals.

PETAL BLIGHT

In a cold and wet summer this Chrysanthemum disease can ruin the flowers. Small water-filled spots appear on the petals, eventually spreading to destroy the bloom. Anemone, Cornflower and Dahlia are affected. Spray with Dithane when buds begin to show colour. Repeat at weekly intervals. Pick off diseased flowers.

GREY MOULD (Botrytis)

Grey mould is a serious disease of the flower garden which strikes when the weather is humid. It can attack a wide variety of blooms; Chrysanthemum, Dahlia, Paeony, Lily and bedding plants are particularly susceptible. Flowers may be spotted at first, but later rot and become covered with a fluffy mould. Badly diseased buds fail to open. Pick off mouldy leaves and flowers as soon as they are seen. Spray with a systemic fungicide.

COLOUR BREAK

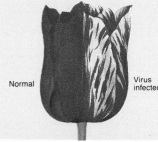

Normal   Virus infected

Petals sometimes possess streaks or patches of an abnormal colour. This colour break is caused by a virus and there is no cure. Tulips are the most likely flowers to be affected; it may also occur in Dahlia, Chrysanthemum, Lily, Viola and Wallflower. The effect may be attractive; multi-coloured Tulip varieties are bred in this way. But in a single-colour bed the effect is undesirable and the plants should be destroyed if you wish to keep the stock pure. The removal of diseased plants is essential where **phyllody** occurs — a virus-like condition which causes the flowers to turn green.

CHAPTER 11

PLANT INDEX